State, Class,
and the Nationalization
of the Mexican Banks

Mefeito, a modern mask in the ancient tradition of Central and South America, was created and produced by Tupac Reinaga, a 35-year-old Argentinian residing in Caracas, Venezuela. The mask signifies the material condition of modern man and the symbolic corruptive power of money. The lips and nose are lighter in color than the "face" of the mask, and the mask itself is designed so that it appears to be constructed of iron. The image created is that of an iron mask with reinforcing bolts to bind or imprison the mask, to which the artist has added Venezuelan coins covering the eyes to depict the impinging effects of a materialist vision. The artistic and philosophical message of the mask can be interpreted as exemplary of the conflicts and struggles that occurred between the Mexican bankers, the Mexican state, and the Mexican people. (Photo: L. Neil White)

State, Class,
and the Nationalization
of the Mexican Banks

Russell N. White

CRANE RUSSAK
A member of the Taylor & Francis Group
New York • Philadelphia • Washington • London

USA	Publishing Office:	Taylor & Francis New York Inc. 79 Madison Ave., New York, NY 10016-7892
	Sales Office:	Taylor & Francis Inc. 1900 Frost Road, Bristol, PA 19007-1598
UK		Taylor & Francis Ltd. 4 John St., London WC1N 2ET

STATE, CLASS, AND THE NATIONALIZATION OF THE MEXICAN BANKS

1 2 3 4 5 6 7 8 9   B R B R   9 8 7 6 5 4 3 2 1

This book was set in Times Roman by Hemisphere Publishing Corporation. The editors were Dave Weber and Marly Davidson, the production supervisor was Peggy M. Rote, and the typesetter was Shirley J. McNett. Cover design by Debra Eubanks Riffe. Printing and binding by Braun-Brumfield, Inc.

A CIP catalog record for this book is available from the British Library.

Library of Congress Cataloging-in-Publication Data

White, Russell N.
    State, class and the nationalization of the Mexican banks /
Russell N. White.
        p. cm.
    Includes bibliographical references and index.

    1. Banks and banking—Government ownership—Mexico—History.
2. Finance—Mexico—History. 3. Banks and banking—Mexico—History.
I. Title.
HG2714.W47   1992
332.1′0972—dc20
                                                    91-20312
                                                    CIP

ISBN 0-8448-1698-1

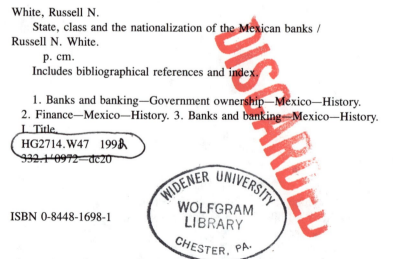

In memory of my grandfather, Lawrence A. White,
a man who exemplified dedication, hard work, honesty,
and a great sense of humor

Contents

Preface   *xi*

Introduction   *xv*

Part One
Definition and Development of the State/Capital Relationship

Chapter 1   **Prerevolutionary Development of the Mexican Banking System**   **3**

Commercial Capital During the Colonial Period and Immediate Postindependence Period   3
The Mexican State   7
The Porfirian Banking System   9
Notes   23

Chapter 2   **Postrevolutionary Finance, 1920–1940: Coincidence of Interest**   **25**

The State, Revolutionary Ideology, and the Party   25
Economic Development and Postrevolution Continuity   32
Postrevolutionary Finance: 1920–1940   33
Development of the Banking System in the 1930s   42
Notes   48

Part Two
Finance Capital and The Consolidation
of Hegemony

Chapter 3 **Postrevolutionary Finance, 1940–1970: Bank**
Capital Consolidation **55**

1940–1949: A Transitionary Period 56
1950–1959: Definition of an Accumulation Model 58
1960s: End of an Era 62
Conclusion 66
Notes 67

Chapter 4 **Finance Capital, the State, and Political-Economic**
Stagflation **71**

Accumulation, Finance Capital, and Desarrollo
Compartido 72
The Lost Sexenios: 1970–1982 76
Finance Capital 84
Conclusion 88
Notes 90

Part Three
The Articulation of Power: The Nationalization
and Postnationalization Period

Chapter 5 **Nationalization of the Banks** **97**

Accumulation, Economic Stagnation, and Financial
Collapse: 1980–1982 98
The Banking System: 1980–1982 101
Political-Economic Developments Leading to the
Nationalization 106
The Nationalization of the Banks 114
Six Analyses of the Nationalization 117
Conclusion 123
Notes 125

Chapter 6   **Postnationalization and the Financial Fraction**   **127**

Immediate Postnationalization Developments   128
The Financial Fraction and the Parallel Financial
      Circuit   134
Stock Brokerage Houses   140
Conclusion   143
Notes   146

Conclusion   **149**

Postscript   **153**

Appendix   **157**

Bibliography   163
Index   177
About the Author   185

Preface

Mexico is a labyrinth. At least that's what I had always been told by numerous experts, authors, and tourists. I must admit, my first recollections of Mexico were rather stereotypical. I remember the unpaved streets of Tijuana, the vendors shrilly and pugnaciously hawking their wares, and the everlasting smells of exotic deep-fried street food permeating my nostrils.

My first "real" academic experience with Mexico was in late 1978. Living in Morelia, Michoacan was nothing less than enigmatic. While participating in a university foreign exchange program, I found myself struggling to learn Spanish. Living with a Mexican family was interesting and always left an inquisitive smile on my face. In short, I was determined to understand this "strange" culture, a culture so contradictory that surrealism permeates every corner.

My passion for Mexico was rekindled every summer when I would travel south with some of my summer earnings. The more I traveled to Mexico, the more confounded I became and the more enduring was my desire to understand the depths of Mexican development. As a graduate student, I studied the development of underdevelopment and I had an opportunity to attend the prestigious Universidad Autonoma de Guadalajara (UAG). Going to school with the Tecos was nothing short of perplexing. My insatiable desire to understand the Mexican labyrinth was increasingly problematic.

On entering the doctoral program at the Department of Political Science at the University of California, Riverside (UCR) in 1982, I was fortunate to find many brilliant minds devoted to demystifying Third World political-economic development. Countless seminars with Ron Chilcote and fellow colleagues focused my attention on the Mexican banking system. The Mexican banks had just been nationalized and this was an opportunity to utilize my studies in political economy to better understand the impermeable maze that confounded my understanding. While at UCR, I became friends with Diana Alarcón and

Eduardo Zepeda, two brilliant Mexican economists who greatly enhanced my understanding of Mexican reality.

As my graduate studies progressed, I broadened my familiarity with Latin America. I became an associate editor with the prestigious journal *Latin American Perspectives*. The journal provided me with an unparalleled opportunity to discuss Latin American political economy with noted scholars. My association with the journal also facilitated access to well-known scholars and intellectuals in Mexico.

My historical studies of Mexico began to focus on the Mexican financial system and the nationalization of the banks in 1983. Upon advancement to doctoral candidacy in 1984 I concentrated all my efforts on studying the nationalization of the banks. I had always been interested in the interrelationships between political economy, finance, and class fractions of capital. Not only was I dissatisfied with the paucity of serious studies on Mexican finance, I also believed that the majority of U.S. scholars utilized American paradigms to describe and explain historical developments in Mexico. In other words, I decided that I had to go to Mexico to further my work on the nationalization of the banks in Mexico. It was fortunate that I was awarded a University of California fellowship for two years. With my fellowship support I was able to live in Mexico for two years and concentrate all of my efforts on my doctoral dissertation.

The research and writing of this book was a long and arduous process, encompassing more than seven years of work. It was always an intellectually enlightening and pleasurable experience. Unfortunately, my initial desire to understand Mexico is still unsatiated. It seems the more I know, the less I understand.

While writing this tome, I met many wonderful people who contributed to my intellectual development and continuously provided immeasurable support. Although there are too many people to acknowledge, I am eternally grateful for the extensive help and support from the following people and institutions: Diana Alarcon; Sabas Alarcon; Sandra Alarcon; Priciliano Bernal; Angela Cornell; Heidi Davidson; Maury Foisy; Chuck Fox; Steve Fox; Fulgencio Menez; Rosemary Galli; Celso Garrido; Julio Alfredo Genel Garcia; Mel Gurtov; Dariush Haghihat; Frank R. Haines; Nora Hamilton; Michael Kearney; Margarita Mazzotti; Maria Lewis Merin; Barbara Metzger; Julio Rodulfo Moctezuma Cid; Carlos Morera Camacho; J. Taylor Phillips, III; Enrique Quintana; Eduardo Turrent Diaz; Mohamed Wader; Aron Weiss; Eduardo Zepeda; Banco de Mexico; The Department of Political Science at the University of California, Riverside; and The University of California. I would especially like to thank Carlos Tello; Roger Bartra; Alejandro Alvarez; Gabriel Mendoza; and the Alarcon family; as well as my parents, Neil and Judy White. A special thanks also to Todd Baldwin, Ralph Salmi, and Taylor & Francis. Above all, I would like to express my sincerest gratitude to Ron Chilcote for his unwavering inspirational encouragement and critical support. Without Ron's support this book would have remained a manuscript. Although I received incalculable support from these collegial associates and friends, I alone am responsible for any and all errors, inaccuracies, and omissions in this book.

Russell N. White

Introduction

Many American academics, analysts, pundits, and scholars have decided that the nationalization of the Mexican banks was a historical act of limited significance. On the contrary, the nationalization of the banks in Mexico has tremendous contemporary significance. Significance "for whom?" one might ask.

Understanding the nationalization of the banks is important for anyone desiring to know more about what is going on in Mexico right now. Finance, particularly in Mexico, has been and is central to the Government's conception and selection of developmental programs. Simply put, the ability or inability to channel financial resources can facilitate or decimate economic growth and development. Not only has the decision to nationalize the banks had a major impact on the definition of the financial structure in Mexico, but it also has affected and will affect the power structure within Mexico. That is why the Mexican government announced in May 1990 that it would privatize the banks.

The decision to privatize the same banking system that was nationalized in 1982 exemplifies the power structure within Mexico. One could argue that Mexico was simply following suit with the rest of the world, manifesting a preference for the private sector. At a less simplistic level, the privatization reflected the power of the financial fraction of capital and also reflected the decision to fortify a new developmental schema or paradigm that focuses on international exports and international competition.

The internationalization of the Mexican economy is an economic reality. The integration of the Mexican economy with the U.S. economy is becoming more concrete every day. American companies are moving production of everything, from autos to computers to agricultural commodities, south of the border. In fact, the U.S., Canadian, and Mexican governments are negotiating a Free Trade Accord (FTA) to form a North American Common Market. Both the nationalization and the privatization of the banks in Mexico are important in this respect because the structure of the Mexican financial system will greatly affect the integration process. The ability of financial groups to restructure organizational configurations to include financial institutions will provide these groups with the power to concentrate and centralize economic control much faster and with much greater efficiency than previously anticipated. Not only will financial groups regain previous abilities to prioritize financial resources for their groups, but they will also be able to use financial instruments and resources to conquer export markets. For example, we will probably see more Mexican companies purchasing U.S. companies (e.g., Vitro). In short, Mexican financial groups will again resemble the Keiretsu of Japan and the Chaebol of Korea. The resurrection of the integration of financial institutions and productive organizations will not supersede the primacy of production, but it will greatly transform the productive structure.

My work on the nationalization of the Mexican banks involved several years of research and writing. I utilized primarily Mexican sources and materials for my work because I believe that most American scholars have used American conceptions and American paradigms and American sources to analyze and understand Mexico. In the process, most American scholars and pundits have not only misunderstood Mexico, but they have also overlooked the significance of the nationalization of the Mexican banks.

Mexico is unique and Mexican history is even more unique. Knowing Mexican history is very important in understanding the nationalization of the banks; I have tried to synthesize a number of important works and ideas to present readers with a Mexican perspective on Mexican history and how it relates to Mexican finance and the history of finance capital in Mexico. Obviously, a lot has been written on Mexican history, but the majority of works in print have ignored Mexican finance.

When I conceived this project, my initial idea was to write an analytical history of Mexican banks and ascertain the relevance of Mexican financial history vis-à-vis the decision to nationalize the banks. The scope of the project was broadened to encompass a historical analysis of the transformation of commercial, bank, and finance capital. In examining the formation and metamorphosis of capital, I also widened the theoretical significance of the project.

The theoretical significance of my work evolved from a simple examination of the role of finance capital vis-à-vis the nationalization of the banks to a theoretical analysis of relations between capital and an analysis of the relations between the State and commercial, bank, and finance capital. By examining the role of the State in relation to capital, I have attempted to address important political conceptions about the nature of the State and the nature of class fractions of capital. By incorporating theoretical issues surrounding the Mexican State and the relations of class fractions to the State, I have attempted to surmount the problems associated with many ideological and dogmatic analyses of the development of Mexican capitalism and the nationalization of Mexican banks.

This book specifically addresses the issue of intraclass political-economic power. Examining the power of the bourgeoisie and more specifically the power and struggles between various fractions of the bourgeoisie provides a very interesting and theoretically rich area for investigation. I am particularly interested in examining the development, maturation, and power of the financial fraction of the bourgeoisie.

Beginning with the classic work of Rudolf Hilferding (1981), *Finance Capital,* the financial fraction of the bourgeoisie has been commonly referred to as finance capital. The genesis, development, and definition of finance capital is a controversial subject, deserving careful theoretical and material examination. In the case of Mexico, the transformation of bank and industrial capital into finance capital is very important in terms of understanding the nationalization of the banks. Although a thorough historical analysis of the development of Mexican finance capital is beyond the realm of this work, a concise theoretical and material analysis will suffice for our purposes of general discussion and conceptual clarification.

The general conception of finance capital was advanced by Rudolph Hilferding (1981). Hilferding defined finance capital as the unification or fusion of industrial, commercial, and bank capital during a particular stage in the development of capitalism (p. 220). Cartelization, capital markets, and the increasing use of banks to create and channel credit and money capital resulted in the fusion or merger of bank capital and industrial capital. Finance capital, the fusion of bank and industrial capital, results from and perpetuates the domination of banks (p. 226). Moreover, the specificity of capital as eliminated with the genesis of finance capital. As Hilferding noted, partial forms of capital are unified. Banks, as intermediaries, use loan capital and fictitious capital to create the appearance of money capital by endowing finance capital with the form of bank capital. Gradually, independent branches of production are unified with the hegemony of finance capital (pp. 234–235).

Hilferding's conception of finance capital has been criticized for its theoretical and material inadequacies (Bottomore, 1981; Castañeda, 1982; Hussein, 1976).[1] The most important limitation in Hilferding's definition of finance capital was his use of an abstract theoretical construction to define the specificity of a social structure. It is important to remember that finance capital is a fraction of a social class—the bourgeoisie—and that classes and class fractions are dynamic social relationships, constantly in a state of dynamic transition: forming, combining, recombining, and reproducing conditions of existence. As a theoretical construct, the concept of finance capital is limited to the theoretical world of abstraction. A historical examination and analysis of the specific forms and relations characterizing the reproduction of capital and social class relations can provide a more realistic understanding of the correlation of forces as expressed in the State and the hegemonic bloc.

The genesis of finance capital is related to the development of capitalist relations of production and the corollary combined and uneven transformation of usury, merchant, commercial, bank, and industrial capital. In Hilferding's (1981) words:

> Bank capital was the negation of usurer's capital and is itself negated by finance capital. The latter is the synthesis of usurer's and bank capital and it appropriates to itself the fruits of social production at an infinitely higher stage of economic development. (p. 226)

The fusion or merger process characterizing the formation of finance capital has evolved unevenly. Distinct forms of fusion have appeared, exemplifying the diversity of relationships between bank, industrial, and commercial capital. This complex development has been manifested in quantitative and qualitative juridical relations (e.g., active and passive stock ownership, interlocking directorates) and different valorization, decision making, and organizational configurations (e.g., integrated financial groups, bank-dominated, and industry-dominated entities).[2] The political organization and expression of finance capital's political interests vis-à-vis the State and other class fractions is another very important aspect of the development of finance capital in Mexico.

The political organization of a class fraction does not necessarily coincide with the economic delineation of a fraction. Contradictions can in fact divide a class fraction politically in terms of a coherent organization or in relation to other fractions, classes, or the State. Class fractions can also coalesce around particular issues or during conjunctural periods of crisis, for instance, the nationalization of the banks. Class fractions are in essence a reflection of their social class and hence demonstrate periods of unity and periods of disunity. Class fractions, in sum, are fluid social relations that manifest the dynamism of the social structure.

Class, as herein used, refers to a concretely situated group of individual human beings interacting in dynamic social relationships that are objective and subjective. Historically defined, social classes are constituted in terms of the relation to the means of production, that is, the total process of social production. Objectively defined, a social class occupies structurally delineated positions or locations, according to economic-legal ownership, control of physical means of production, relation to extraction of surplus-value, control of labor-power, family and class trajectory, and various structural elements of everyday life. Subjectively defined, a class is characterized by a sense of community or homogeneity, class consciousness or self-awareness, political organization, and class struggle. These qualities are manifested at different levels and to different degrees in the everyday experiences of social classes. Thus, *klasse an sich* and *klasse fur sich* can be dichotomized for purposes of abstract analysis, but in the material world of social classes, these two distinctions are intricately interrelated. In a similar manner, in terms of levels of analysis, one can define classes in relation to the political, economic, and ideological levels, but classes must be comprehended in relation to the totality of social production, integrating subject and structure. Ultimately, therefore, a comprehensive understanding of specific class contours of a concrete social formation—especially a social formation characterized by a combined and unevenly developed country such as Mexico—necessitates a historical investigation of the concrete social formation, because classes are social relationships constantly in a state of dynamic transition, forming, combining, recombining, and reproducing conditions of existence.

Upon reviewing the theoretical and conceptual significance of classes and class fractions including finance capital, it becomes apparent that the nationalization of the banks was an extremely important development that permanently affected inter- and intraclass relations. President López Portillo's decision to nationalize the banks was a monumental decision that permanently transformed the Mexican social structure and indelibly redefined the politics of class fractions, ultimately affecting the delineation and definition of the accumulation model. By nationalizing the banks, finance capital lost the central institutional mechanism for valorizing capital. In addition, because of the juridical structure of finance capital, the banks often served as holding companies and as such, when the State assumed control and ownership of the banks, the State became the principal owner of the vast majority of corporate assets in Mexico.

The lack of published works on the nationalization of the banks in Mexico is very puzzling. Not only have American scholars failed to understand the significance of the Mexican financial structure, they have ignored it. The absence of published American books on the nationalization of the banks is particularly curious, given the number of books and articles devoted to the subject in Mexico. Throughout modern Mexican history, the development of the financial system has been closely linked with the State and the formation and transformation of finance capital. As a prominent Mexican intellectual noted, the decision to nationalize the banks revealed the most profound political and economic crisis in over fifty years.

The nationalization of the banks manifested the most serious crisis in postrevolutionary Mexico. The decision to nationalize the banks was interconnected with a power struggle to redefine Mexican development strategy. The nationalization is also important because it provides an opportunity to examine the theoretical relevance of concepts such as relative State autonomy in relation to class analysis. Above all, the nationalization crisis offers us an opportunity to examine critical strategic questions about the essential composition of the State and the utility of idealist conceptions of the State.

I have divided the book into three separate sections. Part One examines the empowerment of commercial-usury capital and the formation and transformation of bank capital and finance capital. The coincidence of interests between the State and the fraction of capital controlling the financial circuits defined the development of the productive structure and the distribution of the surplus product.

Part Two analyzes the crisis permeating the social structure and its implications for intraclass relations relative to State autonomy. This section examines various economic institutions and State policies within the context of political-economic power.

Part Three focuses on the nationalization of the banks and the postnationalization period. I look at the transformation of finance capital into the financial fraction of the bourgeoisie. Throughout the work, a comprehensive multilevel analysis is used, incorporating class analysis as a central component. Comparing different analyses of the nationalization of the banks, I reject a priori reductionist paradigms and stagnant ideological dogmatism. Instead I propose that the nationalization demonstrated the political ingenuity of the financial fraction of the bourgeoisie, and not the relative autonomy of the State nor the reproduction of the general interests of capital. That is, the nationalization of the banks and the postnationalization period manifested a political struggle within the power bloc to define and delineate a new accumulation model. Indeed, postnationalization events demonstrate that a new financial fraction had a major effect on the delineation of the financial circuits and the productive structure.

The postscript provides a brief descriptive analysis of the re-privatization of the banks that was initiated in May 1990. The re-privatization is very significant with regard to the questions surrounding finance capital, the financial fraction, and the newly legislated and legitimized financial group. The re-privatization of the banks in conjunction with the legitimization of financial groups will most likely have very important consequences in terms of the integration of Mexico with the United States and Canada. Undoubtedly, the genesis of financial groups will substantially affect Mexico's power structure, future delineation of the State, and ultimately, its future development.

Notes

1. Criticisms have largely centered on the conflation of money capital and bank capital, periodization of finance capital as the ultimate phase of capitalism, attribution of dominance to bank capital in the fusion process characterizing finance capital; presupposition of the existence of coordinated group behavior, eurocentric perspective, absence of contradictions in the fusion–unity transition, and linear conceptualization of finance capital.

2. The three forms in which finance capital appears in Mexico (Castañeda, 1982) are delineated in the Appendix.

Part One
Definition and Development of the State/Capital Relationship

Chapter 1

Prerevolutionary Development of the Mexican Banking System

COMMERCIAL CAPITAL DURING THE COLONIAL PERIOD AND IMMEDIATE POSTINDEPENDENCE PERIOD

The historical relevance of the transformation of the Mexican social structure is extremely significant. It is significant because one cannot understand the nationalization of the banks without comprehending the historical dynamics of social class relations and the corollary interrelationship with the social structure. Simply put, the empowerment of commercial-usury capital and the development of bank capital are historically interconnected with the hegemonic power of finance capital.

Within the context of financial developments, our focus will begin with the Mexican colonial period and the formation and development of commercial-usury capital. During this period, capitalism and capitalist relations of production were constricted and traditional institutions and social relations were reinforced. In other words, a semifeudal social structure conditioned Mexican social relations and the social structure.

Throughout this period, the Church, supported by the Crown, became the most powerful economic corporation. Although the Church financed merchants, Church lending practices were largely based on señorial rentierism, supporting Church interests and simultaneously reinforcing the feudal fiscal system (Larvin, 1985, p. 67; Semo, 1973, p. 122).

Semifeudalist social relations were also extended as a result of territorial aspirations of Spanish nobility participating in the conquest and colonization of Mexico. Grand haciendas were often organized on the basis of precapitalist relations of production and valorization processes (e.g., peonage debt labor, rentierism; Felipe Leal & Rountree, 1982). After the second half of the sixteenth century, "the innumerable *haciendas, estancias, ganaderas, ingenios* and *obrajes* of the Church, and its lending capital that obligated practically all of the grand proprietors, constituted a powerful obstacle to the emergence of a local bourgeoisie" (Felipe Leal & Rountree, 1982, p. 116). At a global level, accumulated wealth extracted by the colonial system was transferred to Spain for conspicuous consumption rather than productive investment.

Regulation and regimentation of the colonial economy restricted the growth of internal commerce and industry. Regional economies tended to be dominated by local *hacendados,* miners, merchants, and individuals who often controlled more than one of these economic activities. Mercantile production thus developed at a relatively slower pace than did the sphere of circulation, because of the dynamics of social relations surrounding the extraction of surplus value.[2] Historically, there were two nonlinear phases characterizing the transformation of commercial capital, a nontransformative and a transformative stage.

Commercial-usury capital appeared in various forms during the first nontransformative phase. In Mexico City, the emergence of a commercial oligarchy was much better defined than in the provinces, mainly because of linkages with international commercial capital.[3] Capital accumulated by grand merchants was often used for speculative purposes and short-term high interest finance. In contrast, commercial-usury capital in the regional and local markets often appeared in "unitary forms," connected with feudal property and the colonial bureaucracy (Cockcroft, 1983, p. 41). Middle merchants controlled the regional and local distribution of goods and used accumulated capital to gradually participate in the sale and financing of regional level production. Thus, agricultural harvests were sometimes dependent on the financial resources of commercial-usury capital, as in the case of Puebla merchants and Veracruz cotton, with merchants performing a financial function similar to a *refaccionario* or lending bank.[4] In other instances, agricultural harvests were independently financed. Commercial-usury capital was sometimes also invested in mining, artisans, or decentralized production (Cockcroft, 1983, p. 178). These productive investments, however, tended to be confined to the local market. During this nontransformative phase, capital was generally invested to exploit and preserve a semifeudal regime rather than to promote and accelerate capitalist development (Cockcroft, 1983, p. 181). Thus, even though the formation of money capital was accelerated, the essential forms of production were not altered and the development of production was generally impeded.

During the second or transformative phase, commercial-usury capital was more directly enmeshed in the transformation of the social structure, that is, in the appearance and delineation of different fractions of capital. However, the transformative character of commercial-usury capital tended to be constricted because of the embryonic nature of Mexican capitalism and the combined and uneven articulation of different modes of production. This latter phase began to occur after 1750 (Semo, 1973, p. 169) with the advent of the Bourbon reforms, independence, the liberal reforms, and the Porfiriato. (Subsequent portions of this chapter will examine each of these elements in greater detail.) Political-economic developments affecting the Church exemplified the divergent nature of these two contradictory phases.

The Church was an important element in the colonial and immediate postcolonial financial circuit (Greenow, 1983; Schwaller, 1985). Churches accumulated large amounts of capital and reinforced some aspects of the colonial structure. Loans were generally secured on the basis of mortgage guarantees and were used for relatively unproductive investments in rural and urban properties. Lending operations progressed to the point that the Church became a major property owner.[5] Church financial hegemony was intricately interrelated with privileges granted by the Crown and a tremendous amount of capital was amassed through donations, sale of services, and interest payments. The Church also benefited from the diezmo, monopoly of lands, management of education and hospitals, indigenous indoctrination, and the political control of rural zones (Cardoso, 1983, p. 29; de la Peña, 1975, pp. 73–74). Ultimately, the power of the Church was severely affected by colonial politics as exemplified by the Bourbon reforms.

From 1765 to 1771, José de Gálvez implemented measures constituting the Bourbon reforms.[6] The geographical division of the colony into *intendencias* was a particularly important measure, affecting political-economic social relations. The political and economic power of the Church and grand merchants was weakened and the political-economic power of regional commercial-usury capital was strengthened. New free trade policies affected distribution and credit patterns.

> During the 1780s the colony received an unprecedented influx of European goods, and with its markets soon saturated both prices and profits tumbled. The very pattern of distribution changed: Mexico City's *almaceneros* dealt directly with provincial traders. Moreover, a new breed of traveling dealers, who bought at Veracruz and sold wherever they found a market, sprang into existence. The lines of credit also changed. The Veracruz merchants obtained their imports from Spanish shippers who, financed in many cases by foreign trading houses, did not expect immediate case payment. By 1807 Abad y Queipo estimated that Mexican merchants owed overseas traders up to twenty million pesos, a debt on which they were charged a 15 per cent discount. (Brading, 1971, p. 115)

The financial power of the Church began to deteriorate. It was weakened by the imposition of the *Real Cédula* (royal decree) taxing real estate exchanges and the capital charges of the *Capellanías y Obras Pías*. Much more devastating was the partial implementation of the 1804 *Ley de Consolidación de Vales Reales*. The law forced the Church to sell most of its real estate and transfer Church loans to the Crown (Lavrin, 1985, p. 36). These extremely important changes affecting Church power also had tremendous implications for the social structure. The advent of Independence also affected social structure dynamics.

The demise of colonial ties created a political-economic power vacuum. The revolutionary break with Spain affected the relative power of important colonial institutions and reinforced the sociopolitical economic bases of tributary despotism. At the same time that efforts were made to consolidate the national political-economic structure there were intense internal struggles to fortify the power of commercial capital. A new period of original accumulation appeared with the fortification of the *latifundium* and hacienda systems, the theft of national lands, colonization of *tierras baldías,* and enormous speculation on the part of commercial-usury capital (de la Peña, 1975, pp. 98–99). The development of productive forces was also impeded by the destruction of the productive base, the dispersion and annihilation of workers, political instability, and the consequent economic disequilibrium (de la Peña, 1975, p. 97).

Although structural barriers constricting the formation and differentiation of classes and class fractions were reinforced, regional commercial capital (and in some instances, grand commercial capital) obtained sufficient political-economic space to transcend traditional economic sectors. New spheres of accumulation were initiated and commercial capital simultaneously fomented transformation of the social structure. Decreasing commercial profits were also partly responsible for this sociostructural transition. For example, many merchants located near mining communities extended credit to the community and financially supported mining operations. The unsuccessful ventures of many silver banks decreased the amount of available credit and *aviadores,* often merchants, filled the void.

> Many an aviador by progressive foreclosure found himself the owner of first a refining mill and then a mine. In mining, as distinct from refining, some aviadores took shares in mines from the outset. They then participated in overall profits rather than charging a discount on the silver. They still, however, received the normal commercial profit on the materials they supplied. (Brading, 1971, p. 150)

Thus, the velocity of transitionary developments was dependent on specific regional socioeconomic structures, that is, the transformative character of commercial capital was much more apparent in Monterrey than in Chiapas.

In synthesis, the transformative character of commercial-usuary capital was indirectly linked to changes in the socioeconomic structure. Extension of the realm of operations for commercial-usury capital was a nonlinear asymmetrical development interconnected with market dynamics, technology, liquidity, and most important, demise of the colonial system.

THE MEXICAN STATE

The Mexican State is a complex amalgamation of class and institutional mechanisms and interests. The State as herein used, refers to the set of public-political institutions that represent, organize, articulate, and implement the policies, activities, and interests of the "general will." Although the State appears to be institutionally separated from the dominant classes and class fractions, exemplifying the general will, the specific confines of the relationship between the dominant classes and the capitalist State—the State and civil society—is dependent on the gestation of historical factors. Thus, the State is not an abstract "thing" or "entity" but a material-institutional expression of historical contradictions manifested in distinct historical forms of class conflict within a concrete social formation. Hence, the relative autonomy of the State and the State itself, are historically dynamic reflections of the civil society manifesting the unequal interests and power of classes and class fractions. Therefore, the State must not be conceived in either structural or instrumental terms, but instead must be conceived in its historical materiality as an arena of class conflict within a concrete social formation. In other words, the historical transformation of classes and class fractions can exercise direct and indirect power vis-à-vis the social State. The State also has the potential to utilize its constantly changing relative autonomy in relation to social classes. A concrete example of the class–State dynamic was the nationalization of the Mexican banks. Now that I have conceptually defined the State, I will examine the historical development of the Mexican State in its various historical manifestations.

The immediate post–Independence social formation (1821 to 1854) was politically anarchistic. During this period the State did not exercise central or national power. The State manifested a political, economic, and ideological dispersion of power. Political independence in 1821 did not bring forth a definitively hegemonic fraction. Rather, an unstable equilibrium existed between progressive elements (doctors, lawyers, small rural proprietors, and provincial merchants) and regressive elements (clergy, grand merchants, and grand landowners; Felipe Leal, 1975, p. 9). Although the State existed as a formal juridical-political entity, there was no apparent socioeconomic governing base. In response to this situation, the military assumed a strategic role. As is often the case, the military was not an objective governing force. Throughout this period, the military tended to support the clergy and grand landowners. Nevertheless, the military was far from unified, as manifested in the almost constant political instability. In contrast with the general instability characterizing the post–Independence period, the liberal-oligarchic State manifested historical changes of the social formation.

The liberal-oligarchic State was consolidated from 1867 to 1914 (Felipe Leal, 1973). The eventual transformation of the social formation and the articulation of different modes of production contributed to the consolidation of a liberal-oligarchic State. This transformation resulted from several important events, including the 1850s Reform and the expulsion of the French. State power was increasingly centralized and concentrated in the executive, whereas the legislature, judiciary, states, and citizenry lost autonomous power. During the consolidation phase, the State was actively involved in the simultaneous genesis and demise of different social relations of production.[7]

The liberal-oligarchic State was an institutional manifestation of the contradictory unity of the power bloc and the dynamism of the social formation. These contradictions were expressed in diverse forms at specific moments throughout the consolidation and demise of the liberal-oligarchic State. Nevertheless, there were at least six general expressions of the contradictory unity of the power bloc and its constituent elements (Felipe Leal, 1975, pp. 16–30). The first expression of the contradictory unity was from 1867 to 1876, when a parliamentary regime exercised governmental power and the power bloc was composed of mine owners, *comerciantes* (merchants and tradesman) and *terratenientes* (large landowners). Terratenientes exercised a hegemonic position. The second expression was a hegemonic crisis from 1876 to 1880 when the State lost power to local and regional oligarchs. The third expression of the contradictory unity was manifested in the recomposition of the power bloc in 1880: Terratenientes lost their hegemonic position within the power bloc, an imperialist fraction assumed control of the hegemonic position, and the regime form changed to an executive dictatorship. The fourth expression occurred in 1890 with another alteration in the composition of the power bloc: Terratenientes experienced a transformation and diversification, a fraction of the Mexican bourgeoisie joined the power bloc, and comerciantes were displaced from the power bloc. The fifth expression appeared in 1908 with the expulsion of the traditional fraction of the terratenientes from the power bloc. The sixth expression, from 1908 to 1914, was the disintegration of the power bloc and the destruction of the liberal-oligarchic State.

At a less abstract level, the constant instability of the postindependence State reflected a critical hegemonic crisis. It was not until Maximilian's demise that presidents Juárez, Díaz, and González initiated conciliatory and cooptive measures to incorporate dominant opposition fractions within the spheres of State power, thereby increasing the legitimacy of the State and consolidating State power. More specifically, the integration of dominant opposition factions within the power bloc was largely a reflection of Díaz's political machinations. Díaz's use of conciliatory–cooptive policies to consolidate opposing dominant interests ameliorated the hegemonic crisis. Now that I have addressed the political aspect of class relations vis-à-vis the State, I shall examine the regulatory role of the State in terms of the Porfirian banking system.

THE PORFIRIAN BANKING SYSTEM

Prior to the development of the Porfirian banking system, credit was a scarce commodity. There was a general absence of credit institutions, a problem compounded by capital flight. Banks were basically nonexistent. The closest thing to a bank was the commercial house, which extended credit on titles and mortgages; participated in commercial paper discounts; received deposits; and in some instances, issued specie. Credit was also available from comerciantes, speculators, usurers, and the Church.

From 1830 to 1860 comerciantes began to consolidate their political and economic dominance. Their dominance was enhanced as a result of their control of external and internal commercial circuits, as well as the demise of colonial consulates and the decline of Church power. Mercantile activity enabled merchants to accumulate large amounts of liquid capital in a relatively short period of time. Merchant capital, as in the colonial period, was invested in numerous lucrative endeavors, particularly interest-yielding investments. With the progression of time and the accumulation of capital, merchant capital tended to invest in associations with hacendados or miners. In some instances, merchants extended their operational spheres to include agriculture and mining. Merchant capital was nevertheless generally invested in commercial activities.

One of the most lucrative means of accumulating capital was extension of loans to conservative and liberal governments. Loans to the State often empowered merchants to extract important political-economic privileges. Privileges included high interest rates (as high as 24 percent per month), import permits, fiscal exemptions, leases for *cases de moneda,* and temporary control of particular state monopolies (Cardoso, 1983, p. 170). Successive regimes were forced to solicit loans from grand comerciantes and extend concessions to obtain credit.[8]

Regional commercial accumulation was often linked to personal or economic relations with regional oligarchs or state governors. Both national and regional comerciantes (e.g., public officials, hacendados, and incipient capitalists) often created dependent client relationships. Monterrey typified a region where commercial activity and accumulation shaped and was shaped by industrial capital.[9]

> Initially, financial resources for investment derived from individual entrepreneurs. Local sources of credit came from the large merchants who maintained rudimentary banking facilities in their stores. The commercial house of the Hernandez, Rivero, Armendaiz and Milmo families furnished most of the city's credit, savings, and loan resources. Sensitive to the investment opportunities in Monterrey and exhaustion of their own assets, several major regionmonto merchants organized or participated in the establishment of Monterrey's financial institutions. (Saragoza, 1978, p. 83).

It appears, therefore, that there were many similarities at the national and regional levels between comerciantes and the respective levels of government. At both the regional and national levels, State autonomy vis-à-vis comerciantes was largely restricted. The State was politically and economically dependent on the financial power of comerciantes. A brief examination of the history and development of the Banco de Avío further illustrates the point.

Creation of the Banco de Avío, the first State industrial promotion bank, was significant, given the prevailing political-economic instability of the State. Although the bank was relatively insignificant in economic terms, its creation and operations were politically important because the success of the bank reflected State instability and political-economic class struggles within and outside of the State.

The bank exemplified efforts to expand the role of the State and stimulate industrial economic development. Bank operations reflected structural limitations restricting the development of industrial capital (Potash, 1983). Although the bank was supposed to stimulate technological change by promoting industrial development, political reality transformed the bank into an ideological instrument.

The bank was constantly the object of struggles between liberals, conservatives, and artisans. Liberals saw the bank as a political instrument of the governing conservatives and as a material threat to their political-economic interests and laissez-faire policies. Conservatives conceived of the bank as a means of augmenting economic growth and the national welfare. Artisans thought the bank was a government tool to restrict textile imports and therein subordinate artisans to the interests of incipient industrialists. Political-economic controversy was compounded by several factors, including constant political instability, an inadequate supply of goods and factors of production, and an inadequate infrastructure. Although the bank survived a precarious existence for several years, it ultimately failed because State autonomy was nonexistent.

Fragmentation of power characterized the liberal-oligarchic Mexican State during this period. The State was a national entity only in the political-juridical sense (Felipe Leal, 1972, p. 56). Not only did the State lack effective control, there was actually numerous semiautonomous local, state, and economic powers.

Throughout the bank's operational history, the State was weak, dependent, and constantly subject to oscillating and momentary political currents. The success of the bank, in terms of fomenting industrial development, was largely structured by the political and economic struggles occurring within and outside the State. The bank was an institutional manifestation of political-economic struggles between various strata. Politically, the bank was unable to transform the unproductive power bloc composed largely of externally oriented commercial capitalists and hacendados. Economically, the bank and its project were unfeasible in terms of the existing relations constituting the prevailing model of accumulation: "It was a project that was launched when no real social force was interested in decisively breaking the productive and accumulative structure predominating during the epoch" (Cardoso, 1983, p. 75).

During the second half of the nineteenth century, the emergence of the capitalists mode of production (de la Peña, 1975, pp. 156–162) stimulated rapid economic growth. The country was increasingly incorporated into the global market and the international division of labor. At the same time, internal regional markets were integrated by several factors, including the progressive expansion of an exchange economy; the expansion of the railroad; integration and transformation of mercantile capital, industrial capital, bank capital, and a proletariat; foreign investment; and the general diffusion of the capitalist mode of production. These socioeconomic changes were substantially affected by the liberal reforms (1855 and 1856), and the restoration of the Republic (1867). These two events unleashed radical changes. Nationalization of ecclesiastic property was also a major contributing element through restriction of Church participation in the credit system and the consequent reduction in the availability of credit.

The Liberal Reform was more than an aggression by parts of the landlord-merchant-industrial bourgeoisie against Church properties and traditions (tithes, diezmo, etc.). It also delivered a telling blow to artisan corporations (guilds), accelerating the separation of artisans from their means of production and their incorporation into the textile industry's wage-labor force. Most significantly, the Reform laid the basis for the final reduction of the peasantry, dispossessing them of their lands and converting them into "free" wage laborers or debt peons. It thus laid the foundations in both urban and rural areas for a speedier development of capitalist forms of production. (Cockcroft, 1983, p. 80)

Finally, victory over the French and the restoration of the Republic enabled Liberals to consolidate a political coalition that engendered relative political "stability," therein promoting modern capitalist development and reorganization of the credit system (Cockcroft, 1983, p. 80).

The Mexican banking and financial system was archaic and inadequate prior to and during the initial years of the Porfiriato. From 1864 until 1880, there were only three private commercial credit institutions in operation: El Banco de Londres y México, El Banco de Santa Eulalia, and El Banco Mexicano.

El Banco de Londres y México was founded in 1864, during Maximilian's reign by two Englishmen (Guilbert Newbold and Robert Geddes) as a branch of the London Bank of Mexico and South America, Ltd. The Chihuahua state legislature authorized Francisco MacManus, a North American, to charter the Banco de San Eulalia in 1875.[10] The Banco Méxicano was also initiated in Chihuahua in 1875. The Chihuahua state legislature granted a concession to mine owners Francisco Félix Maceyra, Antonio Asúnsolo, and Luis Terraza.[11] It was not until after these three banks had been established that the Porfirian banking system began to experience a rapid period of institutionalized growth.

The Porfirian banking system can be delineated into three different stages (Sánchez Martínez, 1983, p. 60). The first was a period of formation and expansion from 1880 to 1897; the second was a period of consolidation from 1897 to 1907; and the third was a period of crisis and decay from 1907 to 1910.

During the formation and expansion of the Porfirian banking system, fourteen emission banks and one mortgage bank were established. Banks were granted concessions under heterogeneous terms and regulatory stipulations. For instance, the federal government authorized a French-Egyptian company to establish the Banco Nacional Méxicano in 1881.[12] The concession stipulated that the bank was allowed to issue bills and establish agencies and branches throughout the country. The concession also stipulated that federal government offices would only accept bills issued by the Banco Nacional Méxicano and the Monte de Piedad. In addition, the bank was exempt from numerous fiscal charges and was awarded the power to manage government exchange transactions, charges, and funds. The bank was allowed to send foreign stockholders tax-free dividends and interest remunerations. In exchange, the State obtained an annual credit line. It is important to note that bank capital, through the Banco Nacional Méxicano, displaced speculative-usurious comerciantes and allowed the State to establish a substantial line of credit at or below market interest rates.

The relationship between the State and the Banco Nacional Méxicano marked a transition that was gradually occurring throughout the economy. Comerciantes integrated with mine owners and hacendados. Bank capital played an increasingly important role in the financial circuit, displacing usurious and speculative commercial capital. Thus, the Banco Nacional Méxicano, a bank whose original capital was four-fifths foreign, was essentially granted the privileges enjoyed by a central bank in exchange for conceding credit to the State. The new arrangement between the State and Banco Nacional transformed State political-financial dependency from commercial-usury national capital to foreign bank capital.

A global economic crisis debilitated the banking system in 1884. The crisis caused a panic when depositors exchanged bank paper for coin, thus decapitalizing the banks. A casualty of the panic was the insolvent Nacional Monte de Piedad. Government officials consequently determined that both the economy and the government needed the services of a secure, permanent, and large financial institution. The end result was the merger of the Banco Nacional Méxicano and the Mercantil Agricola e Hipotecario (a mortgage bank, constituted largely with Spanish capital) into the Banco Nacional de México in April 1884. The State granted the bank a concession in May 1884, stipulating that federal government offices would only accept money issued by the bank. The bank, in turn, was obligated to manage the public debt and provide the treasury with an annual credit line.

The Banco Nacional de México was able to acquire a competitive advantage in the financial circuit, vis-à-vis other banks, as a result of its ability to act as the financial agent of the Mexican government. As the official depository for foreign debt, the bank capitalized on the float. The bank also subscribed to a portion of government bonds, and profited from the sale in the international market. It was also able to capitalize on the distribution of credits obtained in foreign markets and placed in the national market. Thus,the Banco Nacional de México intervened at three important points in the financial circuit: (a) as an intermediary in negotiations between the government and bank syndicates; (b) as a receptor of loans; and (c) as a source of lending capital. In addition, the bank profited from the difference between the constantly depreciated peso and international transactions made in gold.

A few days after the creation of the Banco Nacional de México, the federal government issued the new commercial code containing regulatory clauses pertaining to the banking industry. The new code was rigid; in contrast, privileges granted to the Banco de México were much more flexible.

The paradoxical developments surrounding the emergence of the Banco Nacional and the regulatory rigidity of the commercial code generated a prolonged debate between supporters of uncontrolled emission and supporters of the Banco Nacional emission monopoly. Banco Nacional supporters argued that there was a distinction between the practice of banking and monetary emission. Supporters of the group led by Banco de Londres (defending uncontrolled emission) argued that banking and monetary emission were mutually dependent banking functions. Juridically, the federal concession given to the Banco Nacional was unconstitutional because it promoted a monopoly. The Banco Nacional monopoly enabled it to earn a disproportionate high return on its capital (Rosenzweig, 1974, pp. 809–813). The debate was gradually defused when the Banco de Londres, leader of the group supporting uncontrolled emissions, purchased the concession of the Banco de Empleados and thereby became an emission bank. The federal government also recognized the emission rights of the Chihuahua banks. In an effort to mollify contradictory interests, an ambiguous commercial code was created in 1889.

The commercial code of 1889 was an attempt to ameliorate contradictory and potentially destabilizing confrontations between the State and a section of the newly emergent fraction of bank capital, and within the newly emergent fraction/strata of bank capital.[13] The new code prohibited additional regulatory bank legislation until a study was completed examining the history and practices of Mexican banking institutions, and banking legislation in Europe and the United States. Furthermore, the code stipulated that the establishment of future credit institutions needed prior authorization of the executive and the congress. The banks were free to operate in accordance with previous concession contracts, whereas no additional banking legislation was passed until 1897. In the meantime, seven new provincial banks were granted concessions (Cardoso, 1983, p. 408).

The establishment of provincial banks during the 1890s reflected the dynamics of political-economic processes at the regional and local levels. Hacendados, *henequeros* (henequen farmers), mine owners, and incipient industrialists had accumulated increasingly large amounts of capital and at the same time extended the realm of accumulation to include other sectors, sometimes in collaboration with investors from other sectors. A process of capital concentration, centralization, and differentiation was occurring. Valentín Rivero, owner of an important Monterrey commercial house, simultaneously managed a branch of the Banco Nacional de México, conducted quasi-banking operations in his store, and was a major investor in the Banco Mercantil (Saragoza, 1978, p. 113). In a similar manner, at the same time that many important Monterrey commercial houses (e.g., Milmo, Armendaiz, Hernández, and Trevino) continued to accept interest-bearing deposits and extend short-term credits, larger groups (e.g., the Garza-Sada "Cervecería Group" rapidly used capital accumulated from commercial enterprises to invest in banking. "Garza Sada and his cohorts were notably present in the formation of the city's banks . . . " (Saragoza, 1978, p. 102). Prior to 1890, 11 of the 12 elite families in Monterrey accumulated their capital in commerce, mining, or sugar refining. Between 1890 and 1910, 7 of the 12 elite families extended the sphere of accumulation to include banking or finance (Saragoza, 1978, p. 131).

> Thus, the availability of capital proved crucial to the merchants' ability to augment their commercial hegemony and to initiate or collaborate in new industrial adventures. The success of those efforts enhanced the advantageous economic position of Monterrey's merchants. The traders' influence and manipulation of local finance institutions and credit facilitated further investment and diversification of interests. (Saragoza, 1978, pp. 257–258)

The second phase (1897 to 1907) of the Porfirian banking system was a period of consolidation and specialization for the banking industry. This phase was initiated with the passage of the general law of credit institutions in March 1897. The law was an attempt by the federal government to regulate and standardize the establishment and operations of emission banks, mortgage banks, and refaccionario banks. The primary objective was to standardize bank concessions.

Secretary of Finance Limantour obtained congressional consent to write the law. He constructed a commission, composed of three lawyers, two financiers, and a representative from the Banco de Londres. Limantour was simultaneously obligated to conduct formal negotiations with representatives of the Banco Nacional in regard to a June 1896 law authorizing the establishment of emission banks in the states and territories. In exchange for accepting the law, the bank obtained an extension of its concession-contract for an additional fifteen years, and in turn extended an additional 500 million peso line of credit to the State without securing any special guarantees. The Banco de Londres also took advantage of the situation and obtained an extension of its concession and authorization to increase its capital to 100 million pesos.

There were essentially three elements constituting the 1897 law. First, the law renewed executive power to authorize the extension of bank concessions. Second, it specified various operational requirements for each of the three types of banks. A pluralistic system was initiated for emission banks. The Banco Nacional was allowed to issue up to three times the amount of its existing capital, whereas the other emission banks were restricted to emitting no more than a specified proportion of their existing capital or precious metals. The Banco Nacional and the Banco de Londres were also allowed to conduct operations throughout Mexico, whereas the remaining emission banks were restricted to conducting their operations in a specific region, state, or territory and could not circulate their bills beyond the local area of emission. The law renewed the Banco Nacional's privilege to operate as the government bank. Finally, it was stipulated that any emission bank could exercise commercial banking operations for a period not to exceed six months. Mortgage banks provided long-term credit for up to 40 years and refaccionario banks supplied intermediate term credit for up to two years.[14] The third element of the 1897 general law also attempted to promote expansion of banking establishments throughout the country. Bank capital, bank shares, and bank dividends were exempted from federal and local taxes for those banks that were the first to obtain a concession in a jurisdiction where there we no other bank branches in operation.

In essence, the 1897 law was promulgated in the interests of promoting a national credit system with specific types of credit institutions to satisfy short, intermediate, and long-term credit needs of different economic sectors. The objective was to efficiently support an expansive economy. The juridical and regulatory intentions, however, must be differentiated from the actual results. As noted by Rosenzweig (1974, p. 819), it was peculiar that banking laws designed to clarify legal and public policy questions were in fact transformed into negotiating instruments to obtain and concede political-economic privileges to specific banks. The transformation of laws into negotiating instruments raises a question as to State autonomy vis-à-vis banking establishments. (This question will be addressed in greater detail in the last section of this chapter.) It is apparent that the regulatory role of the State was anything but objective. The regulatory role of the State reflected the political-economic power of specific factions of bank capital as compared with other factions of bank capital. Another manifestation of this fact was that the law, written by representatives of major banks, was based on a system of preexisting privileges for particular foreign-financial groups. Secretary of Hacienda Limantour expressed the dynamics of the system very well:

> The center of our diverse banks, is and should be the Banco Nacional de México, everyday we should make it stronger and more powerful, and more perfect, through this power and the force of our banking system. (Sánchez Martínez, 1983, p. 70)

The second phase of the Porfirian banking system was expansive. Banking activity was one of the most lucrative and fastest growing sectors of the economy. Tremendous profits were accumulated as a result of laws that guaranteed state privileges, protection, and minimal regulation. Most of the banks established in this period were commercial-emission banks.[15] Emission banks tended to make loans on the basis of political privileges and connections and tended to ignore stipulations in the 1897 general law concerning the amount of emissions, duration of loans, and so on.

A disproportionate number of the banks authorized to initiate operations during this period were emission banks based in the provinces.[16] A natural problem emerged. Mexico City banks controlled the majority of circulation capital. This phenomenon developed as a result of several factors, including the circulatory privileges previously conceded to the two emission banks and the consequent restriction of state bank currency, and the concentrated proportion of commercial activity in Mexico City.[17] In 1895, for instance, the Banco Nacional, the Banco de Londres, and the Banco Internacional Hipotecario (primarily owned by British, British-French, and North American capital) controlled more than 66 percent of bank capital. The Banco Nacional and the Banco de Londres, alone, issued 80 percent of the bills in circulation (Sánchez Martínez, 1983, p. 81). Both of these Mexico City banks effectively controlled the circulation of state bank bills, which were thereby rendered valueless and discounted or accumulated in large quantities and presented to state banks for immediate payment in metal. The first measure restricted the circulation and valuation of state bank bills, whereas the second and third measures negatively affected state bank liquidity and operations.

The proliferation of state emission banks after the promulgation of the 1897 law affected power relationships. State banks began to exercise an increasing amount of political and economic power as the number of state banks increased and state banks formed alliances. The power of state banks also increased as a result of the creation of the Banco Central Méxicano (jointly owned by foreign bank capital and associated state banks).[18] Another factor was the signing of agreements at the first bankers' meeting (1904). State bank power was increased by a plan incorporating various prostate bank elements, for example, par exchange (Rosenzweig, 1974, p. 828).

A specialized credit system, as intended in the 1897 general law, did not develop, and regulatory problems became a de facto norm. Although the 1897 law did create a national banking system, composed of emission, mortgage, and refaccionario banks, bank activities were often extended beyond legal operational boundaries. Thus, some emission banks extended long-term credit to the agricultural sector. This practice was partially due to the mortgage and refaccionario banks' preferential concession of loans to the larger haciendas. Emission banks also tended to roll over short-term credit, therein extending intermediate and long-term credit. In a similar manner, mortgage and refaccionario banks often functioned as commercial banks, providing short-term credit for industrial purposes. The new law inadequately addressed important considerations and affected the balance of power between state and national banks. Improper regulatory oversight resulted in increasingly apparent contradictions and power struggles among the various banks and bankers.

The third and ultimate phase of the Porfirian banking system was characterized by crisis and decay. In 1907, the economy was already entering the second crisis of the twentieth century, a global crisis that affected the viability of the export model. The global economic crisis of 1907 particularly affected the Mexican agro-export sector, the primary clientele for the regional and state banking system (Cosio Villegas, 1974; de la Peña, 1975; Solís, 1981). The crisis was compounded by international economic events. Declining prices and international demand substantially reduced internal economic growth and caused liquidity problems for some segments of the export sector. Some banks had committed large sums of capital to hacendados and henqueros with long-term repayment terms.[19]

In February 1908, Finance Secretary Limantour declared that a majority of banks were financially unsound. Insolvency reflected managerial and regulatory malfeasance stemming from unstable capital bases, fictitious capital, inadequate loan and investment guarantees, and insufficient liquidity (Sánchez Martínez, 1983, p. 73). Limantour's comments led to an assembly of bankers to discuss and promulgate a new set of reforms.[20]

A particularly important element of the 1908 reforms was the foundation of a joint public-private project, the Caja de Préstamos para Obras de Irrigación y Fomento de la Agricultura. A primogenitor to the postrevolutionary developmental banks, the Caja was initiated to finance irrigation projects and agricultural and countryside improvements. Although the Caja was conceived primarily as an institutional means of transferring intermediate and long-term financial support to the agricultural sector, in practice its loans were largely given to businessmen and hacendados linked to the Banco Nacional, Banco de Londres, and Banco Central (Sánchez Martínez, 1983, p. 74). Moreover, the Caja largely functioned as a means for emission banks to unload long-term, often improperly secured, mortgage loans from their portfolios. In other words, the Caja served to facilitate the powers of national emission banks and bankers.

The effects of the 1908 reform were ineffective in ameliorating contradictions of the banking system. Emission banks continued to issue money that fueled inflation, whereas the cost of credit increased and the supply of credit was reduced. The economic crisis made it virtually impossible for most bank debtors to repay their loans, thus accentuating the financial precariousness of the banking system. Emission banks were also unable to restructure their portfolios because there were not enough mortgage and refaccionario banks to absorb emission bank intermediate and long-term loans. These problems, coupled with the inefficiencies of the Caja and portfolio problems of the Banco Central (Turrent Díaz, 1982, pp. 57–58), meant that the intended expansion of institutions conceding intermediate and long-term credit was realistically impossible to achieve.

By 1913, the Porfirian banking system was essentially bankrupt. The solvency of the system during these ultimate years was eroded by the Revolution, global depression, and Huerta's forced loans.

During the Porfiriato, banks acquired a tremendous amount of power within the sociopolitical dynamics of the Mexican economy and social formation. The control of social capital, the power to control and channel credit, and the ability to issue or create money and instruments of value facilitated and augmented the power of bank owners and administrators. This political-economic power was accentuated because bankers had the power to selectively promote the interests of other fractions or economic sectors. Shifting power relationships manifested intrastrata/fraction/class confrontations occurring throughout the social formation, which shaped these confrontations. Within this context, an important question emerges as to the degree of State autonomy vis-à-vis the banking system.

Two contradictory sociopolitical economic blocs controlled the Porfirian banking system. There were also two parallel financial circuits: an externally oriented financial circuit and an internally oriented financial circuit. Each of the two financial circuits experienced relative growth and diminution, reflecting the expansion or reduction of each bloc's respective sociopolitical power. The externally oriented circuit, controlled by foreign capital, tended to definitively influence the dynamics of the banking system.

By 1910, foreign capital exercised participatory control in twenty-eight of the fifty-two existing bank and commercial institutions, and controlled 76 percent of total capital (Ceceña, 1970, p. 54). French capital controlled eleven banking institutions and 45 percent of bank capital in the hands of foreign institutions. North American capital also controlled eleven institutions, but only controlled 18 percent of the total foreign controlled capital. British capital controlled four institutions, and 11 percent of total foreign managed capital. German capital controlled two institutions and only 1 percent of the foreign managed bank capital (Ceceña, 1970, p. 57). These ratios clearly demonstrate the high degree of capital concentration and economic-financial control exercised by foreign capital, particularly French capital. It is also worthwhile to note that several members of the Porfirian regime were closely involved with foreign-controlled bank operations.

A number of notable public officials and relatives of public officials participated in the administrative operations of foreign-controlled banks. Porfirio Díaz, Jr. was a member of the administrative council of the Banco Internacional. Julio Limantour, brother of Secretary Limantour, was also a member of the Banco Internacional's administrative council. Gabriel Mancera, President of the Congress, was a member of the Banco Internacional's administrative council. Pablo Martínez del Río, President of the Congress, was a member of Scherer-Limantour. Joaquín Casasús, President of the Congress, was a member of the Banco Central's administrative council. Pablo Macedo, President of the Congress, was vice president of the Banco Nacional, Cía, and the Banco de Fomentación, and a member of the administrative council for the Caja. Pablo Escandón, governor of Morelos, was a member of the administrative council for the Banco Nacional. Rosendo Piñeda, Undersecretary of Foreign Relations, was a member of the Banco de Londres administrative council. Roberto Nuñez, Undersecretary of Finance, was a member on the administrative councils of the Banco Nacional and the Caja. Guillermo de Landón y Escandón, the mayor of Mexico City, was a member of the administrative council of the Banco Mexico de Comercio e Industria. General Manuel González Cosio, Minister of the Navy and War, was president of the Banco Hipotecario.[21] Participation by these individuals in foreign bank operations suggests that many administration officials (and family members of administration officials) had material interests linked to the success of the external financial circuit and foreign bank capital.

Foreign bank capital exercised various degrees of political-economic hegemony throughout the Porfiriato. During the first phase of the Porfirian banking system, foreign bank capital was essentially given carte blanche political privileges and financial powers by the State. Díaz's 1884 congratulatory letter to De Teresa expressed the essence of the relationship between foreign bank capital and the State quite eloquently:

> At the moment of the celebration of this arrangement between the government and the Banco Nacional, it pleases me that I have procured the conciliation of both parties, and we should congratulate the nation that you and your dignified partners have understood, promoting in this manner, the acceleration of the government's progress and a greater amplitude of liberty for those establishments to dedicate to their ordinary operations without fear nor pain. (Rosenzweig, 1974, p. 809)

Throughout this period, the State not only exercised minimal regulatory control but actually promoted the political-economic interests of foreign bank capital, as exemplified by the State's extension of extraordinary privileges to the Banco Nacional. During the second phase of the Porfirian banking system, in contrast, the hegemony of foreign bank capital was subject to the political vicissitudes of the contradictory dynamism of the power bloc. Thus, the 1897 general law, in its juridical and political expressions, was simultaneously advantageous and disadvantageous for foreign bank capital. Specifically, foreign bank capital was able to participate in the formation of the legislation through representatives of particular foreign-controlled institutions and indirectly through the influence of científicos. The Banco Nacional and the Banco de Londres were also able to retain previously conceded privileges and allowed to establish new branches throughout the country. State banks, in contrast, were granted concessions in most of the states.

The most important aspect of the 1897 law was the creation of a rival internally oriented financial circuit, constituted largely of national capital, serving hacendados, latifundistas, and regional industrial, commercial, and mining interests. These state banks were also empowered to issue money, therein affecting the political-economic power of foreign controlled banks, especially those located in the capital.

A decisive development in favor of the regional-state banks—and the internally oriented financial circuit—was the creation of the Banco Central Méxicano. The suggestion to create the Banco Central emanated from Díaz (Felipe Leal, 1975, p. 26), and the initial capital was largely foreign, although state banks also contributed a minor proportion. The Díaz regime, did not, however, provide the Banco Central with extensive political-economic support, as shown by the demise of the institution in 1909. On the surface, foreign bank capital control of a banking institution facilitating the expansion and profitability of the regional and state banking system is somewhat perplexing, if not paradoxical. That the proposal to create the bank emanated from Díaz and that the 1897 legislation was promulgated within the historical context of the political dispute regarding the 1884 and 1889 commercial codes suggests that the participation of foreign bank capital in the Banco Central was promoted by the Mexican State on behalf of the general interests of the Díaz regime, bank capital, and the incipient bourgeoisie.

During the ultimate phase of the Porfirian banking system, the regional and state banking system began to experience the initial stages of insolvency. Foreign-controlled banks, in contrast, were able to augment their power due to better portfolio management and risk diversification, institutionalization of the Caja, and the 1905 Monetary Reform.[22] Even though the 1908 reform was ineffective in terms of its intended objectives, its promulgation signified an important modification of the political relations within the power bloc, as manifested in the official recognition of the inefficiency of the traditional agricultural sector and the restriction of credit to this sector. The creation and institutionalization of the Caja also exemplified the political dynamics of the power bloc. Although the Caja was supposed to assist the agricultural sector, in practice it operated on behalf of foreign bank capital and the externally oriented financial circuit. Thus, the 1908 Reform and the other previous regulatory reforms were, in essence, attempts to structure and regulate credit and lending practices, within the confines of a particular model of accumulation and on behalf of a particular strata/fraction of a class fraction in the process of formation, that is, bank capital.

> At the end of the Porfiriato, the Banco Nacional de México and the Banco de Londres and México maintained the management of more than half of the total bank assets, and in accordance with what the statistics seem to indicate, 45 percent was obligated in commercial loans and less than 10 percent in mortgage loans. The rest of the banking system, for its part, was in more precarious conditions, having continued financing inefficient latifundiest agriculture. . . . (Sánchez Martínez, 1983, p. 89)

In sum, State relations with bank capital and banking institutions were complex and tended to facilitate the expansion of the externally oriented foreign-dominated financial circuit. State actions also facilitated the creation of a competitive internally oriented financial circuit largely servicing national capital, especially the agricultural sector. Throughout the Porfiriato, however, foreign bank capital was conceded unparalleled political-economic advantages with regard to the regional-state banking system. In analyzing State autonomy, political and regulatory State policy must be examined within the context of the dynamic transformative character of the Mexican social formation; the contradictory composition of the power bloc; and the ability of the Porfirian regime and its representatives (the científicos) to create a political-structural equilibrium among contradictory and contending strata/fraction and class forces. Thus, although the State was able to obtain a number of concessions and benefits from its support of the development and consolidation of foreign bank capital's financial hegemony (independence from commercial-speculative capital; low-interest loans; and financial institutions capable of promoting and sustaining rapid expansion of the capitalist mode of production), State autonomy was nevertheless extremely constrained and often nonexistent. Hence, social class dynamics as well as domestic and international structural forces restricted State autonomy. The triumph of an externally oriented accumulation model and the phenomenal control of the financial circuits by foreign bank capital exemplified the dialectical interplay of class and structure in Porfirian Mexico.

NOTES

1. The Church played an important role in the colonial fiscal and production system (e.g., *diezmo* and *encomienda;* Greenow, 1983; Schwaller, 1985) and ultimately promoted and reinforced quasifeudal social relations. The diezmo was a 10 percent tax, primarily on agricultural products.

2. Small localized markets were often dominated by commercial-usury capital. These merchants often participated in illegal or semi-illegal activities (e.g., contraband).

3. Grand merchants frequently represented Spanish concessionaires from Sevilla and participated in the *Consulado de México.* The Consulado was an organization that enabled its members to control imports, manage exports, profit from the price differentials, and accumulate enormous capital reserves from the 200-year-old monopoly on external trade (de la Peña, 1975, p. 66).

4. Refaccionario banks existed primarily during the Porfiriato. The specific characteristics of these- banks will be examined in a later portion of this chapter. Literally translated, *refacción* means financing, banking, or loan.

5. In Tlaxcala, for example, 65 percent of the *fincas* were mortgaged to the Church, with the amount of taxes and pledged obligations reaching more than 42 percent of the total value of the fincas (Semo, 1973, p. 176).

6. These reforms included the imposition of *intendencias* (an administrative geographical area), installation of an unsuccessful bank, an increased degree of free commerce, and the creation of new consulates.

7. Examples of the State's intervention in the production and destruction of social relations include the following: (1) the promotion of primitive accumulation through the dissolution of indigenous and ecclesiastic property; (b) the promotion of incipient industrial interests through the construction and support of a modern infrastructure; (c) the recision of the *alcabala* (an internal commercial tax system); (d) the promotion of a banking system; (e) the fomentation of an export-oriented accumulation model; and (f) the progressive expansion of capital reproduction.

8. See Marichal (1980) for an analysis of the role of foreign credit.

9. For a microanalysis of the individual histories and activities of comerciants, see Cardoso (1981, 1983); Cerutti (1983); Couturier (1985); Huerta (1985); Lavrin (1985); Morales (1985); Saragoza (1978); and Urías (1985).

10. The bank was given a two-year tax exemption and was obligated to open an annual credit line for the State. The bank was founded with the intention of financing local mining activity.

11. The establishment of this bank provides an example of miners extending the realm of their accumulation to include banking and financial operations.

12. Local investors supplied a fifth of the initial capital.

13. Although foreign bank capital was clearly a fraction of capital, a national fraction of bank capital did not yet exist. Thus, fraction/strata will be used to refer to this group.

14. These banks (which did not yet exist at the time that the 1897 law was promulgated) had the authority to issue bonds and generally operate as commercial banks.

15. In 1897, Limantour authorized the establishment of six emission banks in the states of Mexico, Sonora, Coahuila, San Luis Potosí, Sinaloa, and Veracruz. An emission bank was founded in Jalisco in 1898. In 1899, emission banks were authorized in Guanajuato and Tabasco. In 1902, emission banks were authorized in Hidalgo, Tamaulipas, Michoaca, Oaxaca, and Morelos. In 1903, three emission banks were authorized in Querétaro, Campeche, and Guerrero. The Banco Agrícola e Hipotecaro (1900) and the Hipotecario Agrícola del Pacífico (1900) were the only two mortgage banks founded during this phase. Finally, four refaccionario banks were established: Central Méxicano (1898); Banco Comercial Refaccionario de Chihuahua (1902); Mexicano de Comercio e Industria (1906); and Refaccionario de la Laguna (1907).

16. Twenty of the twenty-six newly established banks were emission banks, all established outside of Mexico City and in accordance with the 1897 general law, legally prohibited from circulating bank bills outside of the respective region of operation.

17. In 1897, 86 percent of national credit transactions transpired in Mexico City (Sánchez Martínez, 1983, p. 86).

18. The Banco Central Méxicano contractually institutionalized the acceptance and exchange of state bank bills in Mexico City (Turrent Díaz, 1982, pp. 57–58).

19. Three banks in particular (Yukatán, Mercantil, and Yukateco) had liberally lent long-term capital to the henequeros. With the advent of the crisis, these lending practices created liquidity problems for those banks with unbalanced portfolios. The Banco de Campeche also experienced liquidity problems in 1908 because of politically based financial practices with the Governor of Campeche.

20. The 1908 reforms officially attempted to correct the inadequacies of the 1897 general law. Emission banks were (a) restricted to conducting commercial discount-deposit operations, (b) prohibited from conceding credit to administrators and stockholders during the first year of operation, (c) prohibited (except for the Banco Nacional) from establishing new branches, and (d) encouraged to convert to mortgage or refaccionario banks to increase the provision of intermediate and long-term credit. Two emission banks were converted into refaccionario banks. The Banco de Michoacan voluntarily changed into a refaccionario bank and was liquidated in 1911. The Banco de Campeche also changed into a refaccionario bank because of its lending practices and corresponding portfolio distribution. Finally, all banks were ordered to accept and exchange emission bank bills.

21. Creel, Landón y Escandón, Pineda, Macedo and Casasus were all members of the científicos.

22. For an examination of foreign bank capital's coup with the implementation of the 1905 Monetary Reform, see Sánchez Martínez (1983, p. 55), Rosenzweig (1974, pp. 872–885), and Torres Gaytán (1980, pp. 85–115).

Chapter 2

Postrevolutionary Finance, 1920–1940: Coincidence of Interest

The 1910–1920 Revolution was a combined and uneven revolution (Gilly, 1971), characterized by intraclass and interclass struggle.[1] In other words, the petty-bourgeois political revolution was also a peasant social revolution that reproduced political segmentation, creating power fragmentation and a power vacuum.[2] These developments contributed to a transitory Bonapartist regime led by Alvaro Obregón (Aguilar Mora, 1982; Bartra, 1975; Gilly, 1971; Semo, 1978). Although the Revolution transformed the liberal-oligarchic State and produced a profound rupture within the Porfirian social structure, the postrevolution structure nevertheless retained a semblance of continuity with the prerevolution social structure (Katz, 1981, pp. 320–321; Semo, 1978, pp. 232–233).[3] Thus, social relations reflected the dynamics of the social order. That is, postrevolutionary social relations reflected the political transition from a rural society, based on semifeudal relations, to a capitalist society incorporating a military bureaucratic petty bourgeoisie. Given these social dynamics, an examination of the significance of the Revolution vis-à-vis the State is in order.

THE STATE, REVOLUTIONARY IDEOLOGY, AND THE PARTY

The Mexican Revolution was a political revolution as well as a cultural and ideological revolution of extraordinary complexity. Positivism influenced the conceptualization of the Revolution and its corresponding goals. The grand utopias of an independent Mexico were to be order and progress—as manifested in the Constitution and shaped in the course of implementation. Postrevolutionary regimes structured civil society, classes, class alliances, and the State in terms of order and progress.[4]

Culturally, the Revolution consecrated a structural logic of power incorporating a dialectical interplay between authoritarian repression and populist manipulation (González Casanova, 1985, p. 77). Political culture was (and is) based on the appropriation and manipulation of historical memories and quotidian struggles through mimesis, concessions, coalitions, corruption, and repression (Eckstein, 1977; González Casanova, 1985, p. 63). The Revolution, for instance, was and is part of the national consciousness as a result of the tradition of struggle and revolutionary experience. Because the State and the official party embody "the Revolution" and reproduce the corollary political culture, the State therein represents and sanctifies the contents of "the Revolution." Thus, the State—the material manifestation of the national Revolution—is an autonomous representative of a conciliation-based coalition preserving and reproducing its class character within a culturally and ideologically neutral nationalism.

> Neither the white that declare themselves Indian, nor the bourgeoisie that declare themselves socialists constitute the only forms of expropriation and assimilation of others' ideas. The mimetic act also occurred during Independence with Catholic religious symbols. . . . Although the mimetic process is characteristic of the leaders, it is also of the masses. Popular movements, and the policy of the masses in Mexico, have resulted in the expropriation of antagonistic general ideas and conversion into a public moral norm, law, objective or program of liberty, of independence, or of social justice. (González Casanova, 1985, p. 70)

At a less abstract level, political regimes have used revolutionary ideology to legitimate policies plainly antithetical to the principles of the Revolution. Inequality was not ameliorated but legitimated in the name of progress and order.[5] Indeed, State raison d'etat promoted capitalist development and industrial modernization. Thus, the myth of the benevolent, autonomous State devoid of particular class interests became one of the most important obfuscating principles of revolutionary ideology.

> The regime emanating from the Revolution proposed the realization of a capitalist model of development, founded in the defense of the principle of private, enterprising property and in the conciliation of social classes, obligating all groups to live together under the same political regime, but procuring in every moment the promotion of the capitalist class, of that which the development of the country was to depend, under the vigilance and with the support of the new State. (Córdova, 1973, p. 34)

Initially, a strong interventionist State, promoting social class harmony and modern industrial capitalist development, was restricted to ideological social discourse. The War had destroyed most of the country's economic base and resulted in financial insolvency and a large external debt. Moreover, national sovereignty was threatened by external political and military forces (Katz, 1981). Internally, the revolutionary leadership was fragmented, and peasants, the proletariat, *caudillos,* and *caciques* remained mobilized.[6] To consolidate its hegemony, the petty bourgeoisie constructed de facto and de jure alliances with revolutionary and reactionary social classes, fractions, strata, and groups.

The early postrevolution State was a state in the process of formation structured by a political crisis necessitating a Bonapartist solution (Hamilton, 1982). President Carranza's inability to establish a social base for the revolutionary State-in-formation led to a major political crisis. Although Carranza was able to use political and military means to restrict the power of several contending factions (e.g., the peasantry, ultrareactionaries, the clergy), he was unable to control the radical military elements and caudillos. Failure to establish hegemonic control on behalf of a particular fraction or coalition was also restricted by the material contradictions inherent in a combined and uneven revolution wherein the executive had to placate a fragmented petty-bourgeois/bourgeois leadership, a mobilized "radical" military, conservative landed interests, and reactionary local caudillos and caciques. Ultimately, Carranza attempted to use revolutionary ideology to subordinate the mobilized radical elements of the Revolution and therein form a personalist coalition with the old Porfirian landowning class. The coalition was based on material and ideological concessions to control contending fractions and groups. Obregón's *Agua Prieta* coup (1920) attempted to resolve Carranza's political crisis and instability, through imposition of a Bonapartist regime.

Obregón surmounted the political crisis that had plagued Carranza through the construction of a Bonapartist regime. The future científicos of Mexico established a new regime exemplifying features of classical postrevolutionary Bonapartism and sui generis Bonapartism (Gilly, 1983, pp. 319–320).[7] The regime combined petty-bourgeois Jacobin socialism and populism—using third forces mainly composed of the middle classes—to reconstruct and relocate the State above social classes, thereby protecting the popular masses and simultaneously respecting capital (Bartra, 1975, p. 16). Although Obregón encouraged foreign capital to invest in Mexico, the State was not immediately reintegrated within the sphere of international capital (Katz, 1981). Foreign capital, particularly American capital, continued to affect political-economic developments, for example, pressures of the International Bank Committee, the petroleum tax, and consequent redirection of petroleum investments (Hamilton, 1982, pp. 69–71).

Obregón's Bonapartism combined concessions, demagoguery, repression, and Machiavellian political machinations to stabilize the proto-bourgeois State. Social bases contributing to the genesis of relative political-economic stability and the hegemony of proto-bourgeois interests were constructed and developed through the absorption and elimination of independent political entities. Socially, Obregón controlled popular mass organizations through bureaucratic mechanisms linked to the State, that is, the Mexican Regional Workers Confederation (Confederación Regional Obrera Mexicana: CROM) and the National Agrarian Party (Partido Nacional Agrarista). Politically, Obregón initiated a program to "professionalize" the military by reducing the power of local military caciques, therein enhancing the regime's support base.[8]

Obregón and the military controlled, organized, and directed the State apparatus. The State apparatus was the axis of the new power bloc and the primary impetus in the genesis and expansion of a national bourgeoisie. The State apparatus was largely controlled by petty-bourgeois constitutionalist army officers, members of the liberal professions, and careerists of diverse origins. The power bloc integrated various leaders of the State apparatus with the petty-bourgeois/bourgeois agrarian fractions and owners of large and intermediate industrial and mining enterprises. The military was thus a quintessential element within the power bloc. As an institution, the military generated political and administrative officials at the national and state levels, directed the institutionalization of the State-in-formation, and ultimately transcended petty-bourgeois class logic through the use of the State and the Bonapartist regime to legitimate primitive accumulation and the autogenesis of a national bourgeoisie. Although the military was the preponderant sociopolitical force during Obregón's Bonapartist reign, there was nevertheless a dialectical interplay between military-politico figures and caudillo-caciques.

> The army, widely politicized since its birth in full revolutionary struggle, followed no one more than the caudillo, or said in other terms, anyone that wasn't a caudillo could not govern the army and the Republic or integrate a new political organization in a country disorganized by civil war. The caudillo, in turn, could not be anything but an individual of the military, whose prestige was linked to his war biography, brilliant military victories, transcended to the political world. (Córdova, 1973, p. 263)

Obregón's Bonapartist regime reflected the Mexican polity's "constitutive moments" (Gilly, 1985) as manifested in the interrelationship between liberal-democratic and traditional-personal forms of dependence and political participation. The cacique–caudillo–masses relationship also reflected a transitionary agrarian/industrial society. During this transitionary phase, military caudillos typically communicated with the popular masses through mediators, that is, a host of hierarchical chiefs, caciques, and politicos (Gilly, 1985), and through ideological mediums—a communicative process that would be institutionalized under Calles and succeeding regimes. Although Obregón was administering the Bonapartist State-in-formation, the State and State apparatus were increasingly structured outside of traditional relationships. This change resulted from the modern institutionalization of the State-in-formation, the centralization of executive power, and demise of the the military caudillo.

The attempted coup of the Huerta entourage and the advent of the Calles regime generated profound changes in the structural dynamics of the State and political system. The Huerta episode resulted in a restructuring of the power bloc. Military caudillos were largely purged from the State apparatus and power bloc. At the same time, fractions of the industrial and agrarian bourgeoisie were appointed to positions of increasing relevance within the power bloc (Bartra, 1975, p. 18). Of greater significance was the Calles regime's assumption of power. Often referred to as "the strong government," the Calles regime expressed the general interests of the modernizing bourgeoisie (or "revolutionary bourgeoisie," as they were also called) in their totality.

A Bonapartist regime was no longer a structural necessity. Although the Calles regime—including the Maximato—continued to manifest Bonapartist characteristics, there was a significant transformation of the social structure.[9] The immediate postrevolutionary situation—characterized by an absence of a hegemonic class or fraction—was gradually transformed during the Calles regime by the progressive annihilation of contending political factions (Meyer et al., 1977). Another contributing factor was the increasing materialization of a vertically and horizontally integrated class alliance based on the promotion of an industrial model of accumulation and a corollary set of agreed upon rules (Meyer et al., 1977, p. 284), that is, the New Economic Policy (NEP). These changes signified the initial transformation of the petty bourgeoisie as well as the formation of a national bourgeoisie and corresponding hegemonic project.[10] Given these sociostructural changes, Calles was able to initiate the institutionalization of the State through the expansion of the State apparatus, the centralization of power, developmental public projects, social reforms, and the foundation of the National Revolutionary Party (Partido Nacional Revolucionario, PNR) (Córdova, 1973; Gilly, 1971; Hamilton, 1982; Krauze, 1977; Ochoa Campos, 1976; Zevada, 1971).

Calles's modernization of the State was largely the result of increasing sociopolitical stability and economic growth that occurred during the end of Obregón's regime and the initial years of Calles's regime. More important, the incipient bourgeoisie increasingly exercised a hegemonic role in the power bloc. Not only did the State effectively promote the formation of "revolutionary capitalists" through the encouragement of revolutionary generals to "trade in their guns for capital," the State actually served as an important recruiting ground for self-enrichment (Córdova, 1973, pp. 376–379; Lieuwen, 1968, pp. 90–92).

Bribery and corruption were common means of placating military-political opponents. For instance, General Abelardo Rodríguez (president, 1932–1934) obtained his initial wealth from gambling, hotel, and bar operations. Many governors, caciques, and revolutionary veterans were similarly integrated into "the new rich" through control of local and regional economic activities.

> To create entrepreneurs among the ranks of the same revolutionaries seemed to completely coincide with the "fever to accumulate fortunes" (Naranjo), that was manifested with all its vigor during the Calles regime, ultimately producing beneficial effects for the system: given all of the infringements and the degree of anxiety that could be contained, the procedure was founding a true institutionalization of the art of self-enrichment, that is, its normalization and peaceful regulation; it's true that in large measure the economic activities of the "new rich" were fundamentally unproductive; however, the transformation of revolutionaries into entrepreneurs opened means through which the politically ambitious could channel their anxieties . . . (Córdova, 1973, p. 379)

Although the State promoted capitalist development and bourgoise interests, continuity with the autonomous precepts of revolutionary ideology were retained through the use of social reforms and the creation and development of an official political party.

Calles created the PNR in 1929 to facilitate the transfer of presidential power through the institutionalization of contending political factions and the centralization and negotiation of political decision making. Foundation of the PNR signified the institutionalization of the personalist-caudillo power structure within a single political party. More important, the PNR was a hierarchically organized party of politically contentious leaders and factions; it was not a mass party. Thus, in practice, the PNR performed a horizontally oriented power mediating function (Bartra, 1975; Gilly, 1985). It incorporated and subordinated regional politicos and simultaneously disorganized political interests contrary to the interests of the established regime. Ideologically, the PNR espoused nationalist and constitutionalist themes and promoted agrarian-worker interests through moderate State-initiated reform projects.

The 1938 transformation of the PNR into the Party of the Mexican Revolution (Partido de la Revolución: PRM) reflected the dynamics of social class/

State relations. Under Cárdenas the State actually adhered to its revolutionary rhetoric, promoting agrarian-labor interests through the organization, mobilization, and integration of popular sectors. The administration also implemented redistributive social policies. However, the contradictory nature of Cárdenas's worker-peasant based progressive alliance was ultimately manifested by the popular sectors' loss of independence vis-à-vis the State. The State's appropriation of worker-peasant organizational independence was partly the result of an incorrect conception—on the part of worker-peasant organizations and the Cárdenas Administration—of the State as an autonomous revolutionary entity, neutrally arbitrating the class struggle. The limits of State autonomy, however, were readily apparent with the course of time (Hamilton, 1982).

> The leadership of these organizations failed to develop an alternative ideology to that of the revolution, which had been appropriated by the state and given considerable credibility by the actions of the Cárdenas government. The failure of the labor leadership to envision goals beyond those of the revolution, and the assumption that the state could continue to implement those goals, weakened or eliminated the rationale for an independent labor and peasant movement. (Hamilton, 1982, p. 183)

The advent of the PRM also reflected the maturation of the institutionalization of the revolutionary process. Cárdenas's semicorporative institutionalization of the progressive alliance within the structure of the PRM resulted in a further loss of autonomous power for peasant-labor organizations. The increasingly sophisticated institutionalization of the structural logic of power absorbed the contradictions permeating the State. Cárdenas's integration of a national revolutionary alliance—consisting of four vertically separated social groups (peasants, labor, popular sector, and military)—transformed the structure and composition of the official party through the formal institutional incorporation of the popular sectors into a controlled support structure. The support structure represented and legitimated the praxis of an ideologically neutral class State. With the incorporation of popular sectors into the PRM, official ideological discourse swung to the left. The ideology of the PRM was composed of an eclectic blend of neo-liberal, socialist, Marxist, and national revolutionary principles and doctrine. Party ideology recognized the existence of class conflict while promoting the consolidation of a semicorporative political organization that vertically and horizontally controlled social classes. Realistically, the PRM represented a de facto disorganization of social classes and the de jure organization of social classes as participatory sectors in the official party of the national revolution (González Casanova, 1985, p. 118).

Further institutionalization of the paternalistic, authoritarian relationship between the semicorporative sectors constituting the official party and the State continued to reflect the dynamics of social class relations. As exemplified in the 1946 transition of the PRM into the Institutional Revolutionary Party (Partido Revolucionario Institucional: PRI), the historical development of bourgeois hegemony was a material reality. For example, one of the party slogans was changed from "for workers' democracy" to "democratic and social justice" (González Casanova, 1985, p. 126). The promotion of "socialist education" was changed to "advanced and nationalist education" (González Casanova, 1985, p. 126). The foundation of the party was changed from a coalition based on a class alliance to a "political association of citizens" (González Casanova, 1985, p. 126). Structurally, power was further centralized within the central committee and the president of the party and state delegations replaced local assemblies and bases (González Casanova, 1985, pp. 126–127).

Reorganization of the official party and the ideological expressions of the Revolution coincided with the increasingly apparent contradiction between the political-economic praxis of the State and official rhetoric. State intervention in the accumulation process demonstrated that a coincidence of interests existed between the State and different fractions of the bourgeoisie.[11] As the class character of the State was consolidated, relative State autonomy was relegated a politically symbolic function within the realm of ideological social discourse.

ECONOMIC DEVELOPMENT
AND POSTREVOLUTION CONTINUITY

The Revolution disrupted the Porfirian model of enclave economic development. Economic activity was negatively affected by the mobilization of combatants, the destruction of infrastructure and property, and political and financial instability. Statistically, in terms of gross domestic product (GDP), the sectoral decline of the economy was devastating.[12] The immediate postrevolution economy was actually sustained by bank money (i.e., forced loans and bank bills), and accumulated goods consisting mainly of herds and seed (Torres Gaytán, 1980, p. 136).

The Mexican economy stagnated during the 1920s and fluctuated widely in the 1930s. During the 1930s, dramatic economic instability resulted from the Great Depression and increasing State economic intervention. Reactivation of the national economy in 1933 was largely the result of stabilizing financial policies and increasing international economic activity. Consistent economic expansion during the 1930s was largely the result of the Cárdenas administration's expansive fiscal and monetary policies.[13] Statistically, the immediate postrevolution economy was virtually stagnant. Gross domestic product increased an average of 1 percent annually from 1921 to 1935. What is important to note, however, beyond the statistical quantification of economic trends, is the political aspect of economic accumulation.

The Revolution interrupted and reinforced the Porfirian modernization model based on agro-mineral exports. Socioeconomic continuities with the Profiriato remained within the limits or boundaries of "the Revolution." Although the Revolution was a political revolution with a petty-bourgeois agrarian thrust, the general hacienda/ranch system remained relatively unaffected until the Cárdenas agrarian reforms. Although the first few presidents redistributed land for politically symbolic reasons, many large hacendados regained or maintained control of land through government assistance or through violent displacement of peasant occupants by private military-police forces.

Another element contributing to postrevolution continuity was the survival of much of the prerevolution economic elite. In Monterrey, for instance, capitalists entrenched in commerce, finance, and industry retained control of their economic resources. The Monterrey regional elite actually benefited from postrevolution nationalist policies.

> The sources of the elite's economic power, coupled with the nature of the revolution, resulted in the survival and continuity of Monterrey's leading capitalists. (Saragoza, 1978, p. 254)

A similar phenomenon occurred in the state of Hidalgo. Regional power of large landowners was not threatened by the Revolution. Many of the politically active *rancheros* assumed leadership positions in different revolutionary factions and recruited their employees. Other local rancheros joined particular revolutionary factions in order to economically destroy rival rancheros.

> These internal rivalries continued in the immediate post-revolutionary period, with terratenientes that had fought as officials in the victorious carrancista faction establishing their own areas of influence. . . . Many of these "revolutionary" rancheros became regional strong men and had small contingents of armed soldiers . . . (Schryer, 1986, p. 25)

POSTREVOLUTIONARY FINANCE: 1920–1940

The Revolution severely affected the liquidity and solvency of the financial system.[14] Political and economic instability disrupted the operation of financial circuits through the generation of clientele mistrust, speculation in silver pesos, contraction of credit, accelerated disintermediation, and extra-bank credit operations by comerciantes and industrialists (Sánchez Martínez, 1985, pp. 17–18).

The Porfirian legal framework regulating banking institutions continued to delineate the juridical boundaries between the State and banks through June 1915. Huerta used the 1897 General Credit Law—conceding privileges to emission banks—and modified the framework regulating currency circulation to fortify relations between the State and banks. Nevertheless, by mid-1914, the banking system was basically insolvent. When Huerta abandoned power in 1915, the financial system was in chaos. Even though private banks lost control of the circulating medium, the historically cozy relationship between the State and bank capital was by no means over. The politicization of economic development and social reform that accompanied the Revolution ultimately augmented the power of bank capital.

Carranza strongly opposed the Profirian banking system. Porfirian banks were antithetical to the revolutionary cause, and they were "the powerful financial enemies of the Revolution." Even prior to his assumption of power in 1915, Carranza initiated confrontational tactics against the banks. In April 1913, he issued his first decree regulating the issue of constitutionalist paper money.[15] Private banks refused to accept constitutionalist paper and Carranza retaliated by decreeing private bank bills fraudulent. In September 1913, Carranza went a step further and declared that revolutionary bank reform would establish a government emission monopoly and government control of the banking system. An October 1915 decree established the Regulatory and Inspection Credit Institution Commission. One of the more important functions of this commission was to examine bank portfolios. The objective was to determine bank compliance with minimum capital requirements. Ultimately, the primary goal was to determine guidelines for liquidating insolvent banks. The commission determined that fifteen of the twenty-four emission banks were bankrupt, with portfolios containing excessive amounts of credit to insolvent clients, shares and bonds of bankrupt industries, and bonds issued by Huerta (Torres Gaytán, 1980, p. 137).

Carranza issued a new decree in September 1916, initiating the liquidation and seizure of all banks operating with insufficient metallic reserves. Officially, Carranza's rationale was juridical, that is, that bank concessions were unconstitutional because the State received no compensation, and the banks enjoyed a monopoly on the emission of bills superior to the amount of metallic reserves (Sánchez Martínez, 1985, p. 32). Unofficially, the decree was based on several additional factors, including increasing economic difficulties; bank speculation against paper money; prior bank alliances with Huerta; and banks' reactionary loyalties (Sánchez Martínez, 1985, p. 32; Torres Gaytán, 1980, pp. 138–139). Noncompliant banks were given sixty days to adjust portfolio reserves.[16]

Insolvent banks failed to comply with the sixty day regulation and consequently were seized in accordance with a December 1916 liquidation decree. The 1916 decree signified partial destruction of the Porfirian banking system and the initial transformation of the revolutionary banking regime.

In actuality, bank policies of the Carranza administration were largely ineffective in destroying and transforming the Porfirian banking system. Seizure councils were to administer and liquidate seized banks. The members of these councils often incorporated the same bankers within the respective council. The impasse was "clarified" in April 1917 with the announcement that the bank situation was undefined and that the liquidation would be exclusively administrative (Turrent Díaz, 1982, p. 84). The "undefined" situation was compounded by Carranza's contraction of 55.5 million pesos in forced loans to provide resources for the government (a sum that was equivalent to two-thirds of total bank system reserves; Torres Gaytán, 1980, p. 140). Finally, Carranza demonstrated the political limits of his bank policy in a September 1919 speech by alluding to the possibility that banks would be allowed to renew prior operations in the near future (Turrent Díaz, 1982, p. 85).

The final element of Carranza's bank policy was the creation of the Banco Unico de Emisión (a central bank). Congressional debate on the inclusion of a constitutional clause delineating a State bank monopoly on emission revolved around the question of the degree of State control over the central bank, that is, the political power of the State vis-à-vis the private financial system. Representative Múgica's arguments expressed the political nature and consequences of the debate. Múgica argued that the creation of a government-controlled bank signified the destruction of the enemies of the Revolution.

> The death of the rest of the banks that are the sworn enemies of the Mexican people, because we have seen how all of the banks functioned in the Republic, not only when they tried to combat the Revolution, but when they have tried with this intention to favor the property owner, we have seen them make disastrous operations and produce the ruin of citizens in a few months . . . in this assembly there are businessmen who know how these banks function and how they have ruined the country. . . . Are we going to take this lying down? No, señores, for once we shall establish in the Constitution a State Bank that will benefit the nation and will avoid, above all, that the same government concoct combinations resulting in the bankers' benefit and in the nation's harm . . . (Sánchez Martínez, 1985, p. 35)

Passage of the measure established the juridical basis for State rectorship of the monetary and financial circuits, and significantly augmented potential political power of the State in relation to the private banking sector. Economic constraints prevented realization of the project until 1925.

Postponement of the central bank compounded financial difficulties. A credit and liquidity crunch (combined with monetary instability), affected productive investment, capital formation, and market expansion. These phenomena, in conjunction with an unstable exchange parity, benefited the export sector and "banking institutions without concession."[17] Commercial capital also profited from depreciation differentials between silver, gold, and the dollar.

The Revolution and the nationalist bank policies of Carranza weakened the banking system. The economic power of banks was reduced by the large number of insolvent banks, State seizure, administrative "liquidation," and "banking establishments without concession." Nevertheless, banks still retained ample political power, exemplified by the appointment of bankers to the administrative seizure councils and the inability of the State to liquidate the old system. Even more revealing, however, was the ability of bank capital to initiate the genesis of an historically important political alliance with Obregón.

The antecedents for a bank–State alliance were actually established prior to Obregón's assumption of the presidency. Attempts to ameliorate conflicting relations between the first postrevolutionary regime and future regimes were manifested in provisional President Huerta's 1920 presidential address. Huerta called for a legal project to regulate credit institutions and promote the "solid construction" of a new financial system with a wide circumference of action (Sánchez Martínez, 1985, p. 43). In addition to Huerta's conciliatory maneuver, the principal banks submitted a proposal to the government in 1920, suggesting that the State relinquish its seizure of the insolvent banks and establish the rules for balancing bank portfolios prior to the reinitiation of normal operations.

Under Obregón, banks seized by Carranza were returned to the previous owners in 1921. The juridical existence of these institutions was recognized, and a law called for the finance secretary to qualify and categorize banks within thirty days and referred to the normalization of bank assets.[18] These measures were only partially implemented, largely because of the inability of the government to settle its debts with the banks. The result was that the liquidation dates were prolonged until 1930 (Torres Gaytán, 1980, p. 158; Sánchez Martínez, 1985, pp. 44–45).

Politically, one of the more significant aspects of this legislation was the government decision not to consult bankers prior to the formation of the legislation. At one point, many bankers became alarmed that the larger banks were secretly negotiating with the President. Their fears were allayed by assurances from a finance subsecretary that bankers would be consulted about the contents of any pertinent legislative project.[19]

The Obregón regime also failed to create a central bank. Economically, the problem of insufficient start-up capital resulted from precarious international relations and domestic economic stagnation (i.e., questions regarding the external debt and the petroleum conflict; Turrent Díaz, 1982, p. 105). Political disunity was also a factor. Moreover, institutional disunity prohibited agreement on the specific doctrinal definition and legal characteristics of the central bank (Turrent Díaz, 1982, p. 111).[20]

A budget surplus in 1924 created the opportunity for a central bank and bank reform. Finance secretary Pani's bank reform was a multifaceted program. Specifically, the program consisted of four basic objectives. These goals constituted the agenda for the first bank convention in February 1924: (a) legislation to promote bank credit, (b) bank rehabilitation, (c) foundation of a central bank, and (d) establishment of a government-controlled national bank system. In a December 1923 convocation, Pani noted that it was necessary to reform the existing bank legislation "to give all banks the possibility to develop for their own benefit and in favor of the most efficient national economic life . . . " (Sánchez Martínez, 1985, p. 53). Pani also noted that the bank convention was necessary because (a) bank legislation was inconsistent with "real circumstances," (b) constant conflicts between the finance secretary and the banks harmed industry and commerce, and (c) it was important to harmonize particular and general interests (Krauze et al., 1977, p. 31).

The first bank convention promoted a coincidence of interests between the State and banks. Gerando de la Fuente (chief of the finance ministry credit department and president of the convention) opened his address on a positive and conciliatory note. The bankers were invited to participate in the resolution of sociopolitical problems. The new conciliatory stance radically modified previous finance policy. Fuente went on to note that the amelioration of ill feelings would be a "great triumph." During the course of the convention, bankers and economists discussed legal and practical problems facing the financial system.

The presence and active participation of two former Porfirian cíentificos— Enrique Creel and Miguel Macedo—exemplified, to a certain extent, continuities between the prerevolution and postrevolution financial system. One of the six sessions was particularly indicative of this continuity. During the February 28, 1924 session, a polemic emerged concerning compliance with the liquidation clause in the 1921 Ley de Desincautación. Creel (Banco de Minero de Chihuahua), representing small banks with precarious portfolios, debated Rodolfo Garza (Banco de Nuevo León), representing large bank interests. The moderator, it is important to note, was Pani, who performed a conciliatory role, combining and directing the various parties toward a harmonious resolution of contradictory interests. Ex-científico Macedo was appointed by the government to draft the new general credit law (Krauze et al., 1977, p. 32). At the conclusion of the convention, Creel cryptically closed with an historically appropriate note:

> The Banks of the Republic represented here, have grand hopes that the government will lend them its moral, and material support, so that they can function regularly and develop their businesses in harmony with the public interest. (Sánchez Martínez, 1985, p. 56)

The convention was a success. The major achievement was the conciliation of State–bank interests and the initial formation of a long-term alliance between the State and the bankers. Harmonizing public and private interests in the name of economic growth and social reform turned bankers into "revolutionaries." Pani's concession of a moratorium for those banks with portfolio problems (i.e., small bank interests) harmonized intrabank interests. The convention also resolved that the government would pay its bank debts, create the National Bank Commission, and establish a central bank (Banco de México). The material expression of the success of the convention, however, was the promulgation of legislation regulating and reorganizing the financial sector.

The January 1925 General Credit Law was the first of many new laws constituting the Calles administration's "legislative assault" on public and private finance.[25] Notable elements of the new law included (a) elimination of the tax exemption privilege by stipulating that all banks had to pay taxes, (b) foreclosure of the plural emission system by assigning specific functions to the Banco de México, (c) control of the concentration-centralization processes through the restriction of banks' acquisitions of other banks' stock, (d) promotion of national bank capital interests, (e) government control of foreign bank capital by regulating foreign banks and foreign bank houses, and (f) consolidation of the State as rector of the national bank system through inspection and regulation.

Foundation of the central bank (Banco de México) was one of the more important achievements. It greatly enhanced the potential for State economic intervention and facilitated the ability of the State to direct development of the financial system.

The integration of the Banco de México's first Administrative Council reflected the coincidence of interests in harmonizing public and private interests. As noted in the Banco de México's official history:

> The Banco de México initiated its operations searching for the maximum support from the public and principal commercial, bank, industrial, and political groups in the country. The integration of its first Administrative Council reflected this policy. (Turrent Díaz, 1982, p. 127)

Perhaps one of the more symbolic examples of the harmonization of public and private interests was the temporary installation of the central office of the central bank in the headquarters of the Banco de Londres (Turrent Díaz, 1982). The inauguration ceremonies for the Banco de México were actually held in the Banco de Londres building with President Calles, the cabinet, "and the highest representatives of the bank, industry, commerce, and worker organizations in attendance" (Turrent Díaz, 1982, p. 133).

The first phase of the Banco de México's institutional existence, from 1925 to 1930, was an expansionary institutionalization period. During this period, the bank confronted a series of obstacles and limitations affecting its ability to perform central bank operations. The bank lacked operational experience, sufficient resources, and most importantly, public confidence. These problems were compounded by economic recession (1926 and 1929) and political instability, for example, cristero rebellion, international relations, and Gómez-Serrano uprisings. Consequently, bank operations were restricted.

The bank operated more as a commercial bank than a central bank. Forty-one bank establishments participated in the 1924 Bank Convention and yet only two banks associated with the Banco de México in 1925. Apart from the fact that limited private bank association necessitated increased government subscription of Series "B" shares, limited association also severely restricted the bank's ability to conduct central bank operations.

Limited association essentially created a situation wherein the bank was forced to conduct commercial-rediscount operations with private individuals and the federal government. The bank quickly fulfilled the function of financing the federal government. (By the end of 1927, the bank had loaned the federal government 11.5 million pesos; more than double the legally stipulated amount, i.e., 10 percent of paid capital.) Its operations with the private sector, in contrast, were essentially commercial.

Instead of centralizing credit, the Banco de México was a privileged competitor in the financial community. The Banco de México's competitive operations generated conflictive relations with private banks.[22] The competitive commercial operations of the Banco de México alienated some members of the banking community and generated positive results for the bank and the national economy.

The bank rapidly increased its importance within the banking system. In terms of deposits, by 1928 the central bank was the third most important bank in the country, after the Banco de Montreal and the Banco Nacional (Turrent Díaz, 1982, p. 154). The bank was also profitable.[23] In terms of beneficial effects for the national economy, one of the more important consequences of the Banco de México's competitive operations was the reduction in prevailing market interest rates.[24] In part, the reduction in interest rates was possible because the central bank increased the available supply of credit. The reduction in interest rates, however, was also a reflection of the marginalization of usury capital.

Although the Banco de México was more of a commercial bank than a central bank, foundation and operation of the bank significantly transformed the Mexican financial system. As noted in a study by Jaime Gurza, the bank served as a bridge between the transitionary Mexican economy and the transitionary Porfirian banking system (Manero, 1957, pp. 184–185).

Among the objectives in creating the Banco de México was the reestablishment of an effective monetary system and the reorganization of capital mobilization congruent with the revolutionary program of development (Anderson, 1968, p. 116). Prerevolutionary promotion of agro-export interests was gradually displaced by the promotion of industrial-commercial interests and State developmental projects. Foreign ownership was largely replaced by national and State ownership. However, foreign capital retained control, for a limited period, of some institutions, for example, Banco Nacional (Granados Chapa, 1982, pp. 77–83; Loyala Díaz, 1984, p. 13).

During the first phase of its development, private bank interests were incorporated within the Banco de México. The composition of the Administrative Council exemplified the consensus and collaboration between the State and private capital in relation to the gestation of the financial system (Quijano et al., 1983, p. 195). A general consensus existed among top policymakers—Pani, Gómez Morín, De Lima—that the banking system was to be the "agent of development" (Meyer et al., 1977, p. 283). National organization of the banking system, Calles explained in his 1926 Presidential Address, constituted a strong base for future sustenance of Mexican prosperity (Ochoa Campos, 1976, p. 149). Private interests, Calles affirmed, understood the importance of collaboration.

> Private interests also recognize the indispensable necessity of collaborating with the Government and among particular bankers the sentiment is slowly being established that the private bank, far from being detached from public finances, or representing interests antagonistic to Government interests, forms part of the national credit system that is integrated with the money, the credit and the public finances. . . . (Ochoa Campos, 1976, p. 133)

Calles reaffirmed the importance of the harmonization of social and individual interests with the 1928 revision of the 1884 civil code. The 1928 revision, according to Calles, corrected the excessive individualism of the 1884 code (Córdova, 1978, p. 365). Perhaps the quintessential manifestation of the socio-economic collaboration between the State and capital was Pani's creation of the concept of the revolutionary capitalist (Córdova, 1973, p. 362).

The relationship between the State and bank capital was generally cooperative, yet ultimately undefined. The class character of the State remained questionable. That is, the State clearly had a visible degree of autonomy due to the nature of political developments characterizing the postrevolutionary social formation. Relative autonomy was in part due to the fact that the State was still in a process of formation. Moreover, the financial-economic base of the State was relatively weak and State-run financial institutions enhanced the State's economic base. A greater economic base, in turn, enhanced State power to define and direct developmental policies delineating the production and distribution of future national wealth. State autonomy vis-à-vis bank capital was reflected in the creation and competitive operation (with regard to private commercial operations) of the Banco de México.[25] State autonomy was nevertheless simultaneously compromised.[26]

Bank capital exhibited similar vacillating tendencies. Economically, the banking system was largely insolvent. Banks were affected by the destruction of the means of payment, low levels of liquidity, public distrust, and capital flight. Politically, the banks exhibited determinative power in some instances with regard to the State. Although banks were discredited during the Revolution (because of Porfirian privileges and Huerta alliance) and attacked by Carranza, they were nevertheless able to retain sufficient power to regain operational status and initiate and influence the formation of bank policy during the Obregón regime.

Neither the State nor bank capital had decisive power. Nevertheless, there was a general tendency toward an augmentation of the power of bank capital. The relationship between the State and bank capital exemplified a vacillating character, with the State exercising determinative hegemony in specific instances, and bank capital exercising determinative hegemony in specific instances. Collaboration between bank capital and the State in regard to policy initiation and implementation simultaneously exemplified the political-economic weaknesses of the State and bank capital. Both the State and bank capital were in processes of formation.

A succession of political changes in State–bank relations became increasingly clear throughout postrevolutionary history. Carranza's antagonistic nonalliance with the banks was replaced by Obregón's conciliatory efforts, which were succeeded by Calles's new alliance with the banks. The contradictory, antagonistic relationship between bank capital and the State was transformed into a collaborative relationship that superficially benefited the Revolutionary program. President Calles summarized the situation well when he explained, in 1928, that there was a renewal of the ascendant march of the banks (Zevada, 1971, p. 90).

DEVELOPMENT OF THE BANKING SYSTEM IN THE 1930s

The banking system experienced important structural changes during the 1930s. Several laws provided the Banco de México with essential instruments to conduct central bank operations. Laws were also passed to restrict its competitive commercial operations. A number of new national credit institutions were also created, substantially increasing the ability of the State to influence the direction and operation of financial circuits and economic activity. Private bank operations were expanded and State–bank interrelations became increasingly complementary.

The reforms, affecting the organic law regulating the Banco de México and the credit law, reflected the inability of the Banco de México to operate as a central bank and conduct national monetary and financial operations.[27] Low levels of liquidity, public diffidence, and speculation affected monetary stability. Speculation was particularly important in contributing to the devaluation of the peso.[28]

Private banks contributed to financial and monetary instability by participating in speculative profitmaking. Bank speculation was partly related to decreasing profitability. The Depression and progressive reduction of bank operations reduced commercial operations. Another factor was that large amounts of capital continued to be held outside of the banking system and many potential borrowers possessed insufficient loan guarantees.[27] Thus, client deposits decreased.

> Bankers often supported these speculations, pledging external transactions or playing the margin, destining by these operations, public funds against the public's funds, and thus compressing the workers' real income, to deprime the value of the money. (Torres Gaytán, 1980, p. 179)

Banking operations reached disastrous proportions in May 1931. The combined actions of the Exchange Regulatory Commission (Comisión Reguladora de Cambios) and a newly formed bank block or "union" reduced the severity of the situation (Torres Gaytán, 1980, p. 189). The union proposed that the government permit the bankers to establish an extra-official exchange control. Bank clients were then invited to participate in the block by purchasing and selling foreign currency through the banks.[30] In essence, the finance ministry, in collaboration with the banks, created a support system promoting the unification and sustenance of quotation prices, thereby enabling banks to augment their liquidity (Torres Gaytán, 1980, p. 189).

Economic and financial difficulties necessitated reform of the monetary order and the operations of the Banco de México.[31] The July 25, 1931 Calles Law attempted to rectify the inadequacies of the monetary system. The principal elements of the law were (a) the demonetization of gold as an internal means of payment, (b) the constitution of a monetary reserve to cover foreign-exchange losses, and (c) the establishment within the Banco de México of an autonomous Junta Central Bancaria (a central bank directorship), which assumed control of money and exchange operations previously exercised by the Banco de México (Cardero, 1984, pp. 17–18; Manero, 1957, pp. 186–187; Ramirez Goméz, 1984, p. 364; Torres Gaytán, 1980, pp. 194–195; Turrent Díaz, 1982, pp. 253–254).

The political and economic effects of the Calles were significant. Creation of the Junta Central Bancaria reflected internal bureaucratic bank politics. Pani was largely responsible for the foundation of the Banco de México and the integration of its personnel. Montes de Oca, the new finance secretary, endeavored to replace Pani's people. It has also been argued that Montes de Oca was resentful and distrustful of Pani's institution and its programs and policies (Turrent Díaz, 1982, p. 254). The retirement of the Banco de México's monetary and exchange functions was thus the political culmination of Montes de Oca's prior efforts, manifested by the 1927 prohibition of the coining of silver and the 1930 creation of the exchange and monetary commission. Political organization of the junta provides additional support for the bureaucratic perspective; the secretary of finance possessed an absolute veto over junta resolutions (Turrent Díaz, 1982, p. 254). The composition of the junta, however, raises the possibility of additional explanations for the creation of the junta. There were seven junta members: Montes de Oca; Luciano Wiechers, vice president of the Administrative Council for the Banco de México; Gaston Descombés, Banco Nacional de México; O.B. Emeno, Bank of Montreal; James Stewart, Canadian Bank of Commerce; William Richardson, National City Bank; and Alfonso Castello and Melchor Ortega, Banco Nacional de Crédito Agrícola (Turrent Díaz, 1982, p. 254). Five of the seven members integrating the new Junta were representatives of private banks and three of the five were representatives of prominent foreign banks. Although Montes de Oca retained veto powers over committee resolutions, the integration of foreign and national bank capital within the administrative committee determining national monetary and exchange policies manifested the influence of bank capital and the continuation and expansion of the collaborative State–bank relationship.

The Banco de México's organic law was reformed in April 1932. The objectives were to (a) complement the March monetary reform, (b) coordinate commercial and bank activities, and (c) better define the Banco de México's special character as a central bank within the banking system. The reform curtailed the bank's operations with the public and delineated emission guidelines, operations with the federal government, rediscount operations, and prohibited operations (Turrent Díaz, 1982, p. 194). A complementary law, decreed in May 1932, determined that all banks and foreign bank branches receiving time deposits for up to thirty days were obligated to associate with the central bank. Accordingly, the rediscount function was to serve as an important instrument in developing the monetary system. An equally important disposition announced new regulatory norms for foreign bank institutions and denoted guidelines for the constitution and maintenance of capital and deposits. Three of the six foreign banks found the new regulations restrictive and concluded operations in the Mexican market. The departure of foreign banks (e.g., the Banco de Montreal) was significant because these banks constituted some of the largest and most important credit institutions. More important, however, was the purge of foreign bank capital and the corollary nationalization of bank capital.

With the promulgation of these reforms the organization of a new banking order was beginning to take shape. Probably the most important aspect of Pani's program was the new general credit institution law, decreed in June 1932. Gómez Morín elaborated most of the new legislation, and important bankers enjoying Pani's confidence (e.g., Legorreta) examined Gómez Morín's work (Turrent Díaz, 1982, p. 363). The banking system was restructured in accordance with economic requirements for more extensive intermediate and long-term credit operations. The credit system was also delineated into two institutional spheres conducting different operations: private credit institutions and national credit institutions. The new legislation also defined operations of auxiliary credit organizations and noted the need for financieras (investment banks) to promote capital markets and provide long-term financing for industry and agriculture.

The final legislative element of Pani's program, expounded in August, was the Ley de Titulos y Operaciones de Crédito. Credit operations had previously been conducted solely through discount or lending operations. The new legislation expanded the realm of credit operations through the juridical "autonomization" of credit titles; that is, credit operations were no longer restricted to operations with material guarantees. Qualitative credit controls were now possible with the diffusion of different types of bonds, titles, certificates, and obligations. The global impact of this measure was extremely significant in terms of promoting the development of different types of credit operations. For instance, credit controls could now favor production credit operations over mercantile credit operations through particular rediscount operations (Turrent Díaz, 1982, p. 365).

The private banking system rapidly expanded from 1932 to 1933. During Pani's stewardship (February 1932 to September 1933) the finance ministry extended fifty concessions for new banks and auxiliary credit operations (Turrent Díaz, 1982, p. 370). In part, expansion was the result of a clause in the central bank's new organic law that juridically legitimized State subsidization of the formation of new banks associating with the Banco de México. The bank could loan or discount up to 50 percent of the value of the capital share of new associating banks. State participation in the formation of new banks was necessary, according to Pani, because of:

> the impossibility for the government to supply, integrally or even in a substantial magnitude, businesses' strong deficiencies, that the organization of all democratic civilized countries reserve for private initiative and considering the important influence that the development of the bank industry can exercise in accelerating the solution of the monetary problem and the advancement of the national economy . . . (Turrent Díaz, 1982, p. 370)

A second element contributing to the expansion of the private banking sector was the reorganization program initiated by the new central bank director, Augustín Rodríguez. Part of Rodríguez's program was the rationalization of the number of central bank branches. The plan to close seventeen of the twenty-three branches was designed to replace Banco de México branches with private bank institutions. Banco de México branches would be transferred to local banks, which would absorb branch operations. In those instances wherein such a transfer was unfeasible, the Banco de México would create provincial banks to assume branch assets and debits. Three commissions were formed in 1932 to promote the foundation and expansion of private banks in localities where Banco de México branches were scheduled to be closed.[32] Rodríguez's reorganization program also indirectly contributed to the expansion of the private banking system as a result of the adjustment of Banco de México personnel and salaries. Many former bank employees joined Banco Mexicano.[33]

New legislative reforms to the organic credit institution law were enacted in

August 1936. Reform of the organic law of the Banco de México transformed the bank into a modern central bank. The most significant element of the new legislation was the expansion of central bank control of the money market. The Banco de México was also assigned responsibility for promoting the establishment of new specialized credit institutions to satisfy the economic needs of sectors necessitating credit services (Ramírez Gómez, 1984, p. 372). Ultimately, these reforms attempted to increase the links between private banks, credit institutions, and the central bank in an effort to enhance the congruency of institutional functions. This was accomplished through changes in the regulation of credit organization, investment of capital and deposits, modifications in the evaluative criteria of credit institution assets, and prohibition of the payment of interest for demand deposits in checking accounts (Manero, 1957, p. 214; Ramírez Gómez, 1984, pp. 372–373).

Newly established national credit institutions significantly increased the ability of the State to influence capital and money markets.[34] National credit institutions also established a strong financial base for future financial and economic growth. National credit institutions also controlled an increasingly important share of the total resources of the banking system. In 1930, these institutions (excluding the central bank) controlled 2.7 percent of total resources, in comparison with 21 percent in 1939 (Banco de México, 1978).

These institutions contributed to private accumulation. Nafinsa, for example, purchased and placed bonds and other financial instruments of private banks, industries, and the federal government.[35] The Public Works Bank (Banobras) placed road bonds, indirectly benefiting the tourist industry. The Crédito Hotelero financed private hotel construction. Agricultral banks also conceded more capital to private property owners than to ejidatorios (Felipe Leal, 1975, p. 93). In essence, the financial operations of national credit institutions were reciprocally beneficial for private accumulation and State legitimation. A coincidence of interests was also visible in other areas of the financial system.

The collaborative relationship between the State and private bankers in the construction of an integrated financial system was increasingly manifested in the formation of a tacit alliance between the public bureaucracy and bankers. In some instances it was difficult to differentiate between private bankers and State functionaries. Abelardo Rodríguez, for instance, was President of the Republic in 1932 and one of the founders of the Banco Mexicano; the same bank employed ex-functionaries of the Banco de México. Maximino Avila Camacho, governor of Puebla during the Cárdenas administration and brother of the future president, participated with Espinosa Yglesias and William Jenkins in the centralization of the control of the Banco Comercio. Gómez Morín instigated the formation of a group of Mexican businessmen who purchased the majority of the Banco de Londres y México after the bank's 1934 liquidity crisis. Gómez Morín was also one of the founding members of the Sociedad Financiera Mexicana (Sofimex) and engineered the formation of the Banco Londres/Sofimex group. Montes de Oca, former finance secretary (1927–1932) and ex-director of the Banco de México (1935–1940), and Alfonso Cedillo, ex-director of the Asociación Hipotecaria Mexicano and the Créditor Hotelero (State companies), founded the Banco Internaciónal. While director of the Banco de México, Montes de Oca also worked closely with the Mexican Bank Association (ABM) in engineering bank employee legislation (1937).[36] Montes de Oca's promotion of the interests of bank capital from within the State also occurred on other occasions.[37]

The coincidence of interests between the State and bank capital also occurred at the institutional level. The State, through the Banco de México and Nafinsa, participated in the formation of Crédito Minero y Mercantil (Grupo Cremi). The State also had a close relationship with the Banco Nacional, which also served as the depository institution for government debt repayment. The government supported the Banco Nacional in 1934 when its capital–deposit ratio was low and the Banco Nacional later financed State projects (e.g., agricultural projects that other banks refused to support). The bank was also one of the few banks openly supporting the Cárdenas regime.

State promotion of the capital market also engendered mutual interests. National credit institutions, for example, contributed to the initial equity of newly founded financieras, and the Banco de México supported provincial banks through capital participation to augment agricultural credit (Hamilton, 1982).

The political-economic power of bank capital increased during the 1930s. Major competitors—foreign banks and the Banco de México—departed from the financial market and provided ample opportunity for the expansion of national bank capital. Expansion of bank capital was also the result of the State's creation of a parallel development banking system—national credit institutions—devoted to the support and subsidization of traditional and modern developmental strategies (e.g., Ejidal bank and Nafinsa). Development banks simultaneously promoted the financial interests of bank capital and legitimized State interests. The central bank promoted the formation of new banks and financially supported some banks by subscribing to initial capital. Bank social capital rapidly expanded.[38] The formation of financial-industrial groups was also indicative of a general trend that increasingly relied on bank capital as an integral (and sometimes determinative) component structuring the accumulation of capital.[39]

In summary, this period of postrevolutionary finance reflected the contradictory characteristics of the Revolution and the Mexican State-in-formation. Although bank capital was clearly in a period of formation and initial consolidation, the State still dominated the financial circuits.[40] The potential power of bank capital to affect the policy process, and thus State autonomy, was beginning to materialize. Consolidation of bank capital is examined in chapter 3.

NOTES

1. Although many North American academics and apologists for the Mexican Revolution have determined that the culmination of the Revolution was in 1917, I have chosen to follow Bartra (1982a) and Gilly's (1971) delineation of 1920 as the end of the Revolution. As noted by Bartra (1982a), the Mexican State and dominant classes could not appropriate the "fruits" of the Revolution until 1920. The real nature or character of the Revolution, moreover, was not apparent until the 1920 political conjuncture that delineated the political forces of the Revolution. Gilly (1971, p. 309) also delineated 1920 as "the definitive end of the first stage of the Revolution." He notes that Zapata died in 1919 and that the period following his death until mid-1920 was a period of political transition.

Because an analysis of the actual Revolution is not an objective of this project, the interested reader may refer to any of the following works for greater detail: Brandenburg (1964); Córdova (1973); Gilly (1971); Gilly et al., (1979); Hodges and Gandy (1982); Katz (1981); Felipe Leal (1975); Lieuwen (1968); Loeffler (1982).

2. The petty-bourgeois elements of the Revolution were led by Magaña, Madero, and the constitutionalists, and the peasant forces were led by Zapata and Villa.

3. Examples of the continued reproduction of prerevolution social relations included the perseverance of the hacienda system (Felipe Leal & Rountree, 1982; Schryer, 1986) and Porfirian banking institutions, as well as the participation of científicos in the drafting of postrevolutionary banking legislation.

4. As noted by Córdova (1973, pp. 35–37), the essential characteristics of the dominant ideology—or conversely, the ideology of the dominant class—consisted of several elements: (a) the State as the material location for the organization and development of civil society; (b) private property—conceived as a specific form of appropriating material goods—as the principal base of social organization; (c) Mexico's material backwardness was the referential point for determining developmental policies; (d) civil society was considered incapable of providing order and social institutions and therefore the State had to provide the necessary requisites; (e) the State has responsibility to intervene and arbitrate among social classes and interest groups to resolve conflicts and create equilibrium; (f) the popular masses must benefit from developmental policies; (g) the Revolution promotes social reform; (h) foreign investment must be regarded as a necessary tool of development as long as foreign capital respects the principles of the Carranza Doctrine; (i) nationalism is conceived as an ideology, manifesting the political practice of independence and uniform national development; and (j) political groups directing the State apparatus produce the dominant ideology, benefiting the interests of the dominant class through pragmatic state policies.

5. Obregón, for instance, believed that relative disequilibrium among classes was the natural order of an individualistic society (Córdova, 1973, p. 270).

6. A cacique is a local political boss, often linked to a major local employer. A caudillo, in contrast, is a regional and sometimes national strongman often directly or indirectly linked to the military. See Rosas (1983) and Krauze (1985) for a more detailed discussion.

7. Obregón referred to his political entourage in this fashion at one point (Gilly, 1981, p. 322).

8. The unsuccessful de la Huerta revolt (1923) reinforced the regime's military power with regard to regional forces (Lieuwen, 1968, p. 78).

9. The Maximato refers to the period from 1928 to 1934 when Calles ran the government from behind the scenes.

10. See Rubel et al. (1985) for an analysis of the constitutive elements of a Bonapartist regime and the temporal transitions of the conceptual classification.

11. The coincidence of interests between bank capital and the State will be examined in much greater detail in succeeding sections.

12. From 1910 to 1920 production declined: Mining declined approximately 4 percent per year; agriculture declined at an average annual rate of 5.2 percent per year; stock-breeding declined at an average annual rate of 4.6 percent per year; and manufacturing declined at an average rate of 0.9 percent per year (Solís, 1984, pp. 77–78).

13. Additional contributive elements included agricultural reform, the creation of national financial credit institutions, the nationalization of petroleum and the railroads, infrastructure construction, redistributive income measures, public works projects, support of national industry, and promotion of external trade (Hamilton, 1982; Ianni, 1977; Ramírez Brun, 1980; Solís, 1984; Torres Gaytán, 1980).

14. Several factors created a precarious operational environment for the financial system, including Huerta's forced bank loans (1913), confiscation of bank resources by belligerent factions, rapid depreciation of paper money, inflation, and falsification of bank bills.

15. Politically, the 1913 decree was important because it circumscribed the banks from the revolutionary movement and delineated these institutions as part of the counter-revolutionary offensive. Economically, the decree was important because it augmented the degree of monetary disequilibrium, therein affecting the intermediation process.

16. Carranza did not want to provoke the bankruptcy of these banks because such action could heighten the already precarious financial crisis. Moreover, he did not want to create burdensome juridical questions concerning bank–client relations (Torres Gaytán, 1980, p. 130).

17. Prerevolutionary in origin, "banking establishments without concession" were largely foreign-owned institutions that took advantage of the 1916 government seizure of the insolvent emission banks. Six of the forty-four banking establishments without concession controlled 63 percent of the total assets of the financial system (Sánchez Martínez, 1985, p. 41). Banking establishments without concession were composed of banking houses, foreign bank branches, and commercial house extensions and were regulated by the commercial code and not the 1892 law. Banking establishments without concession performed commercial bank operations and rapidly gained control of the majority of the total debits of the financial system. These institutions controlled more

than 50 percent of the demand deposits in 1923 and approximately 70 percent of the demand deposits by 1924 (Sánchez Martínez, 1985, p. 42).

The unstable exchange parity was due to the depreciation of silver as compared with gold, the depreciation affects on the internal/external price ratio, and speculative activities.

18. The federal government owed the banks almost 53 million pesos and was obligated to pay its debt with bonds maturing in eight years at a 6 percent annual interest rate. The bonds were to be used by the banks, on maturation, to settle debits.

19. Helio Dueñes, a banker participating in the banks' organizational meetings, has suggested that the larger banks were interested in a separate "alliance with the President" and the promulgation of legislation that would benefit their interests (Sánchez Martínez, 1985, p. 44). It is undeniable that the promulgation of the 1921 law benefited the larger, very solvent banks and threatened the smaller solvent and insolvent banks. Implementation of the law was nevertheless hampered by political-economic circumstances.

20. An example of one of the numerous unsuccessful endeavors was Obregón's February 1921 legislative proposal calling for the reestablishment of a private-based plural emission system with executive granted concessions, numerically restricted to no more than eight emission banks.

21. The law divided the various institutions into three distinct groups (credit institutions, bank establishments, and establishments assimilated to banks) and delineated the characteristics and functions of different types of credit institutions, the quantity and type of credit operations, and the guarantees and special authorizations regulating specific operations. Regulatory and inspection conditions were also stipulated (Krauze et al., 1977, p. 34; Ramírez Gómez, 1984, pp. 359–359).

22. Two examples of the antagonism existing between some private banks and the Banco de México were the 1926 conflicts with the Compañia Bancaria, Mercantil y Agrícola de Sonora S.A., and the April 1926 conflict with some Chihuahuaense banks (Krauze et al., 1977, pp. 46–47). José Almada, general manager of the Compañia Bancaria, expressed his dissatisfactions with the Banco de México's competitive operations in a letter to President Calles: If the Banco de México is going to continue the same competitive and combative policy, snatching our customers like they have in Mexicali, we prefer . . . to retire . . . (Turrent Díaz, 1982, p. 46)

23. From December 1925 through December 1928, profits increased at a 21.5 percent annual rate and the portfolio increased at a 42.1 percent annual rate (Turrent Díaz, 1982, pp. 149, 151).

24. The Banco de México set interest rates at 4 to 5 percent below the prevailing market rate to give production and commerce the best possible credit conditions (Turrent Díaz, 1982, p. 153).

25. Pani's ability to reduce the amount of the State bank debt by almost 50 percent was another example of State autonomy (Córdova, 1973, p. 362).

26. Examples included the use of former científicos to write new regulatory legislation, the incorporation of private bankers within the administrative council of the Banco de México, and the initiation and establishment of common interests and alliances between the financial bourgeoisie and the State bureaucracy.

27. The reforms promulgated during the initial years of the decade were also the

result of the affects of the depression, devaluation of the peso, and the desire to control the peso–dollar exchange rate.

28. Speculators used all pretexts, including news, rumors, and legislation, to garner profits and destabilize the peso (Torres Gaytán, 1980, p. 179).

29. In 1928, Gómez Morín estimated that 300–500 million pesos were being stored privately (Meyer et al., 1977, p. 289).

30. Bank customers were also obligated to contribute to bank liquidity by depositing three silver pesos for fifteen days for every dollar the client requested (Torres Gaytán, 1980, p. 189).

31. The financial crisis was exacerbated by the low level of bank reserves, the State's compensatory stimulation of gold and silver exports, and the problem of declining State revenue (Turrent Díaz, 1982, p. 297).

32. In Piedras Negras, the bank promoted the foundation of a local bank, the Banco Fronterizo de México. The Durango branch was absorbed by the newly founded Banco Comercial de Durango. The Banco Mercantil de Chihuahua, largely controlled by the Vallina family, absorbed the Chihuahua, Ciudad Juárez, and Parral branches. Some branches were also transferred to provincial chains that were later part of the Bancomer group. Many branches were also transferred to the Banco Nacional (Turrent Díaz, 1982, p. 272).

33. Epigmenio Ibarra, for instance, became director of the Banco Mexicano and Bernabé del Valle became sub-director.

34. National credit institutions, as defined in the 1932 general law of credit institutions, were credit institutions in which the State intervened and subscribed to the majority of capital and reserved the right to name the majority of the members of the administrative council and approve or veto Assembly resolutions (Ramírez Gómez, 1984, p. 366). The number of institutions increased from three in 1930 to ten in 1939.

35. In 1939, Nafinsa's portfolio included securities from the Banco Nacional de México, Banco de Londres y México, Banco de Comercio, Fundidora Monterrey, Industrial de Orizaba, and Cervecería Cuautémoc (Hamilton, 1982, pp. 207–208).

36. The legislation prohibited employee strikes and collective bargaining as well as linking the solution of employee–employer problems to the State.

37. The director of the Banco de México urged finance secretary Suárez to eliminate the tax on capital exports, protested that private sector loans for the Banco Ejidal would be political and constitute unsound banking practices, and organized financing of the sugar industry in support of the sugar cartel. Alfonso Castillo (general manager of the Banco Nacional de Crédito Agrícola) was an important shareholder of the Banco Azucarero (Grupo Sáenz; Cardero, 1984; Granados Chapa, 1982; Hamilton, 1982).

38. The Banco Mexicano and the Banco de Comercio, for example, had an initial social capital of 500,00 pesos in 1932, which had increased to 3 million pesos for the Banco Mexicano and 10 million pesos for the Banco de Comercio by 1940 (Hamilton, 1982, p. 203).

39. See Hamilton (1982, pp. 287–336) for a concise examination of the history of the formation of some of the economic groups.

40. The Central Bank controlled approximately 50 percent of bank resources, development banks controlled approximately 10–20 percent of these resources, and private banks controlled approximately 35 percent of system resources.

Part Two
Finance Capital and the Consolidation of Hegemony

Chapter 3

Postrevolutionary Finance, 1940–1970: Bank Capital Consolidation

Mexican postrevolution finance was greatly affected by economic events and political forces. The dynamics of Mexican finance reflected social class contradictions inherent within the Mexican Revolution and everything that resulted from the Revolution. Economic expansion as manifested in the development model reflected these contradictions. Economic development was segmented and imbalanced, and policies reflected this disequilibrium through a gradual transformation in the relationship between the private sector and the State. The State began to assume a much more important role in terms of promoting modernization and industrial development.

Exemplary of the gradual transition in State-promoted industrialization (and support for the interests of industrial capital) was the use of private financial institutions to promote the transfer of credit for productive investment. During the Cárdenas period, public financial institutions worked closely with the private financial sector to promote increased financial intermediation by expanding the private financial system. In contrast, State intervention in the financial markets during the 1950s was much more direct. Specialized credit instruments were used to regulate reserve requirements and the ratio of financial resources for productive industrial investment. Financial institutions assumed a very important role during the 1950s for several reasons.

Economic disequilibrium increased the importance of financial institutions, financial instruments, and financial flows. Banks and financial institutions, for example, became more important as a means of integrating economic groups (e.g., Grupo Garza-Sada and Banco Serfín, or Grupo CREMI and Crédito Minero)[1] and as a means of channeling low-cost credit to different entities of an economic group. Different financial institutions were also used to circumscribe government regulations.[2] In short, the growing importance of financial circuits affected the political-economic power of bank capital and changed the relationship between banks and the State. This chapter examines these sociopolitical changes.

1940–1949: A TRANSITIONARY PERIOD

During the Cárdenas administration (1934–1940), an increasingly important precedent was established for State intervention and participation in production and finance. Politically, the regime institutionalized the class struggle within the State. National objectives of social equity, neutral arbitration, and conciliation were subordinated to the specific interests corresponding to private accumulation. Although Mexico was predominantly a rural-agrarian society with an incipient bourgeoisie, State-promoted private accumulation enhanced the political-economic power of industrial and bank capital vis-à-vis the bourgeoisie and the State.

State promotion of industrial capital interests was not, however, an instantaneous development. It occurred gradually with the increasingly pervasive legitimation of the industrialization myth, the legacy of Cárdenas, and the consolidation of the State. The industrialization myth—the idea that development and modernization are attained through industrialization—was the "secret of the populist movement" (Córdova, 1972, p. 66). It resolved the internal contradictions of the revolutionary class coalition and transposed the specific interests of the bourgeoisie into the general will. Private sector representatives, for example, participated on the boards of directors of *paraestatales* (public sector parastate enterprises)—for example, the National Railroad, light company, and social security institute—to legitimate State firms and gain private sector support.

The new alliance between the State and private capital became patently evident during the Alemán administration (1946–1952). Alemán's national development plan provided for State support of the private sector and diffusion of foreign capital.[3] Additional elements included the contraction of real wages and the promotion of capital accumulation. Inflation, full employment of capital resources, a labor surplus, and repression of the labor movement contributed to income redistribution from labor to capital.

World War II also had a tremendous impact on the Mexican economy. The drastic reduction in imports and the increase in nontraditional exports changed the traditional enclave accumulation model, structurally the same accumulation model since 1880. A new accumulation model emerged in the post-1940 period, based on industrial import substitution and an integrated domestic market.

The Mexican economy was in a transitionary phase of rapid economic expansion. State promotion of economic expansion, particularly infrastructure development, augmented manufacturing and agricultural production. Public capital formation also played a significant role in stimulating production and demand. The State, however, had financial problems because of political constraints restricting fiscal reform and the inability to conduct large scale open-market operations. The only solution was monetary expansion and continued reliance on central bank loans.

During this period the financial system grew in quantitative and qualitative terms. Substantial legislative changes transformed the bank system. Three important laws were promulgated during the decade. The first reform affected the regulatory regime of the Banco de México. The second reform (May 1941) amended the general law of credit institutions. A new legal regime delineated six types of credit institutions into two separate markets with different functions and clients. The money market—served by deposit, savings, and financieras—was organized to support the production cycle with the provision of short-term credit, that is, up to a 180-day maturity. The capital market—served by hipotecarias, capitalization societies, and fiduciary institutions—was organized to operate with long-term bonds and obligations maturing beyond 180 days.[4] The third reform (1949) affected general credit institutions, restructuring bank portfolio regulations by creating additional reserve requirements and new credit instruments.

These juridical reforms strengthened the regulatory powers of the central bank and attempted to regulate the development of the financial system through the promotion of a capital market. However, as was historically the case, efforts to regulate the banking sector were limited by the power of the banks vis-à-vis the State. Structural dynamics of the economy increased State dependence on private sector bank capital to finance development. Concretely, division of the capital market and money market was an attempt to delineate short-term and long-term forms of credit and the corollary institutions and clientele. Historically, as noted in chapter 1, several prior attempts to separate these markets and develop investment institutions failed because bankers were unwilling to cooperate and because regulations were largely ignored and not enforced. A fundamental problem in developing a capital market was regulators' misunderstanding of managerial differences between short-term and long-term capital relative to investment banks and commercial banks. In reality, different types of banks were owned by the same firms, and, as exemplified by the portfolio structures, these institutions used a short-term framework, regardless of the juridical classification as a commercial bank or an investment bank.

A second fundamental problem contributing to the ineffectual implementation of these juridical innovations was the introduction of reserve requirements. Reliance on reserve requirements as a major regulatory instrument demonstrated the inability of the State to control monetary policy in a conventional manner, for example, open market operations or rediscount operations. The reserve mechanism was intended to reduce the State's financial dependency on the creation of money and at the same time to use existing liquidity (which had expanded during World War II as a result of capital repatriation and incoming foreign capital), instead of contributing to the level of liquidity. A corollary problem was that the value of the peso was defined by external mechanisms and institutions (e.g., the balance of payments and international financial institutions) that restricted the national character of money capital. The effect restricted the scope of equilibrium operations to the continued reliance on devaluation as an instrument to restore the balance of payments equilibrium, and therein, the value of the peso.

The Banco de México also attempted to use selective reserve requirements and interest rate ceilings and floors to channel credit to specific sectors, for example, agriculture, industry, or commerce. In practice, these instruments were less effective than expected, due to the enormous increase in deposits resulting from incoming foreign and national capital and pent-up demand from the War. Thus, quantitative controls were counteracted by the increase in funds, and qualitative controls were affected by the fact that regulation was limited to a quantitative or countable inspection, on the basis of subjective interpretations of the categorization of lending practices (Torres Gaytán, 1980, p. 269).

1950–1959: DEFINITION OF AN ACCUMULATION MODEL

The industrial growth policies of the Alemán administration resulted in high inflation and large budget deficits. The ensuing crisis delegitimized the political system and structured the policy agenda for the incoming Ruíz Cortines regime (1952–1958).[5] Policy was consequently eclectic.

The Ruíz Cortines *sexenio* (the six-year presidential term) can be divided into three periods (Puga et al., 1976, p. 70). Policies during the first period (1952 to 1954) attempted to reduce inflation through austerity by reducing public sector participation in the economy. In essence, the objective was to reduce inflation and maintain political stability. Private investment, however, decreased in response to contractionary economic policies and the post–Korean War export decline.

The second phase (1954–1956) of the sexenio was marked by an increase in public sector spending. A tacit State–capital alliance aimed at increasing production through increased private sector investment. Equally important was the tacit accord, which clarified the economic role of the State vis-à-vis the private sector.

The third policy phase (1956–1958) combined the goals of the two prior periods. Public policy was oriented toward attaining price stabilization, private sector confidence, public sector promotion of industrial production, and political stability. An important change was the means of promoting industrial production. Greater emphasis was placed on fiscal and credit measures to stimulate private investment, for instance, tax exemptions and subsidies rather than direct public investment.[6]

The López Mateos administration (1958–1964) inherited an economy in recession, and a mobilized independent labor and campesino movement.[7] Efforts were made to neutralize labor protests, ameliorate the commercial balance deficit, and restructure fiscal policies. Additional measures included prioritizing public sector investment for strategic industries, increasing social welfare expenditures, and reorganizing the bureaucracy.

> In summary, the State seemed to be ready to participate in an open and decided form in the planning of development, creating the instances to administer its resources in an equal form and channel them to priority areas. (Puga et al., 1986, p. 93)

Statistically it appeared that the Mexican economy was expanding at a rapid pace and that industrial-based modernization was a definitive trend. An important policy debate nevertheless developed. Economic disequilibrium caused a debate about State fiscal, financial, and monetary policies.

The 1954 devaluation stimulated a definitive political discussion of the future orientation of fiscal-monetary policy and the appropriateness of devaluation as a corrective tool. At a general level, the structuralist–monetarist debate concerned the propriety of inflationary versus noninflationary finance. Structuralists argued that inflation was the only way to finance development, and demand for financial assets was inelastic relative to yield. Monetarists, in contrast, held that an increase in the real yields of financial assets would stimulate the public to increase its holdings of financial assets, which would stimulate the financial markets that, in conjunction with foreign capital, would alleviate the need to resort to inflationary finance therein resulting in price stability and a balance of payments surplus.[8]

The monetarists won the debate. The economy expanded at an average annual rate of 6.7 percent (1956–1970), with relative price stability equivalent to a 4.2 percent average annual inflation rate (1956–1970; Guillén Romo, 1984, pp. 28, 35).[9] Although inflation remained low, political stability was relatively constant, the exchange rate was stable, and economic growth was impressive, the balance of payments and the government budget continued to register deficits. Savings and investment were substantially increased by relying on foreign investment and foreign loans, subsidies, tax exemptions, low tariffs on public goods and services, and increasing real rates of return on financial instruments.

There was a close correlation between changes in the accumulation model and financial policies and priorities. Bank financing was generally extended to those sectors generating the highest profit rates because they were able to comply with financial requirements. Thus, State-promoted sectors and branches were able to obtain a greater share of total financing because they were able to take advantage of reduced production costs and protectionist measures to augment profits. Credit for the industrial sector declined during the 1950s, and within the industrial sector producers of consumer goods received an increasing share of credit. The share of bank credit for commerce remained constant. Agriculture, in contrast, received more bank credit over the decade.

The changing structure of agricultural finance was exemplified throughout the economy. Private banks financed risky agricultural projects because the State guaranteed the profits. Private banks also loaned to large capitalist agricultural operations. In contrast, State financial institutions loaned to sectors that the private banks would not support because of insufficient returns or the likelihood of nonrecoverable returns. The State, in other words, indirectly subsidized the private accumulation of capital by restricting its operational realm. The increasing participation of public sector banks in financing agriculture, in conjunction with the dramatic increase in the amount of direct foreign investment in the agricultural sector, also reflected the increasing transformation of the agricultural sector.[10]

Private banks, in contrast, tended to lend capital to large private enterprises located in the northern part of the country. According to a study by de Albornoz (1966), 70 percent of private bank lending capital distributed to the agricultural sector was conceded to large private agricultural endeavors (cited in Cardero, 1984, p. 62). Private banks provided capital to these clients because large private agricultural operations were good credit risks and because the State created mechanisms (e.g., *fideicomisos:* trusteeships) to ensure that private bank investments and profits were guaranteed.

An important change that was linked to the new accumulation model was State finance. There were substantial changes in financing the government budget deficit. The amount of government securities in bank portfolios doubled from 2 billion pesos in 1950 to 4 billion pesos in 1959 (Banco de México, n.d., p. 17). The most important change was the distribution of these securities among the different institutions. Over the course of the decade, private bank portfolios held a greater share of government securities, whereas the percentage held by State banks declined.[11]

Privatization of State finance corresponded with the coincidence of interests typifying bank-State relations in the postrevolutionary period. The significance of transferring the absorption of State debt from public credit institutions to private institutions was two-fold. First, the continuing inability of the State to obtain sufficient financial resources to alleviate its perpetual budget deficits reflected the inability to initiate fiscal reform. Second, the State was able to dramatically expand the means of payment, the issue of financial obligations, and the level of private bank financing. An important aspect of the expansion of the means of payment was the introduction of nonmonetary debt instruments. State deficits were financed by private banks through bank intermediation, which reflected the universalization of the social cost of State-promoted accumulation.

The most important aspect of the continuing expansion of the bank system was the general reorganization of the entire system. Although no new private banks were created, the number of bank branches nearly tripled from 322 in 1950 to 963 in 1960. The bank departments of savings and fiduciary banks also increased from 236 in 1950 to 1,414 in 1960 (Cardero, 1984, p. 65). Three new national credit institutions were created: the Patronato del Ahorro Nacional (1950), the Banco Nacional de Transportes (1953), and the Financiera Nacional Azucarera (1953; Ramírez Gómez, 1984, pp. 390, 397). It is interesting that the number of bank institutions declined from 248 in 1950 to 244 in 1960. More important, however, was the diminishing number of institutions that controlled an increasing percentage of total resources, that is, concentration and centralization. Thus, in 1950, fourteen banks controlled 60 percent of total resources, whereas only seven banks controlled the same percentage of resources in 1960. In a similar manner, forty-two banks controlled 75 percent of total resources in 1950, compared with twenty-six institutions controlling the same percentage of resources in 1960 (Cardero, 1984, p. 65). The same phenomenon was occurring among financieras.[12] A final element of the systematic reorganization was the dollarization of the financial system.[13]

A rapid dollarization of the banking system occurred in the 1950s. This phenomenon was demonstrated by the increasing importance of obligations, as a percentage of financial obligations, denoted in foreign currencies. Total system foreign currency obligations increased from 25 percent of financial obligations in 1950 to 38 percent of financial obligations in 1959 (Banco de México, n.d., p. 22).

The distribution of resources among the various financial institutions also changed during the decade. In terms of total system resources, private banks expanded the most.[14] Among private banks, financieras grew the fastest.[15] The rapid expansion of financieras was in large part a reflection of an integrated banking network and differentiated regulatory regime that affected different types of financial institutions differently.[16]

These integrated financial networks were able to transfer resources through interbank lending.[17] Funds were distributed among different institutions of the same network to obtain the most efficient rates of return and to circumvent regulations that treated different types of financial institutions differently.[18]

Another example of special regulatory provisions for financieras was a State authorization permitting financieras to issue guaranteed financiera bonds in the absence of a guarantee. The State indirectly guaranteed financiera bonds with the condition that the proceeds from these issues were to be re-invested in government securities. Ultimately, State authorization of nonguaranteed financiera bonds exemplified a trend that would become much more pervasive in the 1970s (e.g., one percent in 1959).[19]

Financieras constituted one of the most dynamic elements of integrated bank networks. Originally, financieras were supposed to provide long-term credit for industrial production. Legislative reforms, however, enabled financieras to capture short-term resources, exempt from interest rate regulations. The juridical classification of financieras was also changed in 1941, transforming auxiliary institutions into money market institutions. The unparalleled expansion of financieras was also the result of unrestricted financial participation in businesses and the unrestricted extension of consumer credit. In other words, financieras developed into an important intermediary between the financial, commercial, and productive circuits.

> Financieras assumed a determinant role: affecting in advance, the realization of the value of real capital in the financial sphere . . . that in the process, postponed and displaced the presence of money capital, affecting production, distribution and consumption circuits. (Cardero, 1984, p. 73)

The lending practices of financieras tended to favor the production and commercial spheres. Fifty percent of financiera credit was distributed to the productive sphere and 41 percent was for commercial activity in 1959.[20]

1960s: END OF AN ERA

The López Mateos administration (1958–1964) confronted serious political and economic problems. Worker and campesino social unrest[21] was reduced through repression and a policy called "social stabilization" that restructured independent union movements and paraestatales. Declining private investment was compounded by the Cuban "threat" and the leftist discourse of the López Mateos regime.

Capital flight and reduced private investment were nothing less than the material manifestation of the increasing power of the bourgeoisie. The bourgeoisie wanted political stability and continued subsidization of accumulation in the name of industrial development. The power of the bourgeoisie manifested structural coincidence and subjective class forces. The ever-present "crisis of confidence," in combination with the concrete coordination of policies and positions advocated by peak associations (e.g., the Mexican Bank Association [ABM], the CONCAMIN, and the Confederación Patronal de la Republica [COPARMEX]) exemplified the power of the bourgeoisie.[22] Structurally, internal and external economic stagnation increased the need for private investment. In addition to the situational strength of the private sector, the power of the bourgeoisie had increased as a result of postwar economic expansion, industrial development, and modernization. In essence, the bourgeoisie were in a position to condition or influence the exercise and realm of State power. In other words, relative State autonomy was increasingly constricted by structural-class forces.

The Díaz Ordaz administration (1964-1970) continued to support the economic premises of stabilizing development while simultaneously confirming the importance of political order.[23] Above all, the administration promoted private investment by guaranteeing political stability, augmenting demand through public sector investment and external loans, utilizing noninflamatory rhetoric (i.e., non-leftist), and encouraging foreign investment (Newell & Rubio, 1984, p. 108). Public sector investment rapidly increased as did the contraction of foreign loans and sectoral imbalances. The State's democratic facade was a farce, and its ability to promote development produced sectoral imbalance, economic disarray, and political capitulation in favor of the interests of the domestic and international bourgeoisie. Relative State autonomy was further eroded by the increasingly apparent stagnation of the stabilizing development accumulation model.

Balance of payments disequilibrium and sectoral imbalances were serious problems confronting the Mexican economy during the 1960s. Imports continued to exceed exports (Solís, 1981, p. 92). The current account constantly registered deficits ranging from $156 million in 1962 to $632 million in 1968 (Green, 1981, p. 28; Newell & Rubio, 1984, p. 293). Public sector foreign debt increased from $64 million in 1960 to $5 billion in 1969 (Green, 1981, p. 24). Direct foreign investment increasingly played a more important role in the economy, expanding from $1 billion in 1960 to $2.5 billion in 1969 (Gaytán, 1980). These developments reflected sectoral imbalances characteristic of the

ISI stabilizing development accumulation model (Rodríguez, 1983; Ros & Vásquez, 1984; Solís, 1981).

The distribution of credit was interconnected with the problem of economic disequilibrium. Private banks primarily lent to dynamic, profitable sectors and many important companies were often part of an economic group closely connected to a private lending institution. Institutional specialization in the sectoral distribution of credit was also another predominant trend.

Private banks tended to lend to the industrial and commercial sectors, whereas public banks provided funding for less lucrative activities. More specifically, savings and deposit banks increased their proportion of credit extended to the commercial sector and decreased the share of credit for productive activities. Financieras reduced the percentage of credit for the commercial and productive spheres and increased the percentage of credit for the government. National credit institutions, in contrast, primarily lent to the agricultural sector, industry, and public works (de Albornoz, 1980, p. 57).

The distribution of resources among financial institutions continued to reflect the underlying dynamics of the banking system. There was a predominant reduction in the amount of resources controlled by the central bank and there was a minor reduction in the percentage controlled by national credit institutions.[24] In contrast, private and mixed banks controlled a greater share of resources.[25] There was also a shift of resources among private banks. Resources controlled by financieras and hipotecarias increased substantially, whereas resources controlled by savings and deposit banks substantially declined.[26]

These statistics illustrate three significant changes in the banking system during the 1960s. The first noteworthy trend was a shift in the growth of resources held by private credit institutions. Second, private and mixed banks controlled more than 50 percent of system resources. A third important development was the emergence of financieras as the predominant private institution.

The rapid growth of financieras was largely due to efforts of the central bank. The Banco de México attempted to regulate the expansion of financieras by limiting the expansion rate of debits to 1 percent per month and subjecting incoming capital to rigorous reserve requirements.[27] Financieras could circumvent the 1 percent rule by placing financiera bonds.

These measures were designed to facilitate three objectives. First, the Banco de México wanted to increase its control of bank system liquidity by controlling the unregulated flow of capital to financieras through the imposition of greater quantitative and qualitative reserve requirements. A second objective was to restructure the maturity structure of financiera obligations, emphasizing longer-term financing. The third objective was to enhance the development of the security market by increasing long-term bank financing of businesses and individuals. A corollary objective was to reduce interest rates by indirectly providing incentives to increase the issue of financiera bonds, an instrument with a regulated interest rate and relative longer-term maturity (de Albornoz, 1980, pp. 43–44).

Financiera expansion also reflected the concentration and centralization dynamic of the private banking system. Twelve financieras controlled 76 percent of financiera resources in 1960, 44 percent of exhibited capital, and 52 percent of profits. The five largest financieras controlled 60 percent of total resources, 36 percent of exhibited capital, and 39 percent of the profit.[28] By 1968 the twelve largest financieras controlled 84 percent of resources, 63 percent of exhibited capital, and 68 percent of profits. The four largest financieras controlled 61 percent of resources, 46 percent of exhibited capital, and 47 percent of profits (de Albornoz, 1980, pp. 64–68).

The same concentration and centralization processes continued in the larger banking system. In 1960, thirteen banks controlled 72 percent of the 1,003 branches and agencies, 80 percent of private bank resources, 77 percent of exhibited capital, and 81 percent of the profits. More specifically, four banks (Banamex, Bancomer, Banco de Londres, and Comermex) controlled 57 percent of the institutions, 63 percent of total resources, 56 percent of exhibited capital, and 61 percent of profits. By 1968, fourteen banks controlled 74 percent of the 1,165 branches and agencies, 69 percent of exhibited capital, 85 percent of private bank resources, and 83 percent of private bank profits. The four largest banks controlled 67 percent of private bank resources, 49 percent of exhibited capital, and 65 percent of private bank profits.

Concentration and centralization among bank groups also occurred during the decade. In 1960, nine bank groups controlled 75 percent of the institutions, 74 percent of private bank resources, 63 percent of exhibited capital, and 71 percent of profits. Banamex and Bancomer, the two largest entities, controlled 38.4 percent of the institutions, 41 percent of resources, 26 percent of exhibited capital, and 34 percent of profits. By 1968, seven groups controlled 81 percent of the institutions, 78 percent of the resources, 66 percent of exhibited capital, and 72 percent of the profits. In comparison, Banamex and Bancomer controlled 41 percent of the institutions, 45 percent of the resources, 32 percent of the exhibited capital, and 40 percent of the profits (de Albornoz, 1980, pp. 64–68).

The implications of the concentration and centralization processes are tremendous. The integration of financial institutions within larger economic groups permitted the establishment and financial support of larger economic entities with stability and liquidity. Bank groups also used interbank loans to skate regulations and enhance profitability and liquidity. Moreover, financial institutions integrated within an economic group could channel capital at preferred interest rates to companies that were integrated within the economic group.[29] The quintessential aspect of these processes, however, was the exponential growth in the political-economic power of the banks.

CONCLUSION

The power of bank capital increased dramatically during the 1940–1969 period. The banking system expanded more rapidly than the economy, and private banks grew more rapidly than public sector banks. Expansion of the banking sector was intricately interrelated with the industrial accumulation model and State subsidization of the accumulation model. A concrete example was the development and expansion of financieras.[30] The number of bank branches also increased substantially as did the concentration and centralization processes. The financial system developed quantitatively and diversified in qualitative terms. Structurally, the most important change was the privatization of financial circuits.

The most representative example of the privatization of financial circuits was the reorganization of State finance. The transition in government financing corresponded with changes in the overall conception of how to achieve modernization. Emphasis was redirected from direct public investment as a primary tool to the use of indirect fiscal and credit measures to stimulate the private sector. The same thing occurred in the banking sector. The relative role of State banks in the financial circuits deteriorated from 1940 to 1969. The State resorted to quantitative and qualitative controls in an attempt to regulate the growth and distribution of credit by private banks. Part of the explanation for the relative withdrawal of the State from the financial circuits was simple economics. National credit institution profits tended to diminish because these institutions were largely involved in unprofitable investments, and the profit margin was relatively lower than the profit margin for private banks. Declining profits were also related to disproportionate ratios of circulating and fixed assets that had to be covered by credit. Nafinsa, for example, was a prime example of the falling rate of profit.[31]

Part of the explanation was undoubtedly political. The private sector expanded at a tremendous pace during the 1940–1969 period. Its economic expansion was simultaneously transformed into political power. A concrete example of the political power of capital was the capitulation of the López Mateos regime's political-economic policies (previously discussed in this chapter) and the redefinition of the realm of State intervention in the economy. Capital's political power was not simply a de facto determinism or an exercise in instrumentalism but reflected the coincidence of interests between the State and capital.

The coincidence of interests was clearly demonstrated by the privatization of government finance. The transfer of financing the deficit from the central bank to private banks, particularly financieras, coincided with the position of monetarists and supporters of stabilizing development. At a deeper level, however, the privatization of debt reflected an increasingly pervasive pattern of declining State autonomy vis-à-vis bank capital. Although the State discontinued its monetization of the debt, financial dependence on the private banking network was simultaneously increased. The net effect of the State's new financial dependence was to reduce its ability to regulate private bank operations. More important was the changing correlation of powers within the power bloc.

Bank capital, specifically finance capital, began to exercise a much more prominent position within the power bloc during the late 1950s and the 1960s.[32] The increasing political power of bank-finance capital resulted from the State's promotion of the finance sector and efforts to promote the capital market; reorganize the productive structure and the financial circuits with respect to industrialization (e.g., the intermediating role of banks as an integrating factor between the productive, financial, and commercial circuits; and the bourgeoisie's use of speculation and capital flight as an instrument to discipline the State); and the reorganization of the financial sector, that is, the concentration and centralization process accompanying the general monopolization and transnationalization of the economy.

In sum, the vertical and horizontal integration and expansion of bank-finance capital enabled bank-finance capital to affect the decision-making processes of the State as manifested in political-economic policies defining the accumulation model and the dynamism of the class structure. Through its influence within the power bloc, bank-finance capital was able to shape the parameters of the financial circuits while simultaneously distorting the productive apparatus and the flow of capital.[33] The consequent distortion of the productive, commercial, and financial circuits contributed to the genesis and reproduction of finance capital.

NOTES

1. Financial-economic groups will be examined in greater detail in chapter 4.

2. Financieras, for example, were permitted to retain lower reserves, a practice that enabled these newly created institutions to play a preponderant role in the strategy of powerful economic groups.

3. In President Alemán's words: "The private sector ought to have all the freedom and be supported by the State in its development, particularly when this is done positively for the benefit of the collectivity. Ownership of real estate ought to be primarily in the hands of the nationals, following the principles established in our charter; but foreign capital that comes to share the destiny of Mexico will be free to enjoy its legitimate profits" (cited in Newell & Rubio, 1984, p. 88).

4. The law also established variable or selective reserve requirements (*encajes legales*). The reserve requirements varied according to the category of the deposit, the geographic zone or specific location of the bank, and the origin of the money (i.e., national or foreign). New control mechanisms were also created, including: selective credit portfolios, obligatory investments in government securities, interest rate structures, money supply measures, and the facility for national credit institutions to channel resources to specific sectors.

5. The Henríquez electoral challenge and consequent repression raised the succession crisis.

6. These stimulative measures undoubtedly contributed to the 60 percent increase in foreign investment from 1952 to 1958 (Puga et al., 1986, p. 76).

7. The political-economic policies of the López Mateos administration will be examined in greater detail in the next section because most of the regime's tenure occurred during the 1960s.

8. Given the importance of these changes in terms of setting the stage for "the Mexican Miracle" and its subsequent collapse, the fiscal-monetary policies that affected the Mexican economy will be examined in a subsequent section of this chapter within the context of State finance and the development of the financial markets.

9. The annual inflation rate was 4 percent from 1956 to 1970 (Guillén Romo, 1984, pp. 28–35).

10. Direct foreign investment increased from $6.1 million in 1954 to $21.5 million in 1958. In a similar manner, the average increase was 16 percent from 1951 to 1953, in comparison with 24 percent from 1955 to 1959 (Cardero, 1984, p. 54).

11. The amount of government securities held by the central bank decreased from 74 percent of government securities held by banks in 1950 to 39 percent of bank-held government securities in 1959. Deposit banks increased holdings of government securities from 11 percent in 1950 to 26 percent in 1959. Financieras holdings of government securities increased from 1 million pesos in 1950 to 668 million pesos in 1959 (Solis & Brothers, 1967, pp. 124–125).

12. Four financieras (of 97) controlled 49 percent for all financiera resources and the top eight firms controlled 60 percent of financiera resources. The top eight financieras were: Sociedad Mexicana de Crédito Industrial (17 percent), Compañia General de Aceptaciones (grupo Garza Sada de Monterrey; 10 percent), Crédito Bursátil (Banamex; 10 percent), Financiera Bancomer (12 percent), Crédito Minero y Mercantil (grupo Bailleres; 4 percent), Financiera del Norte (grupo Garza Sada; 3 percent), Financiera Industrial, (2 percent); and Financiera y Fiduciaria de Chihuahua (2 percent; Cardero, 1984, p. 73).

13. The term *dollarization* is a commonly used word to denote the process of currency substitution, that is, the increased usage of a foreign currency vis-à-vis the national currency.

14. The share of resources controlled by the central bank more than doubled from

5.6 billion pesos in 1950 to 12.2 billion pesos in 1959, but decreased as a percentage of total system resources, from 34 percent in 1950 to 25 percent in 1959. National credit institution resources significantly increased from 3.9 billion pesos in 1950 to 14.6 billion pesos in 1959, and increased as a percentage of total system resources, from 24 percent in 1950 to 29 percent in 1959. Private and mixed bank resources increased the most, from 6.6 billion pesos in 1950 (41 percent of total system resources) to 23 billion pesos in 1959 (46 percent).

15. Financiera resources increased from 917 million pesos in 1950 (15 percent of resources distributed among these private institutions, or 6 percent of system resources) to 6.8 billion pesos (31 percent of these private bank resources, or 14 percent of system resources) in 1959. Savings and deposit bank resources increased from 5 billion pesos in 1950 to 15 billion pesos in 1959, but declined as a percentage of private bank resources, from 82 percent to 68 percent. Finally, hipotecaria resources increased from 190 million pesos (3 percent) to 343 million pesos (1.5 percent of resources; Banco de México, n.d.).

16. Different types of banks and financial institutions were generally part of an overall financial network controlled by one firm. Grupo Comermex, for example, controlled Financiera de Valores and Financiera y Fiduciaria de Chihuahua, and Financiera Bancomer was owned by Bancomer.

17. An example of interbank lending was the practice of channeling short-term fideicomiso loans from savings and deposit banks to financieras, which discounted the deposit banks' portfolio as a contingent debit exempt from reserve requirements.

18. For example, financiera resources expanded rapidly during the 1950s because these financial institutions were subject to less regulation than savings and deposit institutions and could therefore obtain higher earnings. Prior to February 1958, financieras were required to set aside a reserve for demand deposits and time deposits, and the rest of their financial instruments were equivalent to only 1.1 percent of obligations in 1951 and 1957. The majority of financieras' obligations were in time and demand obligations in national and foreign currencies (Banco de México, n.d., p. 76) exempt from reserve requirements.

19. More specifically, the dollarization of local financial circuits, wherein financial institutions captured foreign exchange and the State converted these resources into reserves, assuming the risk of devaluation.

20. Disaggregating the share of credit dispersed for commercial activity reveals that 19 percent was extended to banks, 21 percent for auto sales, 19 percent for real estate development, 8 percent for electrical appliances and goods for the home, 8 percent for machinery distribution, 5 percent for clothing and material, and 21 percent for other commercial credits (Cardero, 1984, p. 72).

21. Workers' demands included increased wages, democratization of unions, and participation in the administration of paraestatales. Campesinos invaded agricultural land and demanded changes in irrigation and credit policies benefiting export agriculture.

22. COPARMEX is a peak organization, founded by Luis Garza Sada in 1929, that represents the interests of the northern fraction of the bourgeoisie.

23. The "father" of desarrollo estabilizador, finance secretary Ortiz Mena, was retained by the new president. In regard to political stability, the President himself stated unequivocally that: "It is necessary and compelling for all, for the benefit of all, to

exactly obey our legal regime. It must be obeyed in every order: that which benefits and that which hurts; that which goes one way and that which comes back . . . ''(cited in Newell & Rubio, 1984, p. 108). The quintessential demonstration of Diaz Ordaz's pervasive determination to maintain order was the 1968 massacre at the Plaza of Three Cultures.

24. Central bank resources increased from 13 billion pesos in 1960 to 33 billion pesos in 1969 but, in terms of system resources, decreased from 22 percent in 1960 to 15 percent in 1969. In a similar manner, national credit institution resources increased from 20 billion pesos in 1960 to 64 billion pesos in 1969, but decreased from 33 percent of system resources in 1960 to 29 percent in 1969.

25. Private and mixed bank resources increased from 27 billion pesos in 1960 to 123 billion pesos in 1969, and as a percentage of system resources, increased from 43 percent in 1960 to 56 percent in 1969.

26. Financiera resources increased from 9 billion pesos in 1960 to 59 billion pesos in 1969, and as a percentage of these private bank resources, increased from 35 percent in 1960 to 49 percent in 1969. Hipotecaria resources increased from 472 million pesos in 1960 to 13 billion pesos in 1969. Savings and deposit bank resources increased from 16 billion pesos in 1960 to 49 billion pesos in 1969 (Banco de México, n.d.).

27. Quantitative controls included a 1 percent reserve in cash and a 19 percent reserve in government securities. Qualitative reserves included 40 percent of credits to be channeled to productive activities, and 40 percent of credits to be channeled to the commercial sector.

28. Sociedad Mexicana de Crédito Industrial, S.A.; la Compañia General de Aceptaciones, S.A.; Financiera Bancomer, S.A.; Crédito Bursátil, S.A.; and Financiera de Norte, S.A.

29. Financial-economic group activities will be examined in much greater detail in chapter 4.

30. More specifically, regulations that permitted these institutions to circumvent State controls in the name of industrial modernization directly enhanced the expansion of private bank networks and their corporate counterparts.

31. In 1961, Nafinsa obtained a 13 percent return. By 1968, the return had declined to 9 percent. At the same time, its profits as a percentage of expenses decreased from 15 percent to 10 percent (Cardero, 1984, p. 103).

32. The genesis of finance capital will be examined in chapter 6.

33. The multiplication of money capital was faster than the valorization of lending capital (Cardero, 1984, p. 127).

Chapter 4

Finance Capital, the State, and Political-Economic Stagflation

Development and diversification of the financial system during the 1940–1970 period was nothing less than extraordinary. The financial system expanded faster than the economy and private banks grew fastest, financing government budget deficits and industrial and commercial concentration and centralization.

Privatization of financial circuits coincided with the idea of modern industrial capitalist development. Rapid expansion of private banks enabled the State to underwrite capitalist accumulation and transfer surplus value between various social and economic sectors. Bank capital expansion not only allowed the State to increase its realm of political-economic operations, it also facilitated the expansion of capital by integrating the productive, financial, and commercial circuits. The structural expansion of bank capital also manifested increasing political power with regard to the State and other fractions of capital. These developments contributed to the success of the new accumulation model of the 1950s.

The stabilizing development accumulation model, based on the proliferation of capitalist relations of production and the expansion of industrial production through State incentives and subsidies, engendered a short-term "Mexican miracle." By the mid-1960s, the miracle was less than miraculous, producing irresolvable contradictions that intermittently resulted in conjunctural crises. During the 1970s, the fiscal crisis of the State, in conjunction with a politically delegitimized and debilitated State, restricted the political and economic maneuverability of the State. A crisis of unparalleled proportions developed.

The crisis of the Mexican State was more than a structural problem. Class factors also affected relative State autonomy. State-promoted economic development generated new fractions of the bourgeoisie and simultaneously fortified and transformed previously existing fractions of the bourgeoisie. For example, juridical reforms during the 1970s promoted concentration and centralization of industry and finance. The State directly fomented the genesis and consolidation of finance capital and the corollary consolidation of monopoly capital as manifested in the formation of integrated holding companies. The transformation of bank capital and the interconnected development of finance capital and integrated economic groups were inversely related to relative State autonomy. In addition, the crisis of the State was compounded by contentious fractions of the bourgeoisie. The increasing incidence of interclass and intraclass struggle and the inability of the State to mediate these conflicts contributed to a degenerative dynamic affecting the entire social formation.

ACCUMULATION, FINANCE CAPITAL, AND DESARROLLO COMPARTIDO

The accumulation model based on State-promoted industrial import-substitution (ISI) significantly transformed the forces and relations of production during the postwar period. Expansion and development of the internal market and capitalist relations were altered by the absorption and elimination of domestic-artisan sectors, the proletarianization of the labor force, and the partial proletarianization of campesinos. A long-term increase in real wages and a tremendous expansion in the production of consumer nondurable goods also characterized the industrialization process. Savings and capital accumulation increased at impressive rates, and the power base of the bourgeoisie rapidly expanded. Although these developments generated a tremendous social surplus, contradictions emerged during the latter 1960s.

During the latter 1960s the productive structure was significantly transformed. There was a shift from consumer goods to the production of durable consumer goods, intermediate goods, and capital goods (Rivera Ríos, 1986, p. 34). One of the more significant aspects of this restructuring was the reorientation of production from personal consumption to the production of durable and capital goods. The wage-goods market had become saturated and consequently less profitable. More important, however, was that the labor force and the internal market were seen as less dynamic in terms of consumption.[1]

Another facet of this structural reorientation was the expanding transnationalization of production, commerce, and finance. Multinational investments increased substantially during the latter part of the 1970s.[2] The transnationalization of finance was exemplified by the increasing utilization of international capital markets. State and private sector use of international capital markets affected financial flows.[3] An important related trend was the expansion of multinational banks.[4] This development was interconnected with the shift in international finance, that is, the privatization of public sector credit.[5]

Several factors accounted for the increasing use of foreign debt in the 1970s. The relative scarcity and high cost of domestic debt was partly responsible. Another element was the rapid expansion of large conglomerate operations and the consequent importance of financing as a means of promoting expansion. The size and liquidity of the local financial market was also reduced by the shift in public preference from quasi-monetary instruments to other financial instruments.[6] The primary factor, however, was financial disintermediation.[7]

Internationalization of domestic bank operations also resulted from greater reliance on foreign loans. The three largest Mexican banks (Bancomer, Banamex, Serfín) initiated Euromarket operations in 1971. Mexican banks also participated in international banking syndicates.[8] Between 1974 and 1978 Mexican banks participated in bank syndicates that supplied Mexico with 35 percent of its international borrowing requirements (Quijano, 1981, pp. 243–244). A significant aspect of this phenomenon was that these banks functioned as private intermediaries between the State and foreign bank capital.[9]

The contraction of foreign debt through private banks was a dramatic change in State–bank financial arrangements. Heretofore, the State had relied on reserve requirements and securities to finance budget deficits. The new arrangement that emerged in the 1970s relied on foreign debt as a major component of State financial strategy.

Privatization of State financial operations also affected the traditional delineation of banking practices between private banks and national credit institutions. National credit institutions provided a greater share of total domestic credit and obtained the majority of their funds from international capital markets and bank syndicates.[10] Foreign credit accounted for more than 70 percent of national credit institution resources at some points during the decade. The use of private foreign credit as a primary source for national credit institution resources increased State subsidization of national credit institution operations, in turn contributing to the fiscal crisis of the State. Resource transfers from the government to the Banco Nacional de Crédito Rural demonstrated the increasing costs of the State's absorption of interest differentials on foreign loans.[11]

Another aspect of the internationalization of private banks was the international expansion of private bank lending operations. In 1978 and 1979, for example, Mexican private banks directly and indirectly participated in loans to the Republic of Honduras, the Banco Real do Brasil, the Chilean Central Bank, and the Republic of Ecuador (Quijano, 1981, p. 257). Thus, Mexican private banks were participating in several different facets of the international expansion of bank capital. The international expansion of Mexican private banks also affected the dynamics of domestic financial circuits.

The privatization of international financial circuits and the international expansion of Mexican private banks substantially transformed the dynamics of State–bank relations, domestic financial circuits, and domestic production. The stagnating and declining capture of domestic resources affected the financial capacity of the State in a period of expanding State economic intervention.[12] Increasing reserve requirements were also less effective as a means of raising capital because international bank operations (e.g., Euromarket lending to paraestatales or national credit institutions) were not subject to State regulation. Moreover, State dependency on private bank international borrowing was a crucial element in the postponement of State financial disequilibrium, even though the international privatization of State financial operations simultaneously contributed to the materialization of financial contradictions.[13] The international privatization of State finance was also interrelated with the creditworthiness of the State and its role as a guarantor.[14] In summary, the historical relationship between the State and private banks continued to develop in a dynamic manner. Although State dependency on private banks greatly increased, the coincidence of interests continued unabated.

The international expansion of private banks affected domestic financial circuits in several ways. As previously noted, the traditional division of labor between national credit institutions and private banks changed. There were also substantive linkage changes between domestic and international financial circuits and the larger economy.[15]

A more significant development was the relative autonomization of domestic financial circuits vis-à-vis the State. As a result of bank access to international capital resources, the time-frame for the financial valorization of capital was reduced and the role of bank capital as an intermediary in the productive and commercial circuits was enhanced by the ability to affect the dynamics of the productive and commercial spheres (e.g., the use of credit cards to augment demand for commercial goods). The ability of banks to transform the financial, productive, and commercial circuits was a manifestation of increasing political power as regards the State. The increasing political power of banks and the autonomization of domestic financial circuits reduced the power of the State to control the monetary sphere. Regulation of the monetary and credit sphere was ineffective because the State could not regulate international bank operations.

The integration of national and international financial circuits also affected domestic production throughout the 1970s. An important development was the greater use of foreign debt by the private sector. Increasing use of international capital markets by Mexican firms was undoubtedly due to several factors, including the relative higher cost of domestic credit, and expectations that the petroleum bonanza would reduce the possibility of devaluation and therein reduce potential exchange losses, back-to-back loans, and the existence of "excess liquidity" (Quijano, 1981, pp. 270–272). An important aspect of this structural reorientation was that the debt service burden substantially increased because of peso devaluations. More important was the indirect transfer of resources through State subsidization of private firm debt service, for instance, back-to-back loan guarantees. A greater percentage of foreign currency reserves had to be used to alleviate the debt-service crisis of private firms. The financial costs of private firms were socialized.

High interest rate policies also contributed to increasing financial costs for business. High interest rates were part of the reason for the dollarization of the economy, a measure to attract international capital ("hot money"). High interest rates were also used to induce people to maintain peso deposits. The net effect was to increase the cost of financial transactions in the domestic credit markets. These increased costs disproportionately affected small and intermediate businesses because of preferential access accorded to large business in international capital markets. The differential in interest rates and disparate financial costs undoubtedly contributed to the consolidation and concentration of private national economic groups.

The financial costs of small and intermediate firms also increased as a result of speculation. Between 1974 and 1977, domestic currency financing decreased in real terms and bank foreign currency operations, as a percentage of foreign currency debits, declined. These developments suggest that banks did not channel all of the contracted foreign currency resources into the internal financial circuits. Some of these resources were used to speculate in exchange markets (Cardero, 1984, p. 164). The net effect was an artificial increase in domestic financial costs.

The internationalization of production, commerce, and finance and the structural reorientation of production manifested a larger phenomenon, that is, the dynamism of the sociopolitical economic structure. Stagnation of the stabilizing development accumulation model manifested underlying political-economic contradictions. Fundamental contradictions revolved around the interaction of two factors: the preservation and continued reliance on primary exports to correct structural balance-of-payments problems, and combined and uneven economic reproduction resulting in serious production and distribution disequilibriums (Valenzuela Feijóo, 1986, pp. 26–30). These economic contradictions generated secondary contradictions, for example, high capital intensity in a few sectors and low productivity in the majority of sectors. Economic contradictions were compounded by political contradictions within the State and between the State and social classes. These contradictions generated a perpetual crisis of social relations of production. Transformation of the productive structure in the 1970s and 1980s aggravated the contradictions of the traditional ISI accumulation model.

The stagnation of the ISI accumulation model and the constant emergence of sociopolitical contradictions—manifested as a crisis of the State—resulted in an attempt to modify the traditional accumulation model and mollify contradictory class antagonisms. Although efforts of the Echeverría administration (1970–1976) to ameliorate the crisis were unsuccessful, the López Portillo administration (1976–1982) temporarily succeeded in rekindling the economy through an "Alliance for Production," political reform, and petroleum. The inability to clearly define a new accumulation model and the corollary restructuring of classes and class fractions typified the decade. A concise analysis of the political regimes, political-economic policies, and the State and power bloc will clarify the importance of this period, relative to the dynamics of finance capital and the decision to nationalize the banks.

THE LOST SEXENIOS: 1970–1982

President Luis Echeverría initiated his presidency with a bang. The president's December 1970 inauguration speech emphasized the absence of uniform economic development, the excessive concentration of income, the marginalization phenomenon, and the importance of a democratic society. Shortly thereafter he sent the Congress several important legislative initiatives. Although Echeverría assured the private sector that his regime would guarantee and respect the rights of businessmen, the private sector was not consulted in regard to a proposed change in tax laws. The failure to consult the private sector resulted in a series of ideological disputes between the President and the private sector.

Echeverría's new model of development, christened *desarrollo compartido* (shared development), emphasized a return to the original Cárdenas accumulation model. The administration propounded reformist national rhetoric, developmental social themes, and increased State economic intervention. Redistribution, the principal element of shared development, was to be based on (a) policies benefiting workers and peasants, (b) increasing control of MNCs and technology, (c) increasing international contacts, (d) increasing State economic intervention, and (e) more revolutionary nationalist rhetoric (Martínez Nova, 1984, p. 168). The true nature of his policies, however, was reflected in the 1971 consolidation policy. In essence, consolidation policy was based on a reduction in the federal budget and restrictive monetarist policy.

> With the economic policy defined for 1971, one of the most important and irre-
> solvable contradictions of the sexenio was initiated: on the one side, insufficiently
> remedied social deficiencies and the necessity to give the national economy a
> more solid base, amplifying the infrastructure and promoting basic production,
> requiring greater State action, increases in public expenditure and greater public
> sector participation in the economy. On the other side, a restrictive monetary,
> credit and fiscal policy, that was counter-effective and impossible to vary (due to
> the interests and force of finance capital), and that in addition, paradoxically had a
> particularly weak sustenance base, resting on reserve requirements that produced
> excessively liquid deposits to finance public expenses and not on the State's own
> income. (Tello, 1980, p. 48)

Reduced private and public sector investment, increased inflation, and slower
growth, in conjunction with restrictive fiscal, monetary, and credit policy, were
somewhat problematic for the reformist regime.

Politically, the Echeverría administration attempted to restore State legitimacy.
The traditional use of revolutionary nationalist rhetoric, promoting campesino-
peasant interests, corresponded with the facade of shared development. Ideological discourse was thus one way of re-invigorating eroded State legitimacy. A
second element was the "democratic opening." The "opening" included electoral
reform, increased flexibility in the communication channels, increased tolerance
of demonstrations and criticism, and populist politics (Martínez Nova, 1984, p.
169). The third endeavor to bolster State legitimacy was a complex and unsuccessful attempt to superficially subordinate the interests of the bourgeoisie vis-à-
vis State interests. The failure to achieve this ultimate political objective was
exemplified by the extremely contentious relationship with the bourgeoisie.

The policies pursued by Echeverría were contradictory in terms of stated and
unstated policy objectives. Contradictions permeated the socioeconomic system. Before examining the developments associated with the crisis between the
State and capital, it is useful to briefly examine the effects of administration
policies on the productive, commercial, and financial circuits.

The administration's antagonistic rapport with the private sector, in conjunction with declining growth and inflation, reduced the level of private sector
investment. The valorization process tended to be based more on inflation and
speculation than on productive investment. Capital flight and speculation affected the capture of resources and consequently the ability of the State to tap
banks to finance budget deficits. The ability of the State to counteract the
cyclical downturn was therein restricted. State orthodox policies also aggravated the problem by destabilizing the treasured principles of stabilizing development, that is, price and monetary stability.

The 1971 recession resulted in large bankruptcies among small and medium businesses and augmented the concentration of resources among large conglomerate groups with sufficient liquidity. The consequent reduction in the production and supply of goods in the domestic market facilitated inflationary and speculative practices. In other words, expansion of the commercial and financial circuits was interrelated with the distortion of the productive structure.

The expansion and contraction of the economy during the 1970–1976 period exemplified the larger socioeconomic contradictions of the accumulation model. Agriculture was stagnant or declining throughout the period. Public sector investment was unable to counteract the historical trend. Agricultural output was in fact unable to satisfy domestic demand. Industrial production continued to expand more rapidly than the general economy. Commerce and services continued to dominate the economy, accounting for approximately 55 percent of GDP.

Economic stagnation and decline paralleled the expansion and development of speculation and rentier capitalism. High interest rates, high reserve requirements, transitions in the acceptance of financial instruments, and the resulting increase in liquidity reduced productive investment and stimulated speculative investment with minimal risk. Exemplary of this phenomenon was the 110 percent increase in profits for publicly held companies registered on the stock market, and the 74 percent increase in the peso value of these same companies' sales between 1972 and 1974. The discrepancy between sales and profits was not due to increasing labor or import costs (Tello, 1979, p. 105).

At a different level, State economic intervention substantially increased. Expansion of the State apparatus functioned partly as a counter-cyclical instrument to fulfill the private sector investment void, and partially fulfilled the shared development strategy to restructure the economy through public sector stimulation and redistribution of wealth. Expansion of the State apparatus and State economic intervention was one of the major points of contention between the private sector and the State.

Confrontations between the Echeverría administration and the bourgeoisie consistently escalated. Initially, political disputes were verbal. For example, Echeverría's endeavor to implement fiscal reforms and a 10 percent luxury tax were opposed by the leaders of various business organizations. Business organizations' vociferous repudiation of these measures and consequent negotiation of the specifics of these measures diluted policy implementation.

State–capital relations began to deteriorate at a faster pace in 1973 with the assassination of Eugenio Garza Sada (the patriarch of the Garza Sada empire), the Chilean military coup, and the acceptance of Chilean refugees. Garza Sada's funeral oration was turned into a political condemnation of the inability of the regime to maintain public order. The administration was also blamed for fomenting social class division by attacking the private sector. Echeverría countered the attacks against his regime and the State by mobilizing PRI contingents across the nation.

In 1975, a new business organization, the *Consejo Coordinator Empresarial* (CCE) was created. The CCE manifested a new stage of political confrontation between the State and capital. Organization of the CCE was a significant development because it coordinated the organizational efforts and opinions of the leaders of commerce, industry, banking, agriculture, and COPARMEX within one organization, but outside of the State apparatus.[16] The emergence of the CCE, in conjunction with the increasingly belligerent attitude of the COPARMEX, exemplified the political contradictions inherent between the State and capital. The largest and most powerful contingents of the bourgeoisie were contesting State bureaucracy game rules.

> In this sense, the major part of the political fractions of the grand bourgeoisie defined the struggle for power within the interior of the State apparatus, utilizing all of the available measures, from political pressure to the power of money, and renouncing the independent struggle from the state apparatus. Thus, their political activity was realized through the bureaucracy and in the state, and not in the parties. (Fragoso, Conchiero, & Gutiérez, 1979, pp. 268–269)

The severity of State–capital confrontations increased during Echeverría's last year of office (1976). Peasants' growing disillusionment with the Revolution and the promises of shared development resulted in the takeover of several latifundios in Sonora. Businesses responded by shutting down operations. The government expropriated 100,000 hectares, and business countered with a national lockout. The CCE then proposed a government program to restrict the realm of State economic intervention, halt nationalizations of private enterprise, and embrace IMF proposals to control the economic crisis. Capital flight reemerged, productive investments declined, and rumors abounded that a military coup would supersede the succession of Echeverría.

The verbal and material demonstrations of political confrontation between the State and the bourgeoisie reflected a larger power struggle within the power bloc. The true nature of the State–capital dispute was manifested in administration policies supporting capital. Ultimately, regime policy measures contributed to the accumulation of capital and the acceleration of the concentration and centralization processes. Former Secretary of Programming and Budget Carlos Tello believed that State economic intervention during the 1970–1976 period promoted capital accumulation.

As in the past, the State's direct intervention in the production of goods and services during 1970–1976 was in no way "competitive intervention, but above all functional with the country's development of capitalism." During this period the State continued to develop a doubly key role for the reproduction of the system: for one part, creating the favorable conditions for private accumulation; for the other, directly intervening in the process of the formation of capital when it was necessary to fortify national development and in this measure to support private initiatives' practices. (Tello, 1979, p. 204)

The probusiness attitude of the Echeverría administration was also astutely confirmed by Roberto Guajardo Suárez, ex-president of COPARMEX:

It can be affirmed that few regimes like the present (President Echeverría) have been more preoccupied about the promotion and stimulation of private initiative. In only three years the administration has dictated more decrees, laws and diverse dispositions, promoting the business sector, than in all of the previous sexenio. (cited in Tello, 1979, pp. 204–205)

Political disputes between the State and bourgeoisie revolved around the tone of official discourse and reformist legislative proposals; proposals that were consistently and effectively countered by the bourgeoisie (Green, 1981, pp. 78–109). The increasingly contentious relations between the bourgeoisie and the State at a superficial level, appear to be illogical, given the State's reformist objectives (i.e., economic expansion and relegitimization) and support of capital accumulation and private initiative. These disputes were the material manifestation of political struggles within the power bloc. As exemplified by the creation of the independent CCE, the State, conceived as an arena of social class struggle, was permeated by contradictory class forces attempting to utilize the State apparatus to fulfill the interests of particular classes and class fractions.

Extremely limited relative State autonomy was in contention. Thus, the Echeverría regime's initiation of a new model of economic development attempted to satisfy segments of the State bureaucracy while supporting capital accumulation.[17] Within the power bloc, the tripartite alliance between the State technocracy, grand bankers, and the new "revolutionary" bourgeoisie (a.k.a. "la fracción de las cuarenta"), based on the implementation of technocratic populism, ultimately resulted in discrepancies, division, political struggle, and political crisis (Bartra, 1978, pp. 48–52).

The political crisis showed because serious discrepancies and fissures appeared between the fractions of the hegemonic bloc. The oligarchy lost trust in the technocracy in that the technocracy lost its autonomy and legitimacy and it demonstrated its inability to absorb, organize and mediate the proletarianized masses of the countryside. The new bourgeoisie, less "new" every day, dispersed itself in a wide scattering of political factions; it lost a certain coherency that had given it security of being coddled and protected by the State and it also lost the confidence in the reformist projects that it had timidly supported; the result was that its alliance with the state technocracy was debilitated in the same way that it had erased the traditional and already scarce political and economic unity. (Bartra, 1978, pp. 54–55)

The López Portillo administration (1976–1982) assumed power in the midst of a serious crisis.[18] Devaluation of the peso and the loss of confidence by the bourgeoisie created a climate of distrust and diffidence.[19] The diffidence and distrust characterizing the pre-election and immediate post-election were rapidly displaced by López Portillo's innovative agenda.

The central organizational theme during the López Portillo administration was the "Alliance for Production."[20] The Alliance was a sophisticated technocratic variation of Echeverría's technocratic populism. Politically, the Alliance attempted to placate confrontational fractions of the bourgeoisie by reestablishing the State–capital social pact on the basis of collaboration and negotiation (Punto Crítico, 1980, p. 74). At another level, the Alliance was based on a pact with labor leaders to accept wage ceilings and a redistribution of social wealth. Economically, the Alliance attempted to reinvigorate the economy by restoring lost confidence. Restoration of private sector investment confidence entailed the delineation of private and public investment spheres, reduction of inflation, reduction of the government budget deficit, fiscal stimuli to enhance capital accumulation, and greater redistribution of the social surplus for private accumulation.[21]

A corollary conciliatory measure was the Political Reform (*Ley Federal de Organizaciones Políticas y Procesos Electorales*: LOPPE). Political reform legalized and incorporated the Mexican Communist Party (Partido Comunista Mexicano: PCM), the Mexican Democratic Party (Partido Democrática Mexicano: PDM), and the Socialist Workers Party (Partido Socialista de Trabajadores: PST) within the electoral process.[22] The LOPPE co-opted particular segments of the left, created division within the electoral left, and divided the electoral left and revolutionary left. The superficial "opening" of the political system increased State legitimacy and simultaneously increased the co-optive power of the State. The State was able to confer or revoke the right of political parties to participate in electoral politics and receive campaign subsidies (Gilly, 1985, p. 74). Aptly summarized by *Punto Críitico*, the LOPPE was a manifestation of the political-economic crisis confronting the regime:

> The Political Reform must be understood in terms of the economic and political crises and the social transformations that Mexico is undergoing. It is an attempt on the part of the government to prevent stronger explosions, to prevent the left which is organized into parties from participating along with the exploited masses in the struggle against the effects of the crisis. In the strict sense, then, the Political Reform is preventive, an attempt to control the possible vanguards by capturing them in a game of relationship to power so that, to the degree they are weak, compromises are exacted and independence is eroded. (1980, p. 75)

López Portillo's successful restoration of political-economic confidence was initially based on a series of legal reforms rationalizing State economic intervention. Officially, the reform was promulgated to organize the country, adopt budget integrated programming, systematize the administration and development of bureaucrats, strengthen political organization and federalism, and contribute to the administration of social justice (Carrillo Castro, 1978, p. 51). Unofficially, the reform was partly an effort to counteract the delegitimized image of a corrupt State apparatus. The reform also attempted to rationalize a State apparatus that had substantially increased during the Echeverría administration, for example, the number of paraestatales increased from 600 to over 900 (Carrillo Castro, 1978, p. 50).

The second major restorative element, in terms of bourgeois confidence, was clarification of public and private investment spheres. The State assured the bourgeoisie that it would continue to promote private accumulation and not encroach on the private sector's historical realm of operation.[23] The rationalization of State economic intervention was also part of a financial arrangement with the IMF. Under the IMF agreement, the regime agreed to reduce public sector deficits, restrict wage increases, limit foreign debt, increase the price of public sector goods and services, reduce government employment, and accelerate the integration of the national and international economies (Guillén Romo, 1984, pp. 54–55).

Although the economy stagnated in 1977, the resurrection of private sector confidence and redefinition of public policies and sociopolitical relations affected production and accumulation. The 1978 recovery was part of an overall developmental schema propounded by López Portillo in his second governmental address. López Portillo delineated three biannual stages of economic development in his second address: economic recovery in 1976 and 1977, economic consolidation in 1977 and 1978, and accelerated expansion in 1980 and 1981 (Pérez & Miron, 1986, p. 206). The developmental plan was essentially nothing less than the petrolization[24] of stabilizing development with a few techno-populist measures, for example, the Mexican Food System (Sistema Alimentario Mexicano: SAM) promoting smallholding subsistence agricultural production to stabilize the political system (Barkin, 1986, pp. 13–16; Hellman, 1983, pp. 97–98). In effect, the State used petroleum income, in combination with international bank loans and direct financial instruments (e.g., CETES and Petrobonos) to reduce its bank financing requirements and simultaneously augment the State's financial autonomy in relation to finance capital. By increasing the availability of financial resources, the State was also able to expand its ability to subsidize infrastructure development.

During the initial years of the López Portillo administration, disequilibrium and contradiction continued to characterize the stabilizing development accumulation model. The current account deficit substantially increased because of endogenous and exogenous factors, including international recession, high international interest rates, incongruent sectoral expansion, and high import coefficients (CIDE, 1982, pp. 11–12). Industrial intrasector disequilibriums resulted in disproportionate expansion of the intermediate goods sector. Agricultural production experienced a brief period of expansion but began to stagnate at the end of the decade. Petroleum replaced agriculture as the primary foreign exchange generating export.

Public and private sector investment was exemplary during this period. The majority of public sector capital was invested in the secondary sector (manufacturing, electricity, petroleum, communications, and transportation). The majority of private sector capital was invested in the tertiary sector (commerce and services).[25] In other words, the State promoted industrial development to rectify sector imbalances, create employment, and subsidize the costs of private sector production, whereas the private sector predominantly invested in the highly profitable commercial-services sectors. This dichotomization, in terms of production and commercial-services, was a historical phenomenon, interrelated with the genesis and development of finance capital, a fraction of capital that obtained a tremendous amount of political-economic power during the 1970s.

The changes in the productive, commercial, and financial sectors affected and were affected by finance capital. In other words, there was a dynamic interplay between structural and class forces. The structural reorientation of the economy—in terms of the internationalization of production and the increasing importance of speculation and rentierism—affected the viability of the ISI accumulation model. In combination with the internationalization of the commercial and financial spheres, the change in the productive structure compounded the inherent contradictions confronting the State. These contradictions were temporarily ameliorated though Echeverría's use of revolutionary rhetoric and the subsidization of private accumulation. Ultimately, however, class contradictions and contentious fractions successfully undermined the ability of the State to act as an impartial arbiter.

FINANCE CAPITAL

Finance capital was able to command a hegemonic position within the power bloc, indirectly influencing the State and political regimes. The almost constant existence of political-economic crisis during the Echeverría regime was temporarily minimized during the initial years of the López Portillo regime. Unparalleled economic expansion accompanying the petrolization of the economy also helped to reduce social tensions. Increasing political power enabled finance capital to enhance its economic power, which added to its political power. For example, State reliance on private financing facilitated the internationalization of financial circuits, augmenting the power of finance capital to manipulate the regulatory regime governing the organization and power of banks (e.g., the creation of multibanks and financial groups).

A superficial examination of the Mexican social formation might lead one to assert that the Mexican Bank Association (ABM) was the political organization and expression of the interests of bank and finance capital. Such a conclusion, however, would be reductionist. Although the ABM represented banks and served as an "independent" institutional mechanism to discuss and negotiate legislative and economic questions and problems with the State apparatus, the ABM nevertheless reflected the political interests of the Central Fraction of finance capital.

The Central Fraction of finance capital—Banamex, Bancomer, and CREMI—exercised hegemony within the ABM, and consequently, the ABM reflected the policies, strategies, and tactical methods of the Central Fraction. Central Fraction hegemony was concretely visible in the selection of officers in the directive council and the election of presidents governing the body.

> The political characteristics of the Central Fraction are expressed clearly in the ABM: grand capacity to influence the State apparatus; organic channels of communication and control over governmental finance policy; political discretion; relative independence of the political bureaucracy; defined economic project; negotiation as a principal method of movement; use of economic pressure before political pressure; absence of a political project; formation of part of the government bloc, etc. It is to say, that the principal characteristics of the political actualization of the ABM are determined by the location of the Central Fraction in the economic structure and in the State. Thus, the Bankers' Association is not a pressure organization, but the organic expression of one of the fractions that belong to the government bloc . . .
> (Fragoso et al., 1979: p. 243)

Politically, there were three distinct fractions of Mexican finance capital: the Northern Fraction, the Central Fraction, and the Forty Fraction (Fragoso et al.,

1979, p. 243).[26] These three fractions had particular historical and economic configurations. The emergence of a specific group within a particular political fraction of finance capital was concretely related to the reproductive forms of capital used to accumulate capital (e.g., commercial-usury, industrial, and bank). Historical origins—that is, the political, economic, and social conditions—also structured the emergence and consolidation of a particular group or fractions. Regional geographic factors, for example, affected the ability of the Northern Fraction (particularly Grupo Monterrey) to maintain its political independence vis-à-vis the pre-Revolution and post-Revolution Mexican State. The same factors enabled the fraction to augment its accumulation through commerce with the United States. Superstructural factors also affected the character of specific groups within the various political fractions of finance capital. For example, particular families historically dominated the development of many financial groups (e.g., Garza-Sada in Grupo Monterrey; Legorreta in Banamex).

The Northern Fraction, dominated by the Grupo Monterrey (VISA, Vidriera, CYDSA, and Alfa) was characterized by its historical origins, economic heterogeneity, political project, and relative independence from the State.[27] Coparmex articulated its political interests and national project. Its national project was based on an ideological conservatism espousing free-market economics, vehement anticommunism, and extremely limited State intervention. Although the Northern Fraction was not completely opposed to State intervention, its negotiation techniques were confrontational and extremely critical of the ideology of the Revolution (e.g., redistribution of land and the maintenance of ejidos; Fragoso et al., 1979, pp. 51–60).

The Central Fraction (composed of Bancomer, Banamex, and Cremi) was characterized by its economic-financial power, hegemonic position in relation to other political fractions of finance capital, and its close working relations with the State. In terms of its relations with the State apparatus, the fraction was centered between the other two fractions. The Central Fraction had a close and direct relationship with the State, whereas the Northern Fraction's relations were much more autonomous and independent, and the Forty Fraction's relations were organic (i.e., the State promoted and nurtured this fraction's expansion).

Politically, the Central Fraction's interests were articulated and organized within the ABM and the CCE. The fraction publicly supported the revolutionary objectives of the State and the political-economic projects of particular administrations. The fraction utilized public and secret negotiation methods to express its interests to the State and defended and justified the necessity of foreign investment (Fragoso et al., 1979, pp. 205–220).

The Forty Fraction (composed of Grupo Desc, Grupo ICA-Atlántico, Grupo

Comermex, Grupo Pagliai-Alemán-Azcárraga, and Grupo Industria y Comercio) was characterized by its organic relation with the post-Revolution State, and its economic and political heterogeneity. The fraction's principal defining characteristic was its historical origin, based on the State's promotion of industrial capitalist interests during the 1940s. The fraction's economic expansion therefore corresponded with the consolidation and fortification of the Mexican State administered by the Avila Camacho and Aléman regimes. Revolutionary ideology was used to champion the interests of "national" capital. The fraction's political interests were articulated and institutionalized through the Concamin, Concanaco, Canacintra, and the ABM. Political intermediation with the State apparatus was also often direct (e.g., ex-president Miguel Alemán, Aarón Sáenz, or Carlos Hank González; Fragoso et al., 1979, pp. 133–142).

A final characteristic of finance capital was the cartelization or monopolization process generally associated with the fusion process. Historically, Mexican capital has always been relatively concentrated.[28] In the 1960s and 1970s, industry and bank capital were very concentrated.[29] Concentration and centralization of capital accelerated during the 1970s. The dynamics of concentration and centralization were affected by the development of multibanks and financial groups, the proliferation of speculative activity, and capital flight. Rapid changes in the banking system during the 1970s were part of a historical trend that had been occurring for thirty years. Although forty-two banks controlled 75 percent of bank resources in 1950, six banks controlled the same amount of resources in 1979. During the same period, moreover, the total number of banks decreased from 248 in 1950 to 100 in 1979. The fusion process accompanying the formation of multibanks was a major cause of this phenomenon. Thus, the number of banks decreased from 240 in 1970, to 139 in 1975, to 106 in 1978, and to 100 in 1979. The reduction in the number of institutions was accompanied by the concentration of resources among fewer institutions. Thus, in 1970, eighteen banks controlled 75 percent of the resources, and in 1979 only six banks controlled the same amount of resources (González Méndez, 1980, pp. 38–39).

A particularly distinct characteristic of the concentration and centralization processes was the relatively slower growth of the two largest banks, as compared with intermediate-size banks. For example, in 1976 Bancomer (the largest bank) owned 23 percent of total bank branches, employed 28 percent of bank personnel, and controlled 24 percent of private bank debits. In 1979, Bancomer's participation in the banking system was less dynamic. Bancomer owned 19 percent of bank branches, employed 22 percent of bank employees, and controlled 24 percent of total private bank debits. In comparison, Comermex, the fourth largest bank, increased its participation in the system. Comermex controlled 8 percent of bank branches in 1976 and 9.4 percent in 1979, employed 7 percent of bank employees in 1976 and 10 percent in 1979, and controlled 7 percent of private bank debits in 1976 and 10 percent in 1979 (Secretaría de Programación y Presupuesto [SPP], 1984).

Another aspect of the concentration and centralization processes was the rapid increase in profitability. Multibank profits increased 27 percent in 1978 and 38 percent in 1979. The average, however, obscures the substantial increase in profits for the largest multibanks and the average level of profits for all multibanks. For example, in 1978, Bancomer's profits were 40 percent, and in 1979 had risen to 62 percent. Banamex profits were less spectacular but nevertheless impressive—30 percent and 39 percent. In contrast, an exclusion of the top fourteen banks reveals that the rest of multibank profits were 16 percent in 1978, and 21 percent in 1979 (Tello, 1984, p. 55).

In sum, the banking system experienced the most radical transformation in its postrevolutionary history. Structural changes (e.g., disintermediation and declining capture of resources) reflected the internationalization of financial circuits and expansion of the power base of finance capital. The concentration and centralization of resources among a declining number of institutions, and the dramatic increase in profits accompanying the consolidation of financial groups and multibanks was directly linked to speculation, devaluation, and the privatization of international lending.

One of the more important aspects of the concentration and centralization processes was the role of the State in the promotion and consolidation of this process. In the 1970s, two very important pieces of legislation transformed the dynamism of the concentration and centralization processes and affected and manifested the political-economic power of finance capital.

In 1970 and 1974, reforms to the General Credit Law promulgated the formation of financial groups and the creation of multiple banks (*multibancos*). The 1970 reform, recognizing the existence of financial groups, enabled these groups to consolidate their holdings and, more importantly, to strengthen and expand their political-economic power. Smaller deposit banks that were not linked to a financiera or hipotecaria were at a definite disadvantage after 1970. The 1974 reform juridically recognized an existing fact. The official intention was to strengthen the competitiveness of smaller banks, promote competition among diverse banks, increase the efficiency of banking operations, and counteract the concentration and centralization processes. However, the reform accelerated the concentration and centralization processes. Increasing bank participation in nonbanking institutions (e.g., stock brokerages) increased bank earnings and power.

In sum, finance capital evolved in historically unique configurations. Different components of the fraction had historically specific forms of fusion and distinct expressions and organizations of political interest. In the real world, finance capital developed in a heterogeneous manner, reflecting the dynamics of the socioeconomic formation and the complexity of everyday life in a constantly evolving social structure. In short, the political organization of the fraction did not necessarily coincide with the economic delineation of the fraction. Although a coincidence of interests can exist in relation to particular issues (e.g., the creation of multibanks), differences also persisted in other realms (e.g., the proper role of the State). However, during crisis periods the contradictions and differences separating the political and economic interests and organization of the fraction reduced the structural impediments inhibiting the unification of the fraction. In other words, crisis periods created structural situations that necessitated the organized articulation of the political and economic interests of the fraction. The period encompassing the nationalization and immediate postnationalization of the banks, for instance, was the most profound political crisis confronting the State and finance capital. It was a period of unequaled opportunity to examine and analyze the dynamics of social class fractions and their relation to the State.

CONCLUSION

The transformation of bank capital and the genesis and aggressive expansion of finance capital during the 1970s was intimately interrelated with the crisis of the Mexican State. The State's political-economic maneuverability was consistently restricted and its relative autonomy compromised as a result of the increasing materialization of political-economic contradictions. In essence, these contradictions reflected a power struggle within the power bloc and between various fractions of the bourgeoisie. Ultimately, however, finance capital was able to exercise hegemonic power within the power bloc.

The hegemonic power of finance capital was reflected in the increasingly pervasive development of speculative rentier capitalism and the inability of the State to design, define, or implement an accumulation model based on productive investment. According to Tello (1979, p. 208), the Echeverría administration's failure to implement a new accumulation model was due to the orientation of the financial system, that is, finance capital. The crisis of 1976 reflected structural problems but was primarily a result of the failure to reform the financial system (Tello, 1979, p. 208).

The increasingly contentious relationship between finance capital and the State was due to structural and class antagonisms and contradictions. The historical State–bank capital relationship, based on a coincidence of interests, was disintegrating as the coincidence of interests became less and less apparent and the distinct interests of finance capital and the State became increasingly patent. State and finance capital conflicts developed over the State's increasing use of the reserve system to finance budget deficits and the State's attempt to circumvent banks' capture of resources through the creation of CETES (treasury certificates) and petrobonos (petroleum bonds). The State's use of CETES and petrobonos to capture additional resources and circumvent banks was an attempt to increase State autonomy vis-à-vis finance capital. Finance capital expressed its unhappiness with State financial maneuvers in an atypical discussion of the matter at the 1978 ABM Convention. ABM President Eraña García unequivocally stated that the effects of State competition for domestic resources and the consequent effects on the capacity of banks to finance private investment was worrisome (Eraña García, 1978, p. 16). Banks were also unhappy about the use of the reserve system to finance State operations and the restrictive effects on the ability of banks to provide credit to paraestatales and bank clients (i.e., unsatisfied credit demand).

In summary, the crisis of the Mexican State was a manifestation of the combined and uneven development of Mexican capitalism and the increasingly pervasive political-economic contradictions exemplified throughout the social formation. The expansion of finance capital and its contentious relations with the State were temporarily ameliorated by López Portillo's Alliance for Production and the petroleum bonanza. The collapse of López Portillo's development plans and the reemergence of political-economic crisis was the beginning of a period of unparalleled class struggle.

The historical development of finance capital and the complexities surrounding the differentiation of finance capital were clearly evident during the 1970s. Changes in the financial sector reflected rapid developments that had been occurring for more than thirty years. Financial concentration and centralization, in conjunction with increased speculation, fomented financial disintermediation and dollarization. These developments were legitimated with the implementation of the juridical reforms implemented in 1970 and 1974. Finally, although finance capital evolved in historically unique ways, State autonomy declined amidst the increasing materialization of the crisis of the Mexican State. As we shall see in chapter 5, the transformation of bank capital and the consolidation of finance capital affected political-economic relations within the power bloc.

NOTES

1. This change, which really began to materialize in full force during the De la Madrid administration (1982–1988), reflected the internationalization of production and capital, and the expansion and consolidation of specific fractions of the bourgeoisie vis-à-vis the petty bourgeoisie, the middle classes, the proletariat, and campesinos.

2. New foreign investment increased an average of 1.9 percent annually from 1970 to 1978. From 1978 to 1981, however, new foreign investment increased an average 51 percent annually (Jacobs & Perez Núñez, 1982, p. 101). The *maquiladora* (assembly plant) phenomenon provides an illustrative example of the transnationalization of production. Another example was the international expansion of domestic companies (e.g., VISA, Alfa).

3. The genesis of international recession and the competitive escalation of international interest rates substantially increased the cost of debt service. More important, however, was the international expansion of multinational banks, the privatization of public sector debt, and the increasing use of international credit to supplant domestic credit (Green, 1981, pp. 111–239; Quijano & Bendesky, 1983). See Christopher Korth's "International Financial Markets" (1983) for an overview of international capital markets.

4. This phenomenon was interconnected with several developments, including the tremendous growth of international capital markets; the demise of the Bretton Woods accord; petroleum price hikes; recycled "petro-dollars"; and the internationalization of production.

5. At the beginning of the 1970s, the demand by multinational firms for financial resources declined. Credit-worthy nations replaced multinational firms as the new bank clients. Governments were motivated to obtain international financing from banks rather than bilateral and multilateral institutions (e.g., IMF) because bank loans were string-free (Green, 1981, pp. 153–154). In the case of Mexico, the attractiveness of international bank loans was enhanced by the insufficient supply of domestic credit and the State's financial disequilibrium. Thus, public sector debt increased from $20 billion in 1976 to $70 billion in 1981 (Jacobs & Perez Núñez, 1982, p. 106). In a similar manner, private sector foreign debt increased from $266 million in 1971 to $5.6 billion in 1980 (Quijano, 1981, p. 275).

6. This development was compounded by the restrictive dollarization of the financial system resulting from higher bank reserve requirements for dollar-denominated accounts (Jacobs & Perez Núñez, 1982, p. 106). The term *dollarization* is a commonly used word to denote the process of currency substitution, that is, the increased usage of a foreign currency vis-à-vis the national currency.

7. Intermediation and disintermediation are economic terms. Intermediation is an institutionalized financial process wherein financial institutions (especially banks) perform an intermediating function, collecting resources from resource holders (e.g., public savings) and distributing resources (e.g., credit to borrowers). Disintermediation, in contrast, is a phenomenon wherein the institutionalized financial process of intermediation is circumvented. Public financial resources, for example, are not deposited in banks but are invested in foreign currencies, sent out of the country and deposited in foreign bank accounts, or used in other nonproductive investments (e.g., speculation).

8. Banamex, for example, was part of the Inter Mexican Bank consortium, composed of: Banamex (36.25 percent), Bank of America (27.5 percent), Deutsche Bank (14.5 percent), and Dai Ichi Bank (7.25 percent). In a similar fashion, Bancomer participated in the Libra bank consortium and Serfín participated in the Euro-Latinamerican Bank syndicate.

9. This situation resembled the State–bank relationship characterizing the Porfirian banking system.

10. For example, between 1970 and 1979 national credit institutions received $4.5 billion in Euromarket loans through Mexican-led or Mexican-associated bank syndicates. In comparison, during the same period, the government obtained $1.7 billion, Pemex received $1.25 billion, the State electrical company borrowed $365 million, and other institutions and groups borrowed $1.9 billion in the Euromarket (Quijano, 1981, pp. 246–247).

11. For example, the amount of pesos transferred from the government to Banco Nacional de Crédito Rural increased from 2.7 billion pesos in 1973 to 10.6 billion pesos in 1977 (Quijano, 1981, p. 252).

12. This phenomenon will be examined in greater detail in subsequent sections of this chapter.

13. An example was the State's subsidization of interest differentials for national credit institution operations or the stabilization of exchange rates. Another aspect was the tacit alliance between the State, productive capital, and international and domestic finance capital, that indirectly supported speculation through the support of a given peso/dollar exchange ratio. State support of an exchange rate involved the sale of foreign currency and the purchase of pesos. This practice was very prevalent in the 1980s (Cardero, 1984, p. 152).

14. The State had a good credit history which was bolstered by the petroleum bonanza.

15. For example, private bank use of international financial circuits to channel resources from the international sphere to the domestic circuits contributed to the financial valorization of capital at the international level and simultaneously enabled Mexican banks to increase access to financial resources, increase the sphere and volume of lending activity, and augment profits.

16. The principle corporatist organizations—Concamin, Canacintra, Concanaco—were organized by and within the confines of the State. These groups organized the bourgeoisie in accordance with the sectoral function of a specific capital within the cycle of social reproduction, for example, the Concanaco organized commercial capital. In essence, these groups organized and represented class fractions and served to promote capitalist development (Fragoso, Conchiero, & Gutiérez, 1979, pp. 268–269). Thus, a symbiotic coincidence of interests between the State and capital developed: The organizations had relative autonomy, there was a forum for political discussion to mitigate State–capital conflicts, and the State could, in the last instance, control different fractions of capital by using divide-and-conquer tactics (e.g., Concamin and Canacintra).

17. This "new" model of economic development was essentially based on a Keynesian market conception of social reality that promoted the interests of the bourgeoisie while simultaneously attempting to recover State legitimacy, under the guise of shared development (desarrollo compartido).

18. This section will examine the José López Portillo administration during the 1976–1979 period.

19. López Portillo's uncontested election was but one example of the political crisis confronting the victorious candidate. The *Partido de Acción Nacional* (PAN) did not participate in the 1976 presidential elections.

20. The Alliance for Production was a tripartite social pact between the State, capital, and labor, based on the ideological coordination of harmonious interests to expand productive investment and employment.

21. Greater detail is provided in the transcription of speeches presented before the ABM Bank Conventions for 1977, 1978, and 1979, in *Memoria* (1977, 1978, 1979).

22. In terms of a political reform, the measure was rather limited because of the restriction of non-PRI participation to the lower chamber of Deputies.

23. As noted by Finance Secretary Ibarra Muñoz, "there are limits to the functions of the public sector: It cannot do everything and administrate everything" (1978, p. 31).

24. Petrolization is commonly used in reference to the development of petroleum production and exports as the basis for economic expansion. For example, petroleum exports accounted for 16 percent of total export income in 1976 and 75 percent by 1981 (Hellman, 1983, pp. 79–80).

25. In 1978, for example, 62 percent of private sector investment was in the tertiary section (Valenzuela Feijóo, 1986, pp. 57–58).

26. Bartra (1982a, pp. 42–56) delineates two political fractions of the financial bourgeoisie: the regional bourgeoisies of Monterrey, Guadalajara, Puebla, and Saltillo; and the revolutionary "new rich" bourgeoisie of Mexico City and the state of Mexico.

27. The Northern Fraction was composed primarily of the Grupo Monterrey, Grupo Industrial Saltillo, and the grand bourgeoisie of Jalisco and Puebla.

28. In 1910, three Mexican banks—Banco Nacional de México, Banco de Londres y México, and Banco Central Mexicano—controlled 63 percent of total bank assets and 47 percent of total bank capital. Industrial capital was also very concentrated during this period. It has been estimated that the ten largest industrial entities accounted for 66 percent of the industrial capital of the 170 largest industrial enterprises.

29. In 1960, 1.7 percent of the industrial companies controlled 75 percent of industrial capital. In the manufacturing sector, the four largest manufacturers increased their share of total value produced from 42.6 percent in 1970 to 45.7 percent in 1975. Comparing sales share of the top 100 Mexican industrial firms with the figures for the same entities in six developed and semideveloped countries (the United States, Brazil, France, Japan, EEC, Argentina) reveals that the top ten firms in Mexico controlled the largest share of the sales of the top 100 firms among these countries, that is, 58.5 percent versus 52.8 percent in Brazil and 41.6 percent in the United States. Using the same firms and comparing the same countries, the top ten industrial firms in Mexico accounted for the largest proportion of total countable capital of the 100 largest firms (73 percent, 56 percent in Brazil, and 39 percent in the United States). Mexican banks also demonstrated a high degree of concentration in the 1980s. The top five banks controlled 65 percent of the offices in the country in 1980. Likewise, these institutions controlled 75 percent of total resources, 73 percent of the capture of resources, and 80 percent of the profits. Comparing some of the largest banks in Mexico with the largest banks in the United States, France, and Brazil exemplifies the high degree of concentration of Mexican

banks' control of resources in 1980. In comparison with the two largest banks in these countries, the top two Mexican banks controlled the largest percentage of total resources and capture of resources (54 percent of resources and 54 percent of capture), whereas in the United States the figures were 32 percent and 33 percent (Castañeda, 1982, pp. 85–90).

Part Three
The Articulation of Power: The Nationalization and Postnationalization Period

Chapter 5

Nationalization of the Banks

The previous chapter examined the crisis and disequilibrium that characterized Mexico from 1970 to 1979. The economy was unstable and public sector investment was increasingly necessary to stimulate and subsidize private investment. State maneuverability and relative autonomy were restricted by speculation, rentierism, capital flight, and the declining capture of domestic financial resources. The situation was temporarily salvaged by the discovery of extensive domestic petroleum reserves and the energy crisis. The result of these two events was an increase in foreign currency income and greater access to international capital markets. Paradoxically, State dependence on finance capital was decreased, even as finance capital consolidated its expansion.

Socioeconomic structural contradictions were temporarily ameliorated by unparalleled economic growth during the latter 1970s and the early 1980s. The power of the bourgeoisie simultaneously increased. In particular, the hegemonic position of finance capital was fortified, affecting the financial circuits and the accumulation model. The increasing incorporation of speculative rentierism and the integration of international and domestic financial circuits exemplified changes in the social structure. Shortly after the collapse of international oil prices, economic prosperity changed to austerity and crisis. As a result, public sector investment declined and the State could no longer subsidize speculative rentierism nor mollify finance capital.

The delegitimating contradictions of the 1982 crisis augmented political-economic differences between different fractions of the bourgeoisie and demonstrated the inability of the State to exercise minimal political autonomy. In other words, the class character of the State and the hegemony of finance capital were clearly visible until the banks were nationalized on September 1, 1982. This dramatic decision provides an unparalleled opportunity to address important questions about the sociopolitical nature of the State and the dynamism of a deposed fraction of the bourgeoisie, that is, finance capital.

97

ACCUMULATION, ECONOMIC STAGNATION, AND FINANCIAL COLLAPSE: 1980–1982

Domestic and international factors produced unparalleled economic expansion during the López Portillo administration (1976–1981 period). Internationally, the energy crisis and the Iranian Revolution reduced the supply and increased the price of oil. There was also a favorable transition in the terms of trade for primary products, as well as a greater supply of credit due to global recession and high interest rates.

Domestically, State legitimacy substantially improved. State coordination and conciliation of class interests created an environment of political stability, a prerequisite for private investment and capital accumulation. Re-legitimization of the State reassured the bourgeoisie that the State was capable of using ideological discourse on behalf of the general interest to promote particular class interests.[1]

Greater State political-economic maneuverability was another important domestic factor. Increased maneuverability of the State resulted from greater financial autonomy and economic expansion. The State was able to expand economic intervention and promote social investment designed to subsidize private accumulation and satisfy social demands, for example, greater employment opportunities through petroleum revenues, bank loans, increased usage of the reserve requirement system, and the use of new financial instruments to obtain resources directly from the public. Economic expansion also contributed to State maneuverability, with regard to the private sector, by generating a tremendous expansion in the amount of social production.[2] Private sector profits were very high and ameliorated intraclass conflicts. The "Mexican miracle" was miraculously revived, at least for a brief period.

The economic boom began to falter in the second half of 1981. A year later it turned into a full-scale recession and financial crisis of unforeseen proportions. The June 1981 reduction of the price of oil marked the initial stages of an economic downturn. The decision to lower petroleum prices was a political decision, creating consternation within the administration and initiating a national debate on economic and petroleum policies (i.e., the Díaz Serrano affair).

The absence of concerted public policies to ensure that the petroleum bonanza generated sustained and autonomous development became patently obvious. Petroleum prices were subsequently raised in July and October 1981, with price volatility reflecting overproduction, insufficient demand, and most importantly, structural disequilibrium. Petrolization had distorted the economic structure and the financial circuits, such that traditional balance of payments problems were compounded by serious inflation, speculation, capital flight, and political strife. In July, the first in a series of economic adjustment programs was introduced to fortify the balance of payments and reduce the public sector budget deficit. Suddenly, in February 1982, the administration implemented more radical, orthodox stabilizing policies to counteract economic recession and maintain public confidence. The petroleum bonanza had come to an end. Consequently, relative State autonomy was substantially restricted and the ability of the State to reinitiate the historical coincidence of interests with the bourgeoisie was affected.

President López Portillo's administration attempted to use technocratic planning in conjunction with political, economic, and administrative reforms to increase administrative efficiency and re-legitimize the role of the State as political-economic rector. As noted in the presentation section of the *Plan Global de Desarrollo: 1980–1982*:

> President José López Portillo has promoted a social reform that actualizes and projects the basic principles of the Mexican Revolution. This reform has been manifest in three aspects: the political reform, that fortified and accelerated the democratization process of the country; the administrative reform, that has modernized the institutions and given them the capacity to better serve the objectives of an integrated development; and the economic reform that, through the concerted forces of the real factors of the country, will continue to promote national independence, a high and sustained increase to give all Mexicans employment and the minimum welfare that a well-organized nation can provide, to therein progress more decidedly in the arrival of an egalitarian society. (1980, p. 17)

The regime, in other words, was able to use revolutionary discourse in combination with various measures to ameliorate the nascent political tensions and class conflict. Through the Alliance for Production and the petroleum bonanza, the State was able to promote the interests of the bourgeoisie by subsidizing private accumulation. The tremendous infusion of petrodollars, in the form of loans and remunerations from petroleum exports, enabled the State to reinvigorate economic confidence and direct the most dynamic period of economic expansion in the country's history. Thus, the public sector borrowed $37 billion from international lending institutions and paid $24 billion in interest on public sector debt. Income from petroleum exports also skyrocketed from $1 billion in 1977 to $16 billion in 1982. Traditional balance of payments problems continued unabated, as nonpetroleum exports stagnated and imports, in the words of the director of the central bank, increased at rates "rarely observed." The commercial balance deficits were not much better than the current account deficits, and the entire situation was aggravated by $36 billion in capital flight and speculative rentierism (Morgan Guaranty Trust, 1986, p. 13; Tello, 1984, pp. 72–77).

The petroleum boom transformed the productive structure. The international economy influenced State opportunities to sustain a petrolized version of the stabilizing development accumulation model. Not only did export prices in primary material markets decline 14 percent (excluding petroleum prices) in 1981, but a serious global recession reduced demand for Mexican exports.

The articulation and integration of the domestic and international financial circuits was also important in contributing to the failure of the petrolized version of stabilizing development. Disarray in the domestic and international financial markets disrupted production and facilitated the transition toward speculative rentierism. Public and private sector international borrowing resulted in $33 billion in debt service payments between 1977 and 1982 (Tello, 1984, p. 77). At the domestic level, the integration of financial circuits dollarized the financial system and promoted capital flight, speculation, excessively high interest rates, insufficient credit, inflation, and the expansion of public sector foreign debt.

> The phenomena of high interest rates, microdevaluations and inflation gave the national financial system a very strong speculative character. The management of foreign currency, in particular its contraction in the exterior and its placement as internal credits for public and private businesses, was an important source of profits for Mexican banks that, in addition, with their foreign branches, could manage the margin of bank reserves and the payment of taxes. (Cardero, 1984, p. 171)

Most important, however, was the power struggle between different fractions of the bourgeoisie and the State. As discussed in chapter 4, the transformation and empowerment of finance capital was the most important phenomenon during the 1970s. During the last years of the petroleum bonanza, the political and economic power of finance capital significantly increased to the point that the State lost control of its ability to direct the policy agenda. The historically important coincidence of interests that defined State relations with finance capital began to deteriorate in 1981 with the onset of an economic-liquidity crisis. Finance capital was more interested in accumulating capital through rentierist practices than investing in productive operations that were more risky and less lucrative. In other words, finance capital negated the principles of the Revolution and the legitimacy of the State to direct the specific manner in which the bourgeoisie accumulated capital.

The political dimensions of the crisis were manifested throughout 1982, particularly with the nationalization of the banks. A brief examination and analysis of the banking system, the heart of finance capital's accumulation structure, is important in understanding the economic and financial underpinnings of the 1982 crisis leading to the nationalization of the banks in September 1982.

THE BANKING SYSTEM: 1980–1982

The distribution of resources among financial institutions continued to reflect the underlying dynamism of the banking system. Central bank resources remained relatively constant and national credit institution resources increased the most during the 1980–1982 period. Private and mixed bank resources significantly increased and then decreased in 1982. These two developments—the increase in national credit institution resources and the decrease of private and mixed bank resources (as a percentage of the total system resources)—were interconnected.

The declining share of private and mixed bank resources, as a percentage of total system resources, was part of the general economic chaos and financial disintermediation characterizing the speculation and capital flight problém. Bank capture of financial resources never recovered from the negative developments of the 1970s. As a percentage of GDP, private and mixed bank capture of domestic financial resources never surpassed the 1973 figure of 26 percent. During the entire petroleum boom, private and mixed bank capture of peso-denominated financial resources barely increased from 22 percent in 1978. The capture of foreign-denominated financial resources, by private and mixed banks, increased from 3.5 percent of GDP in 1978 to 5.2 percent in 1981 (Tello, 1984, p. 47).

Speculation and capital flight caused financial market volatility. Disintermediation was rampant and capital flight was enormous. In 1980, capital flight was 1.6 percent of GDP, and more than doubled to 3.4 percent of GDP in 1981. For the first trimester of 1982, capital flight was $2.6 billion and in the second trimester more than doubled to $5.4 billion (Tello, 1984, p. 47; Ruíz Durán, 1984, pp. 53, 63). In synthesis, disintermediation, speculation, and capital flight affected the capture of domestic financial resources.

The increase in national credit institution resources, as a percentage of total system resources, was also interrelated with the prevailing economic chaos. Foreign credits played a more important role for national credit institutions because it was difficult to capture domestic financial resources.[3] Stagnation in the domestic financial market caused the government to utilize national credit institutions to obtain more credit.[4]

Some very interesting changes occurred among private banks during the 1980–1982 period. The distribution and growth of assets among specific banks was different from preceding periods. Undoubtedly, the most noteworthy change was the stagnation, in real terms, of Bancomer's asset growth. Interrelated with this phenomenon was the dynamic expansion of smaller multibanks and mixed banks, for example, SOMEX, Internaciónal (SPP, 1984, p. 144). The distribution and growth of private bank debits was similar to the case of bank assets. Once again, the largest bank stagnated and small and mixed banks' debits rapidly expanded (SPP, 1984, p. 158). The same phenomenon also occurred for total debits held by private banks. Bancomer's control of total debits decreased from 25 percent in 1980 to 22 percent in 1982. Banamex decreased from 22.6 percent in 1980, to 21.2 percent in 1982. Somex's share increased from 7.3 percent in 1980 to 10.5 percent in 1982 (SPP, 1984, p. 157). The same phenomenon was also reflected in bank loan portfolios. Using an index calculated with 100 equivalent to 1978, in real terms, the largest two banks' portfolios declined, whereas the portfolios of mixed and smaller institutions generally increased (SPP, 1984, p. 175).

Bank capital and profits showed a similar yet distinct downward trend from 1980 to 1982. For this period, capital and profits in real terms declined for most major banks. For the industry as a whole, real capital and profits increased from 10.6 billion pesos in 1980 to 10.8 billion pesos in 1981, and declined to 9.3 billion pesos in 1982 (SPP, 1984, p. 215).

A couple of important aspects affecting bank profitability included the average cost of obtaining resources and the differential between the cost of debits and the return from assets.[5] The cost of debits increased markedly during the end of the 1970s and the early 1980s. Although the CPP was 11 to 12 percent from 1975 until mid-1977, the rate increased from 15 percent in 1978 to 32 percent in December 1981 (Ruíz Durán, 1984, p. 35; Tello, 1984, p. 51). The CPP substantially affected bank profits and was set by the monetary authorities. The monetary authorities regulated the interest rates that banks paid their clients. The monetary authorities did not, however, set the rates that banks charged their customers for loans. In other words, the margin between asset and debit interest rates was not regulated. The interest rate differential between asset interest rates and debit interest rates (i.e., the difference between the interest banks paid and charged) greatly increased from 1979 to 1981. The margin increased from 5.35 percent during the fourth quarter of 1979 to 14.3 by the fourth quarter of 1981. The margin differential greatly augmented profits between 1978 and 1982 (Ruíz Durán, 1984, p. 35; Tello, 1984, p. 51).

> This situation resulted in an increase in bank profits, of 240.5 percent between 1978 and 1982. Monetary authorities' idea to permit and promote high bank returns was that this would capitalize the banks faster, which would elevate the capacity of these institutions to provide credit. However, it didn't happen that way. The paid capital plus the reserves were elevated only 140 percent, relative to a 240.5 percent increase in profits. In this form, elevating profits faster than capitalization, the profit margin increased. (Ruíz Durán, 1984, p. 35)

What is important to remember is that the extraordinary increase in bank profits was greatest for the largest banks because of oligopolistic market control and the volume of operations. Moreover, these extraordinary profits were not so extraordinary for 1982.

Profits from foreign exchange operations significantly contributed to the level of gross profits until August 31, 1982.[6] Foreign exchange operation profits accounted for 48 percent of multiple and specialized bank gross profits. Delineating multiple banks' foreign exchange operations reveals that the average contribution to gross profits was 50 percent. In the case of specialized banks (e.g., Citibank, Financiera de León) the contribution was much lower, averaging 26 percent. The average, however, obscures some banks' extraordinary profits from foreign exchange operations. Banamex's foreign exchange operations, for instance, accounted for 29 percent of gross profits until August 31, 1982. Likewise, Bancomer gained 35 percent of its gross profits from foreign exchange operations. However, 70 percent of Serfín's gross profits were from foreign exchange operations. The foreign exchange operations of Somex were 156 percent of gross profits and the foreign exchange operations of Comermex were 178 percent of gross profits (Tello, 1984, pp. 107–108). Although foreign exchange operations for the two largest banks were below the average, the sheer volume of foreign exchange operations was incredible. Foreign exchange operations for Banamex accounted for 1.2 billion pesos and 2.4 billion pesos for Bancomer, or 43.2 percent of total profits from foreign exchange operations. In sum, foreign exchange operations were important for bank gross profits, in many cases subsidizing losses.

Bank loan portfolios during 1982 were affected by the liquidity crisis and the greater incidence of past due loans. The past due portion of multiple bank loan portfolios increased from 2 percent in 1980 to 3.89 percent in 1982. The incidence and amount of past due loans, as a percentage of a specific bank's total loan portfolio, increased significantly. Most notable was Banamex. The ratio of Banamex's percentage of total past due loans and its percentage of total portfolio was roughly equivalent in 1981, but by 1982, its past due loans accounted for 29 percent of the multiple bank total, whereas its share of the total multiple portfolio was only 19 percent (SPP, 1984, pp. 175–177).

In synthesis, the banking system was very dynamic from 1980 to 1982. In nominal terms, expansion of bank resources and profits was extraordinary. A closer look at specific developments indicates that problems historically confronting the banking system and the economy continued to affect intermediation and productive economic development. The dramatic shift in resources among private and mixed banks and national credit institution resources reflected the general economic chaos and financial disintermediation characterizing the speculation and capital flight problem. National credit institutions were increasingly dependent on foreign capital to finance a greater proportion of State operations and entities. In a similar manner, the capture of resources by private and mixed banks never really recovered its historical dynamism and grew ever more dependent on foreign-currency (Mexdollar) accounts. The problem was that although Mexdollar accounts became increasingly important, in terms of total capture of resources, in reality, the increase in foreign currency resources was often a facade. In other words, banks received pesos and created a foreign currency debit with their customers. In effect, the operation also created a simultaneous foreign currency obligation on the part of the government. The government, in turn, had to generate foreign currency to satisfy bank obligations. Similar developments promoted capital flight.

The capital flight paradox was that the State socialized the financial and economic costs of rentierist practices by assuming greater and greater responsibility for correcting the disequilibriums. Within the confines of orthodox public policy, the State had to supply foreign currency resources to reproduce the entire mechanism. Thus, capital flight was indirectly interrelated with financial disintermediation and speculation. The departure of financial resources and the investment of these funds aggravated the liquidity problem, the credit squeeze, and the speculative process by restricting the opportunities for productive investment. While the nation's resources were being deposited in foreign accounts, the State was borrowing ever greater sums of money from international capital markets.[7] The State, however, borrowed capital at extremely high interest rates with short-term maturities. The problem was compounded by the constant devaluation of the peso and the declining volume and value of Mexican exports, therein affecting foreign currency income, which in turn affected the speculation process as the country's international reserves dwindled.

State policies did not counteract these problems. State policies actually facilitated and stimulated these degenerative processes. These policies ultimately affected everyone's financial costs. As noted by Tello (1984, p. 63):

None of the measures to stop financial disintermediation had an effect. Neither did they detain capital flight and speculation against the peso, nor could they sustain the exchange rate. What they did do was to drastically change the composition of the capture and channeling of resources by the banking system. Also, as a result of this policy, they fully installed a dual monetary system (*patron*) in the Mexican Republic: the peso and the dollar.

These policies also had an indirect impact on private and mixed bank balance sheets. Capital, results, and reserves significantly dropped. Profits dramatically increased in 1980 and 1981, and they essentially stagnated in 1982. The past-due portion of many bank loan portfolios increased and banks supplemented gross profits by profiting from currency exchange operations. Another important development was the channeling of credit to nonproductive sectors, for example, commerce, services, and government.

Bank practices also negatively affected the financial intermediation process and the economy. Tello (1984, pp. 65–68) noted that bank credit practices promoted bank interests and the interests of finance capital, while negatively affecting the financial system, intermediation, and economic production. For example, many banks provided credits at below market interest rates to bank-owned companies and also to companies owned by bank shareholders.[8] In addition, banks automatically renewed credits to companies owned by bank shareholders, provided below market interest rates to real estate operations owned by bank shareholders, failed to constitute provisions or reserves to cover irrecoverable assets, used inappropriate accounting techniques, paid extremely high salaries to executive directors and provided these employees with interest-free credits, and furnished special clients with interest rates above the legal ceiling.[9] In reference to bank credit practices, Tello (1984, p. 66) noted:

> A group of bank shareholders (or one of them) obtains below market credit from the bank for real estate, with which he constructs a building and rents it to the bank, arranging a rent above the market. With this, bank administrative costs are increased, which augments the interest rate of other loans to recuperate the excessive rent rate and the interests not charged in the below market credit. The shareholders, on the other hand, have developed real estate property without using their own resources.

The most contentious bank practice, however, was bank currency exchange operations. According to Tello (1984, p. 65), the speculation and capital flight problem was stimulated by bank exchange operations. Bank opinions and leadership had a multiplier effect. More important, banks "fomented, operated, and instrumented speculation and capital flight" (Tello, 1984, p. 65).

> Thus, high bank profits weren't derived from solid operations. Rather, they depended upon administrative decisions of the authority (for example, to leave asset interest rates unregulated, regulating only the debit; augmenting the margin in the purchase-sale of foreign currency), and they gave them a stagnant financial market relative to the capture of pesos and the increase in the capture of foreign denominated currency. These profits were flimsy, speculative. (Tello, 1984, p. 65)

POLITICAL-ECONOMIC DEVELOPMENTS LEADING TO THE NATIONALIZATION

The 1981 crisis was a serious and severe crisis. The situation, as noted by the U.S. Department of Commerce, was unprecedented.

> Mexico is going through a particularly difficult economic period. Following four years of economic growth in excess of 8 percent, the Government is being forced by the current economic situation to adopt severe adjustment measures. The outlook is uncertain in part because the current situation has no precedent in Mexican history and in part because a new Government takes office on December 1, 1982. (U.S. Department of Commerce, 1983, p. 3)

What was initially referred to as a liquidity crisis developed into a cash crisis (*crisis de caja*), which in turn led to a generalized political-economic crisis of unforeseen proportions. The predominant government analysis of the crisis incorporated a classical orthodox prescription. According to the orthodox analysis, inflation was the problem. The solution required a reduction of (a) excessive government budget deficits, (b) inadequate government revenues, and (c) excessive liquidity. The peso was also overvalued and government revenues were inadequate.

A number of fiscal policies were implemented to direct investment toward priority areas. The idea was to subsidize private accumulation, increase State legitimacy, and increase public sector income. Small and medium industry, for example, received 5.6 billion pesos in public sector financing through the integral support program (*Programa de Apoyo Integral*). Additional programs supported the steel industry, production of general consumer products, employers' increased salary expenses (resulting from the emergency increase in the minimum wage), and increased financial expenditures of private companies (the result of dollar-denominated debts). The government also initiated several adjustment programs to support the economy and renew public confidence in the ability of the administration to salvage the situation. A chronological examination of the events preceding the nationalization of the banks will facilitate a general understanding of the degenerative dynamic.

Political discord and economic disequilibrium prevailed in January 1982 as strikes paralyzed the distribution of food products. In Guadalajara, a reunion of prominent businessmen (Atalaya 82) discussed the situation of economic chaos and confirmed that the government was responsible for excessive inflation and external disequilibriums. Political discord was compounded by the revelation that the consumer price index increased 5 percent during the month. In a similar manner, interest rates increased, and the amount of foreign currency captured by the banking system surpassed the amount of national currency captured. The devaluation of the peso was accelerated and central bank international reserves declined.

February 1982 was a busy month. In February, the administration implemented an adjustment program and verbally defended the peso, and the central bank used its swap line agreement with the U.S. Federal Reserve. On February 17, the administration initiated a new adjustment program. The most notable aspect of the program was the new exchange policy. The central bank withdrew from the exchange market and the peso was devalued by more than 70 percent. The adjustment program also included several additional measures, including: (a) a 3-percent reduction in the public sector budget, (b) a real increase in domestic interest rates, (c) wage increases to offset the effects of the new adjustment program, (d) reduction of trade barriers and elimination of permits for popular consumption goods and goods indispensable for production, (e) increases in price controls, (f) assurances to international lending agencies and banks that Mexico would continue to comply with its debt obligations, and (g) promotion of national products in the border zones.

The February adjustment package restricted economic expansion, accelerated inflation, and augmented speculation and capital flight. Reduced government expenditures and investment mirrored private sector behavior. The inflation spiral continued to debilitate production and promoted speculation and hoarding.[10] An individual or company could make greater profits by purchasing foreign currency—therein speculating that the peso would be devalued—than by investing in productive instruments. The consequent investment in foreign currencies had a negative effect on the price of the peso as compared with foreign currencies, which in turn promoted further devaluation of the peso and a greater return for the speculator. The continual devaluation of the peso also stimulated inflation. Speculation against the peso and capital flight continued unabated.

In March, the February adjustment measures were reiterated and a series of new measures was proposed to stimulate the economy, protect small and intermediate industry, and protect the "popular" economy. The heterogeneous nature of the new measures, combining restrictive orthodox policies and Keynesian stimulative policies, manifested disagreements and power struggles within the State apparatus. Although the February adjustment program satisfied the demands of the bourgeoisie, the retroactive emergency wage increase announced on March 19 reflected anxieties of the proletariat and the importance of the labor unions in terms of legitimacy and stability. After the emergency wage increase, a series of declarations and counter-declarations were made by business leaders and labor union leaders, denouncing their counterparts. On March 24, López Portillo noted that business and the State had to confront the economic crisis, and that workers had already contributed their effort. Contradictory interests within the State apparatus were manifested by the decision to allow employers the opportunity to defer tax payments to the treasury and receive a fiscal credit. An additional presidential decree on March 19 provided a subsidy for employees receiving the minimum wage and up to 30 percent above the minimum wage. These measures temporarily ameliorated tensions.

In April, another orthodox economic adjustment program was announced. Based on a more radical orthodox prescription, the program (a) reduced public expenditures by an additional 5 percent, (b) limited public sector debt to $11 billion for the year, (c) initiated measures to increase public sector income by 150 billion pesos (e.g., raising the prices of public sector goods and services), and (d) limited increases in the amount of circulating currency to the amount of increase in central bank international reserves. The director of the Banco de México, Miguel Mancera Aguayo, reinforced the orthodox tone of administration economic policies with the release of a document analyzing the impossibility of implementing exchange control in Mexico.

The financial side of rapid economic deterioration began to surface in April. The ensuing liquidity crisis was visible. The private sector renegotiated its foreign debt payments with the Bank of America, and the largest private company, Alfa, suspended debt payments to foreign creditors. The State also renegotiated its short-term debt in an effort to prolong amortization of the debt into the long-term future. By May, finance secretary Silva Herzog explained that although the oil shock was responsible for excessively rapid economic growth, high interest rates had caused a financial liquidity problem of short-term duration, and the fundamental structure of the system remained intact (Tello, 1984, p. 97).

In June, the annual Mexican Bank Association (ABM) convention was fundamentally optimistic. Although bankers reaffirmed traditional loyalties to the

Mexican Revolution, the tone of some speeches was somewhat more critical of the government. ABM president Víctor Manuel Herrera blamed the government for inflation and excessive demand. The ABM president's speech was concise, critical, and somewhat defensive. In a similar vein, the Executive Council gave the government its vote of confidence, in support of administration measures to rectify economic chaos. The council was also defensive, as shown by remarks that the banking system fulfilled its social obligations.[11] The council was also critically aggressive in its analysis of the intermediation process. It was noted that domestic savings were insufficient to finance accelerated development. Several factors accounted for the shortfall, including (a) inflation and pre-1979 negative real interest rates; (b) State-issued financial instruments (e.g., CETES) providing superior return and liquidity vis-à-vis bank financial instruments, affecting the competitiveness of bank's financial instruments; and (c) substantial increases in banks' obligatory deposits. The council also noted that reserve requirements functioned more as a means to finance the public sector than as an instrument of monetary regulation. In short, the insufficient supply of domestic savings limited the financial capability of the banks and increased the cost of money.

These preoccupations were carefully formulated within the traditional confines of a loyal and frank dialogue. Although pronouncements were indicative of an increasingly divisive conflict over bank autonomy to define the realm of operations, the council continued to use traditional methods of negotiation through dialogue.

The head of the central bank, Mancera Aguayo, gave a traditional presentation, focusing on events and statistics of the previous year. However, Mancera Aguayo briefly mentioned the February devaluation and linked the central bank's withdrawal from the exchange markets to the inability of the State to continue international borrowing to support the balance of payments deficit. The February developments were initiated by speculators (Mancera Aguayo, 1982, p. 66). The speculation remark was significant because Mancera Aguayo represented the interests of finance capital within the State apparatus. Although not accusing the bankers of speculation, he did acknowledge that speculation was beginning to undermine the ability of the State to manage fiscal, monetary, and economic policies.

Finance secretary Silva Herzog summarized the administration's policies for the previous year and attempted to allay anxieties. Thus he noted that the Banco de México's return to the exchange market was decisive; instilling confidence and overcoming uncertainty and speculation. Silva Herzog also noted that the crisis was under control. In his closing remarks, the secretary noted that the financial system was modern, solid, and efficient and that these characteristics could be proven by serving the country rather than a particular sector or group. More important was the warning, to bankers, that the State provided banks with their concessions:

> We cannot forget that the bank is a service concessioned by the State, a service that should favor the general interests of Mexico. (Silva Herzog, 1982, p. 76)

In contrast, President López Portillo's address was very short, conciliatory, and optimistic; he emphasized that the government and bankers were privileged to be able to serve the public. The least conciliatory speech was presented by the president of the National Bank and Insurance Commission Enrique Creel de la Barra, who was much more aggressive than any of the previous speakers, as exemplified by his reference to bank concessions:

> The fact that the bank is a concessioned activity not only implies the delicacy of its attributions, but also the absolute necessity that its works are adjusted to the policies and objectives of the State, that provides the concession. An elitist bank at the service of a few privileged should not be concessioned, nor does it have a reason to exist. (Creel de la Barra, 1982, p. 98)

An address by incoming ABM president Abedrop Dávila reflected a defensive optimism. Comparing the 1982 crisis to the 1976 crisis, he carefully delineated the seriousness of the 1982 liquidity crisis for business. This crisis was compounded by the debt problem, price controls, and more important, the insufficient availability of domestic credit. Abedrop noted that banks were concerned about their clients and the inability of the banks to adequately meet their financial needs. Banks, in other words, were trying to comply with their social obligation.

The closing address of finance secretary Silva Herzog reinforced the somewhat conflictive, yet conciliatory tone of the convention. Silva Herzog noted that important questions were analyzed realistically, with congruence between what had been said, what was being done, and what would be done (Silva Herzog, 1982, p. 124).

In synthesis, the ABM convention reflected the increasingly contradictory nature of the coincidence of interests between the State and finance capital. Although the tone of the convention was conciliatory, the underlying perseverance and exacerbation of significant differences in the definition of public policies reflected an important power struggle. Discussion of State encroachment on bank operations exemplified the position of bankers, whereas the position of some segments within the State was articulated by Creel de la Barra's reference to bank social obligations and his enunciation of the concessioned status of the bank. These subtle positions reflected a serious power struggle that was just beginning to become visible.

During June, the seriousness of the liquidity crisis was more apparent. On June 30, the central bank withdrew another $200 million from its swap line agreement with the U.S. Federal Reserve. Additional complications occurred with the May–June international loan negotiations. A $2.5 billion loan, signed on June 30, was the largest single loan the country had ever contracted. The loan was used to repay maturing short-term loans. Meanwhile, the bourgeoisie and the middle class increasingly blamed the administration for the economic crisis, reducing State maneuverability and legitimacy.

In August, the entire situation began to unravel and the distinct interests corresponding to contradictory class interests began to materialize. On August 1, the government increased prices of gas, bread, and tortillas. Although the official rationale for these measures was to stimulate investment, production, and balance public sector finances, the measures contributed to inflation and reduced consumer purchasing power. A brief polemic between the labor unions and the business community ensued, with labor noting that the measures were unpopular. Union leadership nevertheless pledged its support for the government and the revolutionary alliance. Business groups declared that the measures were necessary to transcend the crisis. Meanwhile, inflation increased and speculation and capital flight plagued the peso, the balance of payments, and international reserves.

On August 6, Silva Herzog announced a temporary dual parity exchange system vis-à-vis the dollar: another devaluation. The bourgeoisie was largely opposed to the new exchange program. Although ABM president Abedrop noted that the banking system would apply the new policy in an efficient manner, the PAN decried the measure as another devaluation. The Monterrey CONCANACO declared that the program was absurd. The CCE, CONCAMIN, and CONCANACO were hostile toward the dual parity system because it would not reduce capital flight nor resolve the economic crisis, and it would harm business's financial capabilities, reduce production and employment, and result in corruption.

On August 7, López Portillo publicly defended the dual parity system as a necessary policy, since there were no alternatives. The only real alternative was to administer the use of foreign currency and put an end to the speculative business, a counterproductive activity negatively affecting people's income and credit. Nevertheless, approximately 94 billion pesos worth of Mexdollars were withdrawn from the financial system during the first part of August (Tello, 1984, p. 103).

On August 12, the Central Bank and the finance ministry amended the monetary law by stipulating that bank deposits denoted in foreign currencies had to be paid in national currency at the prevailing exchange rate. Credit institutions were also restricted from conducting foreign currency transactions outside of the country.

The amendment to the monetary law was a clear and important attempt by the administration to restrict capital flight and speculation. Previous exhortations, based on revolutionary rhetoric, social responsibility, and national interest, had been ignored. The new regulation manifested the power struggle within the State apparatus and the deterioration of the coincidence of interests. In April, Mancera Aguayo, director of the Central Bank, had propounded the inapplicability of exchange control for Mexico and the inability of a dual exchange rate to reduce capital flight. Attempts to control the exchange market, Mancera Aguayo warned, would provoke distrust and aggravate financial disintermediation. On August 6, the same day that the dual exchange system was announced, the Central Bank reminded banks that clients withdrawing foreign denominated deposits should be paid in foreign currency and that interest payments for these accounts should be paid in foreign currency.

An interesting contradiction had developed. The finance secretary announced a dual exchange market and noted that free exchange would be maintained. Meanwhile, the Central Bank noted that banks should not alter the way foreign-denominated accounts were treated. In short, Central Bank policy was ignored. Although the finance secretary had prefaced his announcement of a dual exchange market with the declaration that the free exchange market would be maintained, the Central Bank reminded banks to pay foreign-denominated accounts in foreign currency. Most important was that the dual exchange market constituted a very loose form of exchange control. At the same time, the Central Bank advisory board reminded banks to use foreign currency for foreign-denominated accounts, promoting speculation, capital flight, and financial disintermediation. The Central Bank legitimized the role of banks in the process of capital flight and speculation. An August 12 amendment to the monetary law, however, showed the inability of the central bank to affect policies. It also demonstrated that certain elements within the State apparatus were attempting to control speculation and capital flight, regain control over the policy agenda, and relegitimize the State's historical direction and control of the economy.

Reactions to the August 12 amendment to the monetary law were supportive or antagonistic. The labor movement was typically supportive. The ABM, on the other hand, took an aggressive stance against the amendment and purchased space in major newspapers, informing the public that banks could pay foreign-denominated peso accounts in foreign currency. On August 16, the finance ministry backed down and partially rescinded its new rules on the transfer of foreign currency. These events resulted in a renewed attack on and revaluation of the peso.

On August 17, Silva Herzog held a conference and attempted to clarify the economic situation, reiterating the existence of a dual exchange market and confirming that foreign-denominated accounts would be paid at a special exchange rate. Silva Herzog also announced that taxes would be reduced to protect individual incomes and stimulate investment, and that the February price control decree would be extended until 1983. He also revealed that Mexico was negotiating with several parties to obtain credit and that Mexico was temporarily halting debt payments. Reaction to the new measures varied. Business organizations basically supported the policy announcements. Labor was concerned about negotiations to obtain financial resources.

These developments revealed a serious tension and divisiveness between the State and finance capital. Public repudiation of the August 12 amendment to the monetary law was a highly uncharacteristic method of political negotiation and conciliation. Silva Herzog's August 17 news conference on foreign-denominated account payments indicated that a definite rift existed between banks and certain elements of the State apparatus. Although his reaffirmation of the August 12 amendment was a political maneuver to reaffirm State supremacy, the offer to provide a special exchange rate for payment of foreign-denominated account payments indicated a resolve by some elements of the State apparatus to pursue a conciliatory policy with the banks. The offer was an effort to placate the interests of finance capital and therein maintain the traditional coincidence of interests.

On August 19 the exchange market was extremely volatile. Some banks limited the sale of dollars, whereas others ran out of foreign currency. In short, anxiety and confusion predominated.

Throughout this period, banks earned tremendous profits from the extraordinary number of transactions. Profits increased with the number of transactions and the buy/sell margin. In other words, greater volumes of speculation and capital flight were positively related to bank profits. Although the exact relationship between bank profits and speculation and capital flight depended on the volume of a specific bank's exchange transactions vis-à-vis a bank's profit structure, there was a definite correlation between profits, speculation, and capital flight. This explains why the banks were so outspoken about the August 12 amendment to the monetary law. In part, the banks had to look out for the interests of their clientele, especially since particular elements were profiting from speculation and capital flight.

By the end of August 1982, banks obtained 49 percent of gross profits from exchange operations. Profits from exchange operations varied among different banks. Although Banamex obtained 29 percent of its gross profits from exchange operations, Banco Internaciónal gained 98 percent of its gross profits from exchange operations. Some banks earned more money from exchange operations than from gross profits. Atlántico, for example, earned 421 million pesos from exchange operations, whereas gross profits accounted for only 20.5 million pesos. In other words, in some cases, profits from exchange operations were used to subsidize operation losses.

On August 23, the Central Bank contradicted a previous policy pronouncement and authorized banks to receive deposits denominated in foreign currency (Mexdollars) with pre-established maturity dates. Although the exchange markets had become temporarily tranquil, the new Mexdollar authorization reinitiated speculation. A period of speculative disarray emerged amid rampant rumors, massive capital flight, and panic buying of dollars. The situation was so bad that many official organizations urged national unity and an end to the vicious rumor campaigns.

On August 31, the day before López Portillo's annual address, the CTM convened its 97th general assembly. López Portillo's speech hinted at the historical proclamation to be announced on September 1, 1982, noting that the country had to be reconstructed with the support of workers and peasants. The CTM's analysis noted that the crisis was a structural economic crisis based on a particular economic development model that caused disequilibrium and structural deformation.

> The origin of the crisis is in the economic structure and in the vices of an economic model of development characterized by external economic dependence, the concentration of wealth and the deformation of the productive apparatus. (cited in Tello, 1984, p. 109)

THE NATIONALIZATION OF THE BANKS

On September 1, 1982, President José López Portillo's sixth and last annual report announced the nationalization of the banks and exchange controls. The report provided the theoretical and material groundwork for the majority of descriptions, explanations, and interpretations of the nationalization of the banks. The report provided significant insights into the official rationale for nationalizing the banks.

President López Portillo opened his argument by noting that a general incongruence existed between government plans, projects, and real factors: a "brutal contradiction." Internationally, the Mexican economy had become vulnerable as a result of high interest rates, protectionism, declining petroleum and primary product prices, increased debt service payments, balance of payments disequilibrium, international economic recession, and reduced tourism. The fundamental cause of the crisis, however, was the manipulated loss of confidence in the peso and the resulting speculation and capital flight.

The loss of confidence generated a financial and liquidity crisis of devastating proportions. Mexicans had an estimated $14 billion in foreign bank accounts and $25 billion in urban and rural property outside Mexico, which amounted to an additional $8.5 billion in capital flight. Mexdollars accounted for $12 billion, and capital flight, during the previous two to three years, had been estimated at $22 billion, with an unregistered $17 billion in private debt allocated to liquidate mortgages.

> In synthesis, the public sector's increasing necessity of foreign currency, to pay for importations and debts, and for individuals, banks and companies that take their capital or dollarize the economy, had aggravated the need for greater external credit to repress these pressures. (López Portillo, 1982, p. 935)

By the end of 1981 and early 1982, these processes affected the inflation rate, accelerated State expenditures, and increased the contraction of external credit. The vicious inflation–devaluation cycle had become perverse.

According to López Portillo, the 1982 crisis differed from that of 1976. The 1976 crisis was the culmination of a developmental strategy, whereas the 1982 crisis occurred during the initial part of a new strategy of growth that had been undeniably successful. In February 1982, the peso was brutally attacked by speculators and there was a drastic decline in international reserves. The Banco de México retired from the exchange market February 17, and the peso was devalued. The government consequently initiated defensive measures through an adjustment program to reduce public expenditures, implement import controls, restructure prices and tariffs in the public sector, and increase interest rates to defend the peso. Another financially orthodox adjustment program was implemented in April. Nevertheless, speculation against the peso continued to be good business. The government lacked sufficient funds to protect or curtail capital flight. Speculation had to stop, even though such action implied political risks.

In August, historic decisions were taken. Foreign currency funds from petroleum sales and external loans were prioritized for imports and debt service, with the remainder earmarked for demand. Foreign creditors announced that short-term debt maturing in August and September would not be rolled over. In addition to a liquidity problem, Mexico now had a cash problem. A dual exchange market was created on August 5 to defend the nation's capacity to pay international creditors. Several emergency measures were initiated, for example, loans and IMF.

The president identified great internal and external evils. Externally, international economic disorder punished developing countries. Internally, three great evils existed: conciliation of free exchange with national solidarity; the conception of the Mexican economy as a right without corollary obligations; and the management of concessioned highly speculative banks, disregarding national solidarity.

These internal evils resulted in the loss of a substantial amount of resources generated from savings, petroleum, and public debt. Mexicans and their banks enriched external economies instead of channeling resources to capitalize the country. Private banks led, counseled, and supported a group of Mexicans to "sack more money from Mexico than the empire." National security had been damaged and the great evil had to be corrected. The State, as in all critical moments, was with the majorities (López Portillo, 1982, p. 939).

The question was between an economy progressively dominated by absenteeism, speculation, and rentierism, or an economy oriented toward production and employment. Speculation was impermissible. Given the extremity of the crisis, continuing speculation would defeat the established constitutional system. The financial crisis threatened the productive structure.

> We have to organize ourselves to save our productive structure and provide it with the financial resources to proceed ahead; we have to detain the injustice of the perverse process of capital flight–devaluation–inflation that damages everyone, especially the worker, employment and businesses that generate employment. (López Portillo, 1982, p. 939)

In support of these critical priorities, two decrees nationalizing the banks and establishing generalized exchange control were promulgated. These measures were required and justified by the critical conditions confronting the country and not as a better-late-than-never survival policy. Bank concessions were terminated and the service was incorporated directly by the Nation. The only change was that the Mexican State was now the administrator. "In sum, we nationalized the banks because it is not permissible that the instrument dominate or condition the proposition" (López Portillo, 1982, p. 940).

These measures benefited the nation; inflation would decrease, and speculation would be confronted. The productive structure would be saved and neither workers nor business would be sacrificed in the adjustment process. Demand had to be reoriented toward the internal market, production increased, and liquidity extended to businesses, enabling them to comply with their obligations. Interest rates would be managed rationally, and credit would be oriented toward productive businesses. "The State will no longer be cornered by pressure groups" (López Portillo, 1982, p. 940). The nationalization and exchange control measures expressed the Revolution and its will to change.

In sum, the President's Sixth Report defended the administration's record and blamed the banks for the genesis of the crisis. The official charge was that the banks had led, counseled, and supported speculation and capital flight, therein endangering national security. The State nationalized the banks to defend the interests of the majority of the nation and promote employment and productive investment. The President also noted that speculation dominated the crisis and threatened the productive structure. Moreover, banks had demonstrated a lack of solidarity with national interests and the productive apparatus. Finally, the nationalization manifested the Revolution.

SIX ANALYSES OF THE NATIONALIZATION

Rather than examine every single analysis and description of the nationalization of the banks, I have categorized analyses of the nationalization, and present a concise synthesis.[12] There are basically six different types of analysis: individual/psychological; political; economic; statization; class; and conspiracy.

The conspiracy theory is an extraordinary explanation of the September measures, claiming that[13] López Portillo and Durazo (the ex-chief of police for Mexico City) were involved in drug trafficking and channeled their operations through the banks. López Portillo had also become a cocaine addict, as exemplified by his psychological behavior manifesting paranoia and euphoria. López Portillo nationalized the banks in order to confiscate records that would implicate the President and Durazo. Although this explanation is rather absurd, it nevertheless merits mention because it exemplifies right-wing efforts to create political instability and delegitimize the nationalization of the banks.

The statization analysis had both left and right variations. The general argument was that the nationalization of the banks was nothing less than the culmination of a historical process of State intervention in the financial markets (Aguilar et al., 1982; Pazos, 1982; Turrent Díaz, 1983). Pazos (1982) noted that after the September measures, the Mexican economy had become socialized and the expression of private property had been minimized. Moreover, the nationalization of the banks had consolidated the government as the premier capitalist.

The individual or psychological explanation of the nationalization focused on the personal characteristics of López Portillo. This analysis emphasized the former president's personal prestige and his sense of history, in other words, wanting to be remembered as a good president (Castillo, 1982; Del Rio, 1982; Hinojosa, 1982; Krauze, 1982; Medina Macias, 1982). Del Rio (1982) noted the popular comparison with the nationalization of petroleum and the natural comparison of López Portillo with Cárdenas. Medina Macias (1982) also noted that the president had a personal crisis as a president in regard to his historical image. Krauze (1982) provided the most in-depth analysis of López Portillo's personal and psychological development within the context of the regime's managerial inadequacy and policy failures.

The economic analysis of the nationalization emphasizes financial aspects of the prenationalization crisis and the culmination of the accumulation or development model. Galindo (1983), for example, argued that from 1977 to 1981, economic expansion determined the specificity of the 1981–1982 crisis. Petroleum served as a means to secure enormous loans from international banks. Capital flight and speculation negatively affected the possibilities for debt repayment. The State, therefore, located itself at the vanguard of the bourgeoisie and sacrificed national finance capital in favor of international finance capital. The nationalization of the banks enabled the State to prioritize debt repayment. Valdés (1983) presented a variation of this theme, based on the fiscal crisis of the State. Valdés argued that banks were nationalized because administration policies caused a fiscal crisis of the State. Public sector finance and economic policies, driven by the IMF, had petrolized the economy, and in 1981, government deficits and external debt failed to sustain previous policies. The nationalization, in other words, resulted from a crisis in State economic intervention strategy. In a similar vein, Fitzgerald (1985) argued that the nationalization was related to the fiscal crisis of the State. The fiscal crisis resulted from the exhaustion of the postrevolutionary industrialization model. Additional contributing factors included the consequent increase in public sector investment and private sector opposition (led by the banks) to the State's increasing role as economic rector. Banks were concerned about State control over the surplus and foreign borrowing, which aggravated internal and external disequilibriums (Fitzgerald, 1985, p. 229). Private banks responded aggressively to public sector fiscal deficits, in the form of capital flight. Capital flight "brought the system into implicit bankruptcy, so that the State was forced to take over the entire banking system and apply exchange controls to prevent a collapse of the monetary system" (Fitzgerald, 1985, p. 227).

The political analysis of the nationalization was the overwhelmingly predominant analysis. The general argument was that the nationalization was fundamentally a political measure and was economically unnecessary (Morera Camacho, 1983). This analysis tends to support or reject the nationalization in terms of the public interest (Landerreche Obregón, 1984), the "revolutionary trajectory of the State" (Lugo Gil, 1983), the recuperation of national sovereignty (Blanco Mejía, 1982), and popular demand (Ramírez, 1982).

There also was the question of State legitimacy. Among the several variations of this focus was Turrent Díaz's (1983) argument that the decree to nationalize the banks was a reaffirmation of the ability of the administration to manage the political agenda, in other words, it was a political answer to a sexenio of economic failure. In a similar manner, Anda Gutierrez (1982) noted that the measure was a reaction to the worst economic crisis in a situation when government credibility was the lowest. Basáñez (1983) also noted that events surrounding the nationalization constituted the third credibility crisis during a succession period. Arriola and Galindo (1983) explained that López Portillo hoped to recuperate lost confidence in order to regain public support. Hellman (1983) argued that the September 1 measures were political symbolism to hide political mismanagement and malfeasance. *Punto Crítico* (1982d) noted that the political objective was the recomposition of State legitimacy. Aguilar et al. (1982) also noted that the September 1 decrees reaffirmed the State's revolutionary nationalist character and simultaneously weakened the left's political struggle. Hamilton (1983, p. 23) noted that López Portillo marshaled popular support for the nationalization to outflank the left and politically appease the population, which was going to receive the brunt of the austerity measures.

Another theme among political analyses was the question of State autonomy. Hamilton (1983, p. 45) noted that the nationalization resulted in the realignment of relations between the State and the private sector, demonstrating State autonomy in relation to dominant class interests. Cockcroft (1983, p. 309) also argued that the nationalization was political, giving the state more nationalist breathing room to manipulate the class struggle. Similar variations of the autonomy theme argued that the State functioned as a guardian of the general interests of the bourgeoisie, protecting the reproduction of capitalist relations of exploitation and capital accumulation (Guillén Romo, 1984). Olson (1984, p. 39) argued that the bank nationalization "was a move which the State reluctantly took against finance capital in order to protect the interest of capital as a whole in maintaining political stability." *Punto Crítico* (1982a, 1982b) also argued that the nationalization created a significant change in the correlation of social forces and that State rectorship was reconfirmed. *Coyoacán* (1983) also noted that the nationalization signified a reaccommodation of State–capital relations, wherein the State represented the global interests of national and international capital, that is, preservation of the necessary juridical, economic, and political conditions for private accumulation.

The most authoritative political account of the nationalization was Carlos Tello's (1984) work.[14] Tello (1986) explained that López Portillo thoroughly examined the idea of the nationalization and selected the fifth option as a pragmatic attempt to confront the severity of the problems confronting the government.[15] Tello (1986) felt that the banks and financial system had constituted a historical problem, restricting the country's ability to transcend the stabilizing development model. The problem was that economic policy was subordinated to the interests of banks and finance. The national economy was in "checkmate."

According to Tello (1984, p. 122), the contradictions and problems permeating the country's style of development exhausted and displaced the ability of the government to make public policy decisions. By the end of the 1970s, problems associated with the financing of development caused the government to cut back its operations. During the 1980s, the contradiction between monetary policy and public sector expenditures limited the realm of public sector activity and contributed to the increasingly oscillatory contraction–expansion process. In short, financial questions affected policy initiatives.

López Portillo's decision to nationalize the banks responded to the failure of conventional policies (e.g., the February devaluation). The situation was compounded by the perverse behavior of exchange markets during mid-1982, which essentially annulled every conventional option except political and economic disaster (Tello, 1984, p. 122).

> The nationalization had a grand importance not only for the management of the conjunctural problems; its transcendence will be permanent. It ended the idea that the State had lost its decision power and its capacity to conduct the development process. . . . But, above all, the State could terminate once and for all the principal adversary that in a secular manner had limited its capacity to maneuver. (Tello, 1984, p. 122)

The financial analysis of the nationalization was the class analysis. This analysis focused on relations between different fractions of the bourgeoisie and the relations of these fractions to the State. This analysis also examined the significance of the nationalization with regard to the productive structure. Basave, Moguel, Rivera, and Toledo (1982) incorporated different levels of analysis in their examination of the nationalization, noting that there were no immediate consequences. At the economic level, the decrees enabled the State to rehabilitate and regulate the economic system against the possibility of bankruptcy and the paralysis of the complete reproduction process. The crisis, these authors argued, was the confluence of the overaccumulation of capital and the fiscal crisis of the State, resulting from overindebtedness and the onset of a recession cycle. In combination, these factors expressed the contradictions of Mexican capitalism and the instability resulting from speculation and capital flight. In terms of general economic policy, the nationalization was an effort to control a crisis that appeared uncontrollable. The expropriation also reinforced a historical process wherein the capitalist State directly intervened in the economy and fortified the monopolization of the economy. At another level, the nationalization changed the power relations within the structural interior of the power bloc and revealed relative State autonomy in a critical period. State capital was strengthened at the cost of monopoly capital. Finally, in terms of political strategy, the measure was reformist. It was also not a popular measure because of the accompanying austerity measures.

Alvarez (1983) also argued that the nationalization "expressed and confirmed a change in the correlation of forces within the Dominant Bloc, displacing hegemony to transnational finance capital. . . . "

Alcocer and Cisneros (1985) examined the change in relations between the State and capital after the nationalization. The nationalization opened a new stage of political confrontation between the State and the financial bourgeoisie and forced finance capital to reorganize its structure and way of functioning. The financial bourgeoisie's traditional mechanisms of accumulation were restructured and a new political project was initiated. The political project attempted to disrupt State mechanisms of social legitimacy by populist concessions through PAN militancy. The economic component of the new political project has been the re-creation of a parallel financial circuit, attempting to subordinate the nationalized bank system to the interests of the financial fraction.

> The bank nationalization initiated a fragmentation process in the government's relations with private initiative, that affected the schema of traditional agreements (*acuerdos cupulares*), those that constituted the mechanisms of legitimating power. (Alcocer & Cisneros, 1985, p. 214)

Bartra (1982b) analyzed the nationalization of the banks as a crisis of hegemony within the power bloc. A conjunctural crisis gradually materialized during the early 1980s in the form of a financial crisis and fractures within the political domination apparatus. The important question, Bartra noted, was: "What unleashed the process?"

> It is evident that almost uncontrollable division and antagonisms had been generated within the interior of the State: the financial sector rejected political direc-

tives; the technocrats turned their back on the populist leaders; the union bureau-cracy seemed to confront the transition team of the new president; the new moral technocrats profoundly disgusted a part of the political class; the president couldn't control his own cabinet; the bickering between small groups for the division of power parcels contributed to the atomization of the decision-making mechanism. Ultimately, an accentuated state of ungovernability in the governing class. (Bartra, 1982b, p. 20)

The majority of the analyses were written shortly after the nationalization. Chapter 6 will show why a thorough understanding of the implications of the nationalization is impossible without analyzing the transformations and conflicts that occurred and are still occurring relative to the State and finance capital. For example, in terms of the constitution of finance capital, what does it mean when one of the central components accounting for the fraction's accumulation of political-economic power—banks and bank holding companies—is taken away by the State? The previous analyses also indicate the real paucity of comprehensive analyses incorporating various levels of analysis, relevant statistics, and a detailed examination of the development of finance capital vis-à-vis the State. In other words, although there are a few serious works on the nationalization of the banks, the majority of analyses are very brief, inconclusive, and oftentimes superficial in an ideological sense.

For example, Bartra (1982b) noted that most of the early leftist analyses were either nationalist or orthodox. The orthodox analyses argued that the State nationalized the banks to maintain the functioning of the capitalist system and save the global interests of the bourgeoisie. The orthodox interpretation adopted an economistic paradigm, so that the political and juridical superstructures are dependent on the capitalist economic base. Although it explains the structural coherence and logical continuity of the State and capitalist development, it does not explain why the nationalization occurred, nor does it examine the concrete change in social relations vis-à-vis the State (Bartra, 1982b, p. 14). In essence, it is a static, a priori, and reductionistic delineation of classes, based on a functionalist conception of social reality.

The nationalist version focused on the government's decision as the vindication of national interests and constitutional values. The nationalist version was based on two models of development–neo-liberal and national popular–and presupposes the existence of a polarized presence within the interior of the State. The nationalist interpretation accepts López Portillo's analysis wholeheartedly. The nationalist explanation does not explain why the nationalization occurred on September 1, 1982, nor can it explain the profound ramifications of social conflict and transformation stemming from the nationalization. As noted by

Bartra, it is essential to progress beyond these paradigms and confront social reality. As of October 1982, it was impossible to arrive at any serious conclusion (Basáñez, 1983, p. 57).

A comprehensive critical understanding of the nationalization has to examine changes in social relations and the productive structure before and after the nationalization of the banks. Classes were not static entities, nor is the State. Examining the immediate postnationalization period is important in terms of theory and politics. One could easily argue that the nationalization was a demonstration of relative State autonomy and then proceed to construct a political position based on reformist ideas about the ability to influence the State during periods of crisis. However, a brief examination of immediate postnationalization events indicates that the nationalization of the banks initiated a period of class struggle by the deposed financial fraction of the bourgeoisie. The financial fraction was and continues to be a powerful political-economic force vis-à-vis the State. An underestimation of the vicissitudes of the financial fraction vis-à-vis the State restricts one's ability to understand the socioeconomic structure in contemporary Mexico, and the ability of the financial fraction to attempt to reconstruct its historical hegemony. In other words, in terms of political strategy, the limited autonomy of the State may be a concept that should be relegated to the specific historical context surrounding the Cárdenas period.

CONCLUSION

This chapter has examined political socioeconomic developments preceding the nationalization of the banks. During most of the López Portillo administration, the State utilized petroleum revenues, international loans, and renewed private sector confidence to stimulate economic expansion, sustain a previously exhausted development model, and maintain a coincidence of interests with the bourgeoisie. These accomplishments occurred at the same time that the State was upholding the Cárdenas pact with labor and the peasantry. At another level, exploitation increased, as manifested by the greater transfer of surplus value to capital. All of these developments occurred during an economic boom of tremendous proportions.

The demise of economic expansion reduced State maneuverability and exposed an artificially sustained yet exhausted accumulation model. Disequilibrium permeated the entire economy. Contradictions began to appear with increasing resiliency at various sociostructural levels. Politically, the financial crisis affected the ability of the State to encourage development and secure the material guarantees of the Revolution. More important, however, was that relations between the State and capital were increasingly strained by the delineation and divergence of interests. The historically important coincidence of interests began to coincide less and less, which in turn affected the ability of the State to fulfill its revolutionary objectives, therein affecting State legitimacy.

An important struggle within the power bloc between elements of finance capital and the State apparatus unleashed a period of political disarray within the interior of the State, as manifested by the political vacuum in 1982 and the increasing materialization of contradictory policies. At the economic level, the financial crisis contributed to a liquidity crisis in the productive sphere, and the consequent distortion affected the transfer of surplus value and the traditional schema of productive investment. The prioritization of financial circuits and the genesis of speculative rentierism undermined the political-economic maneuverability of the State and initiated the delineation of State and finance capital interests. In other words, there was an interrelated dynamic between the financial and productive spheres and the political and economic levels. The ideology of the Revolution was unmasked by the increased power of finance capital and State loss of control over the direction and implementation of public policy. The consequent political vacuum revealed the undeniable power of finance capital to affect the interpretation of the coincidence of interests between the State and finance capital.

The bank system reflected the dynamics of the crisis. As disintermediation increased and the liquidity crisis affected the productive sector's financial costs, banks' sources of income changed. Resources were increasingly captured in the exterior or in foreign currencies, and the banks provided a growing share of resources to the government to finance budget deficits. Problem loans increased and capital and resources declined as profits stagnated. The use of foreign currency exchange operations by banks to augment gross profits indicated the severity of the crisis.

The nationalization raised many important questions. Theoretically, what did the State's nationalization of the banks mean in terms of the hegemony of finance capital within the power bloc? Assuming that finance capital exercised a hegemonic position within the power bloc, how or why did the State nationalize the banks? In terms of the constitution of finance capital, what did it mean when one of the central components accounting for the fraction's accumulation of political-economic power (banks and bank holding companies) is taken away by the State? In other words, what does the nationalization of the banks signify, in terms of conceptualizing the State and classes? Thus, what must be established and linked together into a coherent analysis are the causes producing the decision with the conditions permitting the implementation of the decision and the concrete social forces determining the outcome. In terms of political strategy, the important question concerned the popular conception of limited State autonomy and its relevance in conceiving the State and practical strategic questions. These questions will be examined within the context of the most serious political-economic crisis historically affecting the bourgeois Mexican State, that is, the immediate postnationalization period. The inability of the State to define a new accumulation model and the continuing ability of finance capital in its new form—the financial fraction—to exercise political-economic power vis-à-vis other fractions of the bourgeoisie and the State manifested the dynamism of social classes and the State.

NOTES

1. For instance, the Plan Global (a State-promoted development plan for 1980–1982) was supposed to use the proceeds from petroleum sales to develop the country and increase the distribution of national wealth. However, petrodollars were used to subsidize private accumulation, support speculative rentierism, and service the debt.

2. Increased production, as measured by GDP, averaged 8 percent for the 1980–1981 period.

3. The amount foreign resources obtained by these institutions increased from 44 percent of debits in 1981 to 62 percent in 1982.

4. In 1981, 68 percent of these institutions' credit was extended to government entities. In 1982, the percentage increased to 84 percent.

5. The cost of debits as measured by the CPP (Costo Promedio de los Pasivos) is a reference point system used by bankers to calculate interest rates for loans to clientele.

6. The day before the nationalization.

7. Part of the international capital market resources, especially in the United States, were composed of Mexican resources involved in the capital flight phenomenon.

8. Credit also often exceeded legally permissible amounts and was conceded without sufficient guarantees.

9. The practices of Comermex exemplify the trend (see Ortiz Pinchetti, 1983).

10. A major component of the inflation cycle was the continual devaluation of the peso, the consequent increase in financial costs, and the increase in production costs resulting from higher input costs of imported goods. In a similar manner, increasing interest rates did not stem the speculation and capital flight problem because the earnings resulting from devaluation were greater than the interest rate return.

11. For example, its report noted that the banks were conscious of their place and function within the social structure, for example, commitment and contribution to capital formation to finance development (Informe del Consejo Directivo, XLVIII Convención Bancaria, 1982, p. 19).

12. The delineation of specific elements of a typology is an exercise in arbitrary decision making. Subjective interpretations affect the selection and categorization process. The categorization of specific authors' works as representative of a particular school or genre of analysis on the nationalization of the banks does not mean that the

works cannot be interpreted in a different manner than I have chosen. Moreover, several analyses contain multiple elements permitting one to classify an analysis in different ways. For example, Bartra's analysis incorporates a political-economic analysis intertwined with an examination of the intraclass struggle within the power bloc.

13. Because of an agreement of confidentiality, I cannot mention the name of the government official who discussed this theory with me. However, I can say that he is fairly prominent and indicated that these ideas had circulated among some people in the intellectual and public sector establishment.

14. Tello was a long-time advocate of the nationalization of the banks and researched the secret studies that served as the basis for the nationalization. He was also director of the Banco de México for the last three months of the López Portillo administration.

15. The decision to nationalize the banks was referred to as the fifth option in a series of possible public policy options.

Chapter 6

Postnationalization and the Financial Fraction

The nationalization of the banks shocked everyone. It was a period of intense power struggle. A polemical debate ensued about the legality of the act and the "authoritarian" decision-making process that excluded the administration, the private sector, and the public. The last ninety days of the López Portillo administration was a transitionary period, exemplified by the rise and fall of Tello as director of the Banco de México. The new de la Madrid regime implemented an International Monetary Fund (IMF) agreement based on orthodox recessionary economic policies and replaced Tello with Mancera Aguayo. The developmentalists' famous "ninety days" were over. The de la Madrid regime represented another important transitionary change. Specifically, the new technocratic administration conceptualized, negotiated, and implemented a series of measures that defined the significance of the nationalization of the banks.

The de la Madrid administration defined the structural reorganization of the nationalized financial system and the future role of State economic intervention. More important, the State determined the fate of finance capital, as a fraction of the bourgeoisie. The provisional answers to the quintessential questions concerning finance capital and the nationalization of the banks are ascertainable only by critically analyzing developments within the State and between the State and the financial fraction of the bourgeoisie. Structural and social class developments accompanied the struggle to define the financial circuits and a new accumulation model. As noted by *Punto Crítico* (1982a, p. 3), the complexity of the situation necessitated a rigorous class analysis:

> With the nationalization of the bank, the exchange control and the official promotion of unionism among bankers, the government temporarily struck the Mexican financial bourgeoisie, renewed its ideological clothing to present itself as an arbiter among the class, in such a manner that it opened the political conditions to demand, also of the popular organizations, a sacrifice on behalf of "national

unity." Therefore, the complexity of the situation requires a rigorous class analysis.

Beyond theoretical questions, the nationalization was extremely important in terms of political strategy. The September measures introduced a climate of confusion among diverse democratic and revolutionary actors. There was a patent absence of a generally critical and historical perspective. In part, this absence was because leftist parties and some elements of the labor movement had advocated the nationalization. Adoption of the nationalization proposal was therefore seen by many as evidence that the State was exercising limited relative autonomy. The measures also were espoused and supported by Carlos Tello, a well-known "nationalist/leftist" bureaucrat. Furthermore, many analysts accepted the President's explanation of the nationalization in an acritical manner. Most preliminary analyses also used a nationalist or orthodox paradigm to structure their respective analyses. The point is that the absence of a critical and historical perspective debilitated the ability of the left to understand the nature and ramifications of the nationalization in terms of class and State dynamics. In other words, most of the left supported the nationalization and raised superficially critical questions. The majority of the left assisted the State in legitimating the López Portillo regime and the consequent austerity adjustments implemented by the new technocratic de la Madrid regime. Examination of some of the developments that defined the nationalization of the banks in the postnationalization period will facilitate a critical understanding of the theoretical and strategic questions surrounding the nationalization.

IMMEDIATE POSTNATIONALIZATION DEVELOPMENTS

One of the key questions that surfaced during my examination of the immediate postnationalization period is: Who controlled and controls the decision-making processes that defined the restructuring of the financial circuits? A related question is: Who benefited from the new financial circuit configuration? Furthermore, how are the answers to these two questions related to the decision-making processes that affect the definition of the new accumulation model? This section will examine these questions by comparing the first ninety days of the nationalized bank system, as managed by Tello, with developments during the de la Madrid regime.

President López Portillo named Carlos Tello as director of the Banco de México on September 1. Tello occupied this position until the end of the López

Portillo regime (November 30, 1982). During the now famous "ninety days," Tello implemented a series of measures in accordance with his developmental conception of the nationalized bank system. As noted by Ruíz Durán (1984a, p. 83), the problem was that new monetary and credit policies had to be formulated without altering the institutional order and within the political context of an outgoing administration. Moreover, there was a sense that the change had to be consolidated before the new administration assumed power. Therefore, two basic principles shaped efforts to define and implement policies affecting the new financial system: the creation of popular support and stabilization of the economy and the crisis (Ruíz Durán, 1984a, p. 83). With these objectives, a press conference was called on September 4 to assure the public that their savings were safe and to announce measures to promote savings and productive investment.[1] The objective of these measures was to encourage long-term savings and therein stabilize the banking system.

Another policy objective was the de-dollarization of the financial system. The public responded to these measures and increased deposits, a move that increased the capture of resources from September to November.[2] De-dollarization of the financial system was accomplished by converting dollar-denominated accounts into pesos (Ruíz Durán, 1984a, pp. 86–88). The dedollarization program also benefited dollar-indebted businesses by allowing these businesses to repay their loans at a subsidized exchange rate. In other words, the State absorbed the costs of defusing the dollar-denominated debt problem so that businesses' debt problems would not add to the economic crisis.

Another problem was bank profits. Excessive bank profits penalized productive sectors. The solution was to stabilize the economy by reducing the cost of financial intermediation, therein redistributing bank profits to productive sectors. By reducing the CPP margin, increasing the amount of interest paid for existing deposits, and de-dollarizing the financial system, the authorities reduced the speed at which bank profits increased, from 38 percent for the June–August period, to 24 percent for the September–November period.

In retrospect, the policies initiated during the last ninety-day period reduced financial instability. Financial costs were stabilized. The inflation process was stabilized. The capture of resources was fortified. In short, public confidence demonstrated support for the nationalization. However, these policies were unsuccessful in curtailing the production crisis and halting capital flight (Ruíz Durán, 1984a, pp. 81–117). Part of the problem, as noted by Tello (1984, p. 178) and Ruíz Durán (1984a, p. 116), was that the Central Bank was unable to implement a fully developed and integrated financial policy, partly due to the ninety-day political limitation. As noted by López Portillo, the incoming administration had responsibility for restructuring the newly nationalized financial system.

> It would be committing an imprudent impardonable policy to try to organize the definitive form of the functioning of the nationalized bank system, this corresponds to my successor . . . this regime would be irresponsible if it advanced more in the pending organization, an organization that will be the responsibility of better hands than my own . . . (López Portillo, cited in Tello, 1984, p. 161)

The problem was also compounded by the inability to coordinate Central Bank financial policies with financial policies advocated by the finance ministry.

> Therefore, it is very difficult to evaluate, in an adequate form, the results or qualify them as inefficient. Simply and sincerely, the policies were not permitted to function; there was insufficient time to evaluate the operation. (Tello, 1984, p. 178)

The inability of the Central Bank to coordinate its financial policies with the finance ministry revealed contradictory interests within the State apparatus. The difference of opinion between sectors of the State apparatus had a historical element, the most recent example having been the implementation of incoherent and contradictory policies during the first eight months of 1982. The "ungovernability of the governing class" that had prevailed within the State at the time of the nationalization continued throughout the last three months of the López Portillo administration. A quick look at some of the events that transpired in the fall of 1982 illustrates the point.

A select few persons participated in the decision-making process that led to the nationalization of the banks. Mancera Aguayo and Silva Herzog were excluded from the decision-making circle for obvious reasons. Mancera Aguayo was replaced by Tello on September 1, and Silva Herzog offered his resignation. López Portillo refused Silva Herzog's resignation on the grounds it would have undermined IMF negotiations. Silva Herzog retained his position in the cabinet and flew to Toronto to meet with the IMF and the World Bank. While in Toronto, the finance secretary held a press conference on September 5.[3] Silva Herzog ignored protocol by disputing Tello's developmentalist conception of the nationalized bank system. Silva Herzog declared that bank operations would remain the same.

Tello and Silva Herzog's dispute provided a public view of the internal struggle within the State apparatus to concretely define the role of the nationalized banks. The same struggle surrounded the designation of individual bank presidents to head the newly nationalized banks. López Portillo designated a few individuals with financial experience to direct the largest banks. Ex-finance secretaries Carrillo Flores, Ibarra Muñoz, and Olloqui were selected to direct

Bancomer, Banamex, and Serfín. These men were distinguished and respected former public administrators, familiar with the problems confronting the system. They could guarantee that these institutions were managed in an efficient, honest, and capable manner and would lend credibility to the managerial operation of the nationalized banks. The remainder of the bank presidents were selected by Silva Herzog, with the agreement of López Portillo (Tello, 1986). According to Robinson (1982, p. 49), Silva Herzog "fought to exclude the names of several left-wing economists from the list of the new heads of the nationalized bank." In fact, Silva Herzog threatened to resign prior to his departure for Toronto if a suitable list of names had not been agreed upon (Robinson, 1982, p. 49).

Most of the designated bank presidents were trained at the Central Bank or Nacional Financiera. An ex-banker noted that all of the newly designated bank presidents were acceptable (Robinson, 1982, p. 49). As noted by Tello (1986), the selection of conservative people was a good short-term policy, given the problems surrounding the management of the newly nationalized banks. The uses and practices of the bank could be changed in the long run (Tello, 1986).

Another example of the dispute to define bank operations involved credit card policies. The Federal Consumer Ombudsman issued a report claiming that credit cards negatively affected the inflationary process. Enrique Rubio, general director of the National Consumer Institute, also argued that credit cards encouraged inflation and therefore should be regulated or controlled.

> The bank nationalization is attempting to establish an operation that will really facilitate the just progress of the country, the national project. It is therefore recommendable that all of the banks reexamine the proposition of credit cards and the characteristics of their operation. (cited in *Expansion*, 1982c, p. 74)

However, Carlos Anaya, sub-director of Bancomer, noted that credit cards would continue to serve as a payment instrument.

> This function, noted Anaya, was established in the same form by the private bank as well as the mixed bank before the nationalization, and therefore its objectives should be the same. (cited in *Expansion*, 1982c, p. 74)

Rubio also suggested that the banks should examine the possibility of issuing a single card, since competition was no longer a necessary practice. Bank practices, Anaya argued, effectively prohibited the rationalization of credit cards as well as the consolidation of the banks into a single bank. As noted by Anaya:

> We believe that for the moment it is difficult to coordinate a single card for reasons of systems and operations; this is as complex as the establishment of a single bank institution. On the other side, it is recommendable that the spirit of competition continue to offer better service and have an efficient operation. (cited in *Expansion*, 1982c, p. 74)

The credit card question reflected an overall dispute concerning the managerial operations of the newly nationalized banks. Although Tello accepted the designation of conservative establishment-type directors as a short-term solution to the managerial problem, therein lending credibility to the nationalization decree, the political significance of this strategy had greater ramifications in terms of the political forces that concretely defined bank operations. As noted by López Portillo in his national address on September 1, the nationalization had only brought a change in ownership and the banks would remain the same.

López Portillo's remark was aptly exemplified by the bank director selection process and the succession process at higher managerial levels. For example, Ibarra Muñoz gave up his position as vice president at Banamex to become president of Banamex. The vice president was Rubén Aguilar, the right-hand man of Agustin Legorreta (ex-owner of Banamex). In a similar manner, Augustín Venegas Mendoza, was named as the sub-director for the National Bank Commission.[4] The internal power struggle to define bank operations merely set the stage for future negotiations with the incoming de la Madrid administration. Tello's vision of a developmentalist banking system was restricted by (a) the crisis, (b) heavily foreign-indebted businesses with serious liquidity problems, (c) bank portfolios with delinquent loan portfolios, (d) IMF negotiations, and (e) confrontational private sector activities. Private sector activities were particularly disruptive.

Bankers had planned to call a press conference after López Portillo's Sixth Report and reiterate their traditional support for the President and the Revolution. The bankers were shocked and dismayed upon hearing that the banks were being nationalized.[5] Immediate reactions ranged from dumbfoundedness to declarations and demands. Abedrop, in a short interview, noted that the government had nationalized bank dollar debts (Ramírez, 1982, p. 8). Legorreta reportedly told foreign bankers that Banamex had lent the government $2 billion and couldn't get it back. He supposedly said the "others must have been in the same strait" (Robinson 1982, p. 50). Clouthier (president of the CCE) demanded that the nationalization be submitted to a national plebiscite because the decision-making process had been undemocratic (Ramírez, 1982, p. 8).

Initial shock was quickly transformed into a concerted attempt to defend previous banking practices. Abedrop (ABM president), for example, noted on

September 2 that abundant proof existed that the banks had been patriotic (Quezada & Acevedo, 1982, p. 1). The CCE also argued that Mexican bankers had been very responsible and professional (Uno Más Uno, 1982, p. 1). The ABM also declared that the banks would be turned over to the government without resistance and that the bankers (a) had not favored capital flight; (b) acted legally within the free-exchange system; (c) worked on behalf of clients, avoiding the promotion of capital flight even though it was legal; (d) acted no different than mixed and official banks; and (e) exercised solid, technically competent administration, widely recognized inside and outside of Mexico (Expansión, 1982b).

Soon thereafter, the private sector launched its offensive. Advertisements blamed the government for the crisis and asserted that the nationalization was a totalitarian measure with a socialist trajectory. A vicious rumor campaign precipitated fears that army maneuvers were within striking distance of the capital and that a coup was going to subvert the transition process (International Currency Review, 1982, p. 54).

Reactionary rhetoric was rapidly replaced by an organizational offensive. Bankers held secret meetings in private homes to map out a strategic plan.[6] It was decided that they should call for re-privatization of the economy, removal of exchange controls, return of bank-held shares in private companies to "their legitimate owners," and a clear definition of private and public spheres of activity.

The private sector also organized a series of public demonstrations against the nationalization and the government. In Monterrey, for example, representatives of various business organizations spoke out against the measures. The CCE also organized a one-day employee lockout that was canceled at the last minute. In addition, a CCE-coordinated national assembly planned to examine the decrees. A series of demonstrations around the theme "Free Mexico" were also canceled because the government considered the meetings to be subversive.

During the immediate postnationalization period, bankers differed as to an appropriate political strategy. According to Robinson (1982, p. 49), a Legorreta colleague stated that the banks were "not used to fighting" and that they were timid and powerless. Legorreta and Espinosa Yglesias (Banamex and Bancomer) were not going to do anything, whereas Abedrop and Clouthier would fight the nationalization (Robinson, 1982, p. 49). Indicative of differences among bankers was the decision of 21 banks to purse a legal tack, arguing that the expropriation of the banks was unconstitutional. By October, several bankers involved in the case withdrew their challenge, in particular, Banco Mercantil, Banco Aboumrad, and Crédito Mexicano (Colmenares et al. 1982, p. 155).

In sum, the initial backlash of the private sector against the nationalization and the State was largely disorganized. Everyone was caught off guard. Ideologically, the bankers attempted to defend their previous practices and blame government policies for capital flight and the crisis. Politically, an unsuccessful effort to challenge the legality of the expropriation was launched. Efforts of the industrial and commercial sectors were more radical but nevertheless largely ineffective. Ultimately, ex-bankers waited for the inauguration of the new administration. They would use their traditional negotiation techniques to define the financial circuits. Irma Salinas, ex-member of the Grupo Monterrey family, summed up the situation:

> The nationalization of the banks was the strongest blow the business groups had received. Above all the Grupo Monterrey, because it was through the bank that they collected the necessary money to multiply their own industries.
>
> At the beginning they were stupefied. They believed that communism was around the corner. But these people are well prepared, very capable and experienced, and they organized to counteract the blow. Moreover, they are accommodating. . . . They displaced the conflict to the political level, so that things would return to how they had more or less been before. (1984, p. 34)

THE FINANCIAL FRACTION AND THE PARALLEL FINANCIAL CIRCUIT

The ex-bankers received an important concession in September 1982. On September 4, 1982, Tello announced that the State would sell, at a future undetermined date, private company shares held by the newly nationalized banks. Tello also noted that the proceeds from the sale would be used to help compensate ex-bankers. The decision to sell companies that the banks owned was widely seen as an effort to restore private sector confidence.[7]

The de la Madrid administration (1982–1988) initiated and implemented many important policies that defined the structural reorientation of the financial system. The technocratic regime effectively re-privatized the nationalized bank system by creating a lucrative parallel financial circuit composed of nonbank financial institutions (Instituciones Financieros No-Bancarios: IFNB). A brief examination of some of the measures adopted during de la Madrid's tenure will be helpful.

The actual sale of private company shares held by banks began in May 1984. The banks retained shares in companies that were involved in banking services and sold shares in all remaining financial service companies and nonfinancial service companies. According to government officials, the sale of financial service companies (e.g., stock brokerage firms and insurance companies) would allow the private sector to become involved in the development of financial and capital markets—markets considered to be distinctly different from the nationalized bank system.

An interesting aspect of the sale of these shares was the scheduling of the sale. Ex-bankers were given the first opportunity to purchase shares owned by their former banks. They were also allowed to use indemnization bonds to pay for the shares. Next in sequence were the general shareholders of the company or companies being sold. Ex-bankers were the next group allowed to buy the stock of companies belonging to any bank. Finally, the private sector and labor organizations were permitted to purchase any leftovers.[8]

The sale of bank shares in various companies was an extremely important development. The official rationale for the sale of these shares was economic: The state could not afford to support these companies in a period of economic crisis; shares in companies being sold were unnecessary for the provision of bank services; sale of IFNBs to the private sector would fortify the capital market; and the proceeds from the sale of these shares would ameliorate State financial problems and compensate the owners of indemnization bonds. While State economic problems may have contributed to the decision to sell State shares in various companies, the fundamental reason the State sold these shares was political.

The sale of bank shares in IFNBs signified the willingness of the State to abandon the possibility of integrating a coherent financial system facilitating productive intermediation and social development. In other words, the State renounced its complete control of financial markets. The decision ignored pre-nationalization and immediate post-nationalization historical experience. Moreover, the proceeds from the sale of IFNBs was small, relative to the costs of rehabilitating and balancing the rest of the banking system (Sánchez Martínez, 1985, p. 259). In essence, the State had decided to develop a financial system strictly based on the traditional interpretation of financial intermediation, that is, the acceptance of deposits and the provision of credit (Alcocer, 1984, p. 15; Quijano et al., 1984, p. 16). *Most important, the State had simultaneously facilitated the reorganization of the financial fraction of the bourgeoisie.*

An obvious explanatory element for the sale of shares in IFNBs to the private sector was the re-establishment of private sector confidence. More important was the potential reconstitution of the financial fraction of the bourgeoisie and the ability of this fraction to reconstruct its ability to influence and direct financial circuits on behalf of private accumulation. A brief examination of Legorreta's activities illustrates the capabilities of the financial fraction.

Legorreta (ex-president and owner of Banamex) and a group of ex-directors of the *casa de bolsa* (stock brokerage) Banamex created a business called Inverlat. Inverlat acted as a trustee for the indemnization bonds of exshareholders of Banamex. The principal objective was to trade the bonds for shares in IFNBs, that is, casa de bolsa Banamex and Seguros América Banamex. Inverlat was established as a holding company and, in exchange for indemnization bonds, shareholders received shares in Inverlat. For the purpose of assessing the value of the casa de bolsa Banamex, Inverlat produced a study. The study was used to reduce the purchase price. Inverlat purchased the company for 990 million pesos, even though an intergovernmental commission had assessed the value of the company at 1.5 billion pesos. Beyond obtaining a 500 million peso reduction in the price of the company, Legorreta and associates obtained a loan from Bancomer to enable the group to buy all of the shares of the casa de bolsa Banamex (Granados Chapa, 1985).

Another important initiative that was substantially transformed during the regime change was the indemnization procedure. Initially, the indemnization process involved three cabinet ministries: the finance ministry, the budget ministry, and the ministry of public works.[9] Although it was determined that the amount of indemnization would be based on countable capital, the entire affair was postponed until the new administration took office. Thus, in July 1983, the finance ministry announced that it had determined the rules for the indemnization.

The rules had been changed. The finance ministry was now going to determine the amount of the indemnization. A technical committee (integrating members from the finance ministry, the National Bank and Insurance Commission, and the National Securities Commission) would assist the finance ministry in its indemnization endeavors. Ultimately, it was determined that the indemnization formula would be based on an unspecified formula using adjusted countable capital. The specific bases and criteria for the adjustments were not made explicit, but nevertheless, specific indemnization amounts were determined.

The different method of calculation, based on the adjusted countable capital formula, was significant. Using the adjusted countable capital method, the indemnization for Banamex, Bancomer, and Serfín was 118 billion pesos. In comparison, the original method would have amounted to 47 billion pesos (Tello, 1984, pp. 167–168). In addition, capital gains resulting from the indemnization were tax-exempt. The banks, needless to say, were pleased. Abedrop (former ABM president) declared that the government had acted equitably and listened to the opinions of the interested parties before making the final decisions (Zuñiga, 1983b). The situation, as noted by Sánchez Martínez (1985, p. 237), "seemed to demonstrate the governmental will to reconstruct the terms of its relations with the old bankers."

The de la Madrid administration's first independent measure was the legislative proposal creating National Credit Societies (Sociedades Nacionales de Crédito: SNC). The Bank and Credit Public Service Regulatory Law changed the juridical character of banks.[10] More important was that the new legislation divided SNC shares into series A and series B shares. Series A shares were the exclusive property of the State, accounting for 66 percent of total shares. In contrast, series B shares were available for public subscription, that is, 34 percent of total shares. The maximum amount of shares (*certificadoes de participación patrimonial*) an individual could own was 1 percent of social capital, guaranteeing that no one could exercise disproportionate influence (Sánchez Martínez, 1985, p. 237; Quijano & Bendesky, 1983, p. 368). Shareholders also had access to SNC directive councils (through the consultation commission) and could participate in the section of commissioners for SNCs.

The official rationale for divesting 34 percent of the SNCs was to democratize the financial institutions. Assistant budget secretary Sales Gutíerrez (1983, p. 1) affirmed that the new law attempted to ensure that diverse sectors of the population participated in the direction of financial institutions. The objective was to combat bureaucratization, inefficiency, corruption, and promote public confidence in the institutions.

Many analysts (e.g., Ruíz Durán, 1984, pp. 121–122) argued that the new legislation was a historical regression, opening the door for a profit-based bank system. In retrospect, however, the measure was an "ideological concession" to the private sector (Quijano et al., 1984, p. 16). According to Alcocer (1986), the financial fraction was not interested in purchasing SNC shares because it enhanced their negotiation power, and the 1 percent limitation diluted the power of share ownership. Moreover, according to Alcocer, many ex-bankers (including Legorreta, Vallina, and Espinosa Yglesias) stated in private conversations that they were not interested in participating in the SNCs because they knew that the SNCs would not be denationalized. The ex-bankers also realized that the stock brokerages would acquire a new dimension if they were divested.

> With the nationalized bank the stock exchange acquires other characteristics: the State controls for good or bad the decisions as to who they will lend to, but the banks want, and are going to struggle as well as they can, to have their own instrument, where they can manage their lending capital, their money capital, and make returns. They are not interested to work through the bank, because, among other things, it represents giving the State information: of businesses, their investments, etc. They prefer to work through the stock exchange. Think of it, that two casas de bolsa in this country control 48 percent of stock exchange operations: Banamex and Bancomer. (Alcocer, 1984, p. 16)

Another major policy initiative propounded during the de la Madrid tenure was the National Program of Financial Development (Programa Nacional de Financiamiento del Desarollo: PNFD). The PNFD was announced in June 1984 and enunciated the basis for a general restructuring of the banking system. The Plan, incorporating an analysis of public sector financial policy since 1982, attempted to integrate financial policy objectives with general economic objectives. The fundamental objectives were to recuperate and strengthen internal savings, promote the efficient and equitable assignment of resources, re-orient external economic relations, and fortify and consolidate the institutional structure of the financial system (Sánchez Martínez, 1985, pp. 254–255).

The two key elements of the PNFD were the fortification and consolidation of the institutional structure of the financial system and the emphasis on internal savings. These two objectives, in conjunction with the sale of IFNBs, served as a basis for the creation and stimulation of a parallel financial circuit. The State would control the money markets through its control of the bank system, and the privatized IFNBs would direct the capital markets through their control of stock brokerages and other auxiliary institutions (e.g., insurance companies).

> While in the bank market the interest rate would continue to be one of the principal management instruments, in the non-bank financial market the intent would be to transform the securities market into a long-term financial instrument for small and medium businesses; they would try to develop a secondary market for diverse securities, like the futures market; and promote investment societies and capital risk funds. Another essential aspect referred to the constitution of . . . auxiliary credit institutions as sources of internal savings for financial development. (Sánchez Martínez, 1985, p. 295)

The first revision of the PNFD was the sale of bank-owned shares to the private sector. The second revision was the introduction of new legislation that concretely defined the different financial markets.

The public release of a series of laws that concretely restructured the financial system was delayed because of a "behind-the-scenes debate." Definition of the private sector realm of operations was politically touchy because the new legislation was designed to promote the creation of new IFNBs and support stock brokerages, and leasing and insurance companies (Frazier, 1984b). Originally, drafts of the new legislation permitted nationalized banks to own 49 percent of stock brokerages. Later versions reduced the amount of bank participation to 15 percent. Private financiers, however, fought for zero bank participation. As noted by Jorge Caso Bercht, president of the Mexican Association of Stock Brokerage Houses, "We don't even want them to have 1 percent of stock brokerage firms. . . . We want a total separation, because it's the only way the capital market can grow" (cited in Frazier, 1984b).

The legislative package was sent to the Congress in late December 1984. The approved package consisted of four new laws: the Regulatory Law of Public Service Banks and Credit (Ley Regulamentaria del Servicio Público de Banca y Crédito); the Bank of México Organic Law (Ley Orgánica del Banco de México); the General Law of Auxiliary Credit Organizations and Activities (Ley General de Organizaciones y Actividades Auxiliares del Crédito); and the Investment Societies Law (Ley de Sociedades de Inversión). A brief examination of each of these laws will clarify the political character of the new legislation.

The Regulatory Law for Public Service Banks and credit defined the realm of operations for multiple banks and development banks.[11] Multiple banks would continue to perform commercial bank operations, and development banks would promote investment.[12] Banks were restricted from directly participating in the securities market, except through stock brokerages. They were also authorized to participate in investment societies.[13]

The Organic Law of the Bank of México dramatically transformed relations between the State and the Central Bank. The Central Bank's function was limited to monetary regulation. The reserve requirement system was eliminated as a means of financing public sector deficits.[14] The law also de-linked monetary emission from foreign currency circuits and associated it with internal finance operations. Finally, the Central Bank would now set interest rates and terms for asset and debit operations.

The Investment Society Law authorized three types of investment societies. Common investment societies would work with fixed and variable return securities. A second type would work exclusively with fixed return securities. A third type would organize long-term risk capital. A noteworthy feature of this law was that foreign companies and persons were allowed to participate in investment societies.

The General Law of Auxiliary Credit Operations and Activities regulated leasing companies (*arrendadoras*), general bonded warehouses (*almacenes generales de depósito*), credit unions, and exchange houses (*casas de cambio*). The Law permitted SNCs to participate in leasing companies and bonded warehouses.

The Securities Market Law was also reformed. It stipulated that only legally recognized stock brokerages not connected with banks could operate in the securities market. However, stock brokerages could be either private or national.

The most significant aspect of the new juridical arrangement was undoubtedly the disarticulation of the nationalize bank system. The State gave the private sector, including ex-bankers, the opportunity to form de facto investment banks. By controlling the capital market, these groups could create a parallel financial market with the potential to affect State finance policies. Moreover, in terms of social class relations, the new legislation, in conjunction with previous State concessions, manifested political power of the financial fraction vis-à-vis other fractions. The financial fraction's pre-eminent participation in the capital market also signified the possibility that the financial fraction might regain its hegemonic control of the valorization process and the power bloc.

> The new institutional design opens a space to develop capital flows and valorize capital, a place where the old groups will look to redefine their hegemony in relation to other emergent actors that they find in this new articulation, a possibility to increase their economic and decision power in the realm of economic policy. (Garrido & Quintana, 1985, p. 10)

STOCK BROKERAGE HOUSES

The Mexican stock exchange was the most dynamic exchange in the world. A few statistics demonstrate the point. By the end of 1986, the stock index increased 320 percent over December 1985. In terms of points, the index increased from 11,000 in December 1985 to nearly 47,000 points in December. The value of operations in 1986 was equivalent to 75 billion pesos, that is, 197 percent more than 1985. Stock brokerage profits for 1986 were 55 billion pesos, versus 13 billion in 1895. Countable capital for stock brokerages in 1982 was 3 billion pesos, and by 1986 was approximately 140 billion pesos. Even more suggestive of the importance of these institutions was that 26 companies, with 120 offices, managed slightly less than 30 percent of total public savings. For comparison, in 1982 these institutions managed only 8 percent of total public savings (Acosta, 1987).

The statistics were even more amazing for 1987. The stock index increased from 47,000 points at the end of 1986 to 98,523 points by the end of March. By the end of October 1987, the index was nearly 400,000 and by the end of the year had declined to around 100,000 points. Stock brokerage profits increased more than 60 percent, and the value of daily operations increased to 600 billion pesos, that is, three times the average in 1986. From March 1986 to March 1987, the exchange had an approximate 600 percent return. An incredible increase, given that only 250 businesses were quoted on the exchange and only 120 of these were permanent.[15] In a similar vein, there were only about 200,000 investors in the market (Acosta, 1987). These numbers illustrate the tremendous expansion that occurred in the capital market, but they do not illustrate the distribution of instruments nor the kind of activity that has driven the stock exchange.

The stock exchange was historically active. In real terms, it was stagnant from 1975 to 1978. The peso volume distribution of specific instruments, as a percentage of the total market, was very distinct. From 1975 to 1978, stocks increased an average of 65 percent annually. Qualitatively, an important aspect of the market during this period was its initiation as a speculative mechanism and as a means for finance capital to influence State economic action through the valorization of State financial instruments (Leriche, Quintana, & Bustos, 1987, p. 78).

From 1978 to 1982, the stock exchange performed important functions for the private and public sectors. For the private sector, it placed financial instruments in the market and raised capital at below bank rates and performed an intermediary valorization function for financial groups. The stock exchange also helped the public sector by capturing resources through the sale of CETES and petroleum bonds.

During the 1982 to 1896 period, the peso volume (1978 pesos) of the market increased 55 percent. The peso volume (1978 pesos) distribution of specific instruments, as a percentage of the total market, continued to register trends similar to the 1978–1982 period. Stock shares increased an average of 157 percent annually (Leriche et al., 1987, p. 80).

Structural changes that occurred since 1984 clarify recent developments in the stock exchange since its privatization. An additional perspective on the rapid expansion of the stock exchange is possible by comparing the level of financing provided by the stock exchange with the amount provided by the nationalized banks. In real terms, the amount of financial resources channeled by the bank system increased 12 percent from December 1984 to October 1986. The amount of financing provided by the securities market for the same period increased 346 percent and the level of net effective financing increased 441 percent.[16] In absolute terms, the bank system provided 35.6 trillion pesos in financing for the same period, whereas the stock exchange provided 75.2 trillion pesos in financing, or 9.7 trillion pesos in net effective financing (Leriche et al., 1987, p. 84).

These numbers indicate that the stock exchange expanded rapidly. The market was driven by government debt instruments and the constant need to refinance public sector debt. The State relied on internal debt to finance its budget deficits and repay the interest on the debt. The primary instrument for raising capital was CETES, which was also the most important instrument traded in the capital market. From December 1984 to September 1985, the internal debt increased by 2.6 trillion pesos, 68 percent of which was CETES and 32 percent was provided by the Central Bank (Garrido & Quintana, 1986, p. 30). In other words, the financial fraction managed the debt offerings and purchased a large share of the debt offerings. The essential point is that the financial circuits were converted into a valorization mechanism that redistributed the social surplus through the payment of astronomical interest rates on the internal debt. Thus, approximately 50 percent of the public sector budget was used to service the internal and external debts. Government interest payments for CETES in 1985 were 1.3 trillion pesos, 50 percent of which was paid to private firms. Thus, private firms received the equivalent of approximately 1.3 percent of the 1985 GDP through interest payments on the internal debt (Garrido & Quintana, 1986, p. 30).

Increased reliance on internal debt resulted in the reappearance of State financial dependency. The State once again was financially dependent on the financial fraction. This financial dependence has enabled the financial fraction to accumulate a tremendous amount of capital. It also allowed the financial fraction to indirectly affect State financial and economic policies by constructing a power logic based on the public sector's restriction of credit through bank circuits and the implementation of extremely high interest rates. The financial fraction demanded and received increasingly higher interest rates in order to facilitate the placement of public securities in the private capital market (Garrido & Quintana, 1986, p. 34). The process indirectly contributed to the centralization and concentration of capital by restricting the ability of ill-liquid private firms to participate in the game. It distorted the productive circuits by creating an artificial credit crunch, therein promoting financial liquidity problems and mass bankruptcies. It also transformed the accumulation strategy of large firms. One of the largest companies in Mexico, for example (as of the middle of 1986), was obtaining approximately 50 percent of its profits by participating in the capital market. In essence, the entire productive apparatus stagnated and the logic of accumulation shifted from entrepreneurial productive investments to speculative rentierism. As noted by Garrido and Quintana (1985, pp. 31–32):

> It is to say the increase in the federal government's internal debt, via CETES, has had repercussions on all of the financial circuits, transforming the dispute for economic power between the different fractions into the adoption of a financial struggle among the fractions. The groups that emerge fortified from this process will be those that have greater advantages in the redefinition of the accumulation model.

Given the relative significance of the stock exchange, a quick look at who owns the stock brokerage houses is useful to determine who exercises control over the capital market. Many stock brokerage houses and IFNBs employ and are owned by ex-bankers. Actually, it is not that surprising that these individuals have used their skills in the financial arena, an arena that allows them to reorganize their political-economic power. A quick look at some of the owners of these firms reveals that stock brokerage *Operadora* is partially owned by Eduardo Legorreta and Manual Somoza (Augustín Legorreta's "number two man" at Banamex); Abedrop partially owns casa de bolsa Fimasa; Abedrop is also president of Seguros Olmeca and Eduardo Legorreta is vice-president; Augustín Legorreta presides over Inverlat; Bailleres (owner of prenationalization CREMI) partially owns casa de bolsa CREMI; Abedrop also owns a 20 percent interest in IFI (Acosta, 1985; Fernández Vega, 1985a; Galaz, 1985; Hiriart, 1986).

The final example, Ingeniería Financiera Internacional de México (IFI), is a rather interesting case. IFI is jointly owned by Abedrop (20 percent), Operadora de Bolsa (18 percent), Bancomer (20 percent), and Lazard of London, Paris, and New York (42 percent). The first notable aspect of this new company is the joint participation of international finance capital, the State (Bancomer), and the Mexican financial fraction (Abedrop and Chico Pardo). A second important aspect of this firm is its self-defined objectives. Abedrop noted that it would not be a banking institution but a service society of "financial engineering." According to IFI advertisements, IFI performs banking operations; that is, IFI provides (a) business consultation for expansion and new products, (b) assessment for international commercial and exchange operations, (c) debt restructuring, and (d) assistance in the search for new technologies and partners. It is surprising that, in contrast with Abedrop's declarations that IFI was not a banking institution, an AFP press release from London announced that the Lazard group was about to establish a new business bank in México. The essence of the AFP release was confirmed by Peón Escalante (president of the National Securities Commission). Peón Escalante stated that "if it's true that this business dedicates itself to what it says it will . . . it will have the attributable functions that only correspond to the nationalized banks" (cited in Acosta, 1985).

CONCLUSION

It is apparent that sociostructural factors shaped the definition of the nationalized bank system. Structural factors, such as the proliferation of an internally and externally induced economic crisis (e.g., orthodox economic policies, IMF agreements, and speculation and capital flight) have definitely affected the ability of the State to use the bank in a developmental sense—in the style of Tello. However, comparing the brief developmentalist successes under Tello with successive developments under de la Madrid (e.g., extremely high interest rates and extremely restrictive credit practices) demonstrates that even under the most difficult crisis situations (1982), the bank was used in a somewhat developmental manner. Social class provides a better explanation of postnationalization events.

Political relations between the financial fraction and the State definitively shaped the financial system. The nationalization expropriated finance capital's central valorization mechanism. By nationalizing the banks, the State assumed control of the banks, bank holding companies, and the companies owned by the banks. In other words, finance capital's economic power was substantially affected. Given that finance capital was stripped of its principal valorization mechanism and that political relations with the State were also ruptured: How has the financial fraction been able to initiate its economic recovery?

The financial fraction gained a tremendous amount of political-economic power in the last five years, in relation to other fractions of the bourgeoisie and the State. The analysis of this development is the key to understanding the nationalization and the dynamics of the relationship between fractions and the State.

Initially, after the nationalization, finance capital was objectively a nonentity in terms of its economic integration. Politically, it constituted a fraction that had a political-economic identity based on subjective factors. The ex-bankers reacted in a semicoordinated manner with other fractions of the bourgeoisie and organized a coherent negotiation strategy based on universal identification with capitalist precepts. The State had confiscated the property of part of the bourgeoisie, and the monopoly elements of the bourgeoisie reacted against the State, using political, economic, and ideological mechanisms.

A few elements within the State apparatus had secretly coordinated sufficient power at the specific moment when a conjunctural crisis threatened the legitimacy of the entire Revolution. Part of the explanation as to why López Portillo and Tello were able to successfully coordinate the nationalization project was the political chaos permeating the State apparatus, resulting from the increasing materialization of sociostructural contradictions. The class character of the State was becoming apparent and the contradictions threatened to de-legitimize the very essence of the Revolution, that is, the ability of the State to conceal the bourgeois nature of the State and the Revolution.

Analyses conceptualizing the nationalization of the banks as a reflection of relative State autonomy or as a manifestation of State protection of the general interests of the reproduction of private accumulation are therefore dogmatically stagnant and ahistorical. At a specific moment on September 1, 1982, the Ló-pez Portillo regime exercised relative autonomy by decreeing the nationalization of the banks. This point is worth repeating: The *regime* exercised relative autonomy. The dynamic of social class forces, however, was almost immediately set in motion. The State's apparatus's momentary exercise of relative autonomy unleashed a powerful political dynamic by rupturing the coincidence of interests based on political consultation and negotiation. The resulting demise of the confidence of the bourgeoisie destabilized the State, therein facilitating the financial fraction's struggle to regain its political-economic hegemony. A historically unprecedented attack on the State enabled the financial fraction to initiate the reconstruction of its political-economic power base.

In synthesis, the Mexican State promoted the construction and development of the financial system when it was a privately organized system valorizing capital. Within the context of the most serious conjunctural crisis affecting Mexico in the postrevolution period, part of the apparatus nationalized the banks. After the banks were nationalized, the State proceeded to dismantle the nationalized system by selling the most profitable elements to the ex-bankers and retaining the weakest, least dynamic part. The State's continual chain of political-economic concessions to the ex-bankers manifested the financial fraction's retention of political and ideological hegemony. As noted in *The Wall Street Journal*, "Mexico decided to bow to the private financiers and keep the government-owned banks from owning and operating other financial institutions (Frazier, 1984a)." State concessions also manifested the class character of the bourgeois State and the continuing struggle within the power bloc to redefine the articulation of political-economic power vis-à-vis the concretization of a new accumulation model.

The ability of the financial fraction to better its relations with the State was initially based on political-ideological grounds and eventually encompassed economic measures. The financial fraction received State concessions through political and ideological negotiation. These concessions provided the fraction with the opportunity to reorganize its valorization process through a parallel financial circuit. Once the financial fraction regained ownership of IFNBs and the State had redefined the public and private financial circuits through new legislation, the financial fraction was able to control the capital market and therein affect public sector financial circuits and the redefinition of accumulation.

Naturally, the preceding theoretical analysis has tremendously important implications for political strategy. One of the more important conclusions is that relative State autonomy appears to be a historical anomaly, at least in the case of the contemporary Mexican State. The inability of the Mexican left to demystify the conception of the benevolent bourgeois State, as explicated in the ideology of the Revolution and adopted by various nationalist elements, constricted the ability of the left to undermine the ideology of the Revolution and the hegemony of the bourgeoisie. It also restricted the ability of the left to organically integrate workers, peasants, and the semiproletarianized forces. In other words, although the State was permeable in terms of reflecting social class forces, the left's confusion facilitated the confusion of the masses and the mystification of the class nature of the State. The State continued to represent the interests of the bourgeoisie and also continued to manage the class struggle. The inability of the left to organically penetrate the class struggle resulted from its reactive strategies and incoherent comprehension of the social composition of the Mexican State. The left's theoretical and strategic confusion also resulted from the adoption of Eurocentric Marxist theories of the State. The relative autonomy of the Mexican State was a historical anomaly.

NOTES

1. Specifically, that interest paid on savings accounts would be raised from 4.5 percent to 20 percent; commissions on checking accounts would be removed, irregardless of the amount held in the account; interest rates for new accounts would be reduced; interest charged on loans to productive businesses would be reduced; and interest rates for social interest housing credits would be reduced (Ruíz Durán, 1984a, p. 84; Tello, 1984, pp. 168–169).

2. The amount captured in three months was 76 percent of the amount captured in the previous eight months.

3. This was the day before the newly nationalized banks were scheduled to reopen and the day after Tello had announced several new measures.

4. The Commission was charged with the responsibility of regulating and sanctioning the nationalized bank system.

5. Legorreta (Banamex), for example, reportedly fainted.

6. According to Robinson (1982, p. 49), industrialists began to participate in these meetings a week after the nationalization.

7. Within the context of the overall economy, as administered by the de la Madrid regime, the sale of these companies also complemented the administration's efforts to radically rationalize the realm of State economic intervention.

8. For a partial indication of the number, types, and percentages of companies possessed by the banks, see Ranjel (1982) and Concheiro (1984).

9. The finance ministry was supposed to determine the source of resources for the indemnization. The budget ministry was supposed to determine the form of payment. The public works ministry was supposed to determine the amount of the indemnization (Tello, 1984, pp. 162–163).

10. Ranjel (1982) examined the specific changes that accompanied the creation of the SNC.

11. Development banks are the old National Credit Institutions (e.g., Nafinsa).

12. There was no general legislation for development banks.

13. A bank monopoly on the internal monetary market was maintained and the principle of decentralization was affirmed. In a similar manner, the principle of bank secrecy and the ability of foreign banks to retain representative offices were maintained.

14. The objective was to separate fiscal and monetary policy. The reserve system was largely replaced by an obligatory deposit system, based on a percentage of bank debits.

15. For comparison purposes, the New York Stock Exchange quotes about 1,800 companies.

16. Net effective financing is the amount of placement minus amortization. Thus, this indicator filters out rolled-over debt.

Conclusion

Understanding the nationalization of the banks required a historical sociostructural analysis. Studying the historical development of specific elements—social class fraction trajectories—facilitated an understanding of the totality of the social formation. For example, understanding the social dynamic is impossible without understanding how and why the relationship between specific class fractions and the State changed. Likewise, without understanding changes in the relationship between the State and the bourgeoisie, it is difficult to understand changes in other variables, for instance, policy and regime changes.

The nationalization of the banks was primarily the result of interaction between social classes and the State. To understand the historical relationship characterizing the interdependent formation and transformation of these two variables, a detailed analysis of the structures and forces that shaped the social structure was necessary. For example, understanding why commercial-usury capital dominated financial circuits is incomprehensible without analyzing the articulation of combined and uneven modes of production, the Church, and the absence of a hegemonic fraction. In a similar fashion, the emergence of bank capital cannot be understood without analyzing the sociostructural dynamics that accompanied the internationalization of capitalist relations of production within a nascent socioeconomic formation.

The multitude of determinants that affect and are affected by social classes and the State has also been examined. A general understanding of classes and the State has been outlined by demonstrating the interrelationships between these concepts and the need to examine theoretical concepts in relation to the material social structure. The contradictory nature of social classes, for instance, is impossible to understand in the absence of a historical material analysis. The historical trajectory of bank capital demonstrates the point. The transformation of bank capital into finance capital was a nonlinear process characterized by specific distinctions as to the form of finance capital. In addition to the different forms of finance capital, there were political distinctions that created contradictions within the fraction.

The relative autonomy of the postRevolutionary Mexican State was a similar historical phenomenon. The State-in-formation during the Cárdenas regime was a historical anomaly. The consolidation of the Mexican State during and after the Cárdenas regime affected the autonomy of the State vis-à-vis bank and finance capital.

The historical fortification of bank capital and the genesis and expansion of finance capital was based on a coincidence of interests that simultaneously legitimized the State and fortified the political-economic power of finance capital. The hegemonic position of finance capital within the power bloc eventually resulted in a divergence of common interests with the State. Finance capital did not adhere to the traditional negotiation methods characterizing the historical coincidence of interests between the State and bank capital because it was against their material interests. The failure of finance capital to adhere to the terms of the negotiation process worsened the crisis of the State. The López Portillo regime reacted by symbolically nationalizing the banks. The nationalization, however, did not signify nor demonstrate the relative autonomy of the State. A few elements within the State apparatus secretly coordinated sufficient power at a specific moment when a conjunctural crisis threatened the legitimacy of the entire Revolution.

Part of the explanation as to why José López Portillo and Carlos Tello were able to successfully coordinate the nationalization project was the political chaos permeating the State apparatus. Political chaos resulted from the increasing materialization of sociostructural contradictions. The class character of the State was apparent, and the contradictions threatened to de-legitimize the very essence of the Revolution, that is, the ability of the State to conceal the bourgeois nature of the State and the Revolution.

The ability of the bourgeoisie and the financial fraction to restructure the nationalized bank system in favor of private accumulation and private control of the financial circuits manifested the power of the financial fraction. It also manifested the poverty of analyses incorporating explanations emphasizing the relative autonomy of the State. The reality of the State as an arena of class conflict was ignored in favor of nationalist conceptions. Indeed, the State's continual chain of political-economic concessions to the financial fraction has manifested the financial fraction's retention of political and ideological hegemony. State concessions to the financial fraction enabled the fraction to reorganize the valorization process and thereby affect the definition of the financial circuits and the delineation of a new accumulation model.

The nationalization of the banks was the single most important development in postrevolutionary Mexico. The nationalization reflected the manifold contradictions confronting the State and the recomposition of social class relations. A fundamental contradiction between the redefinition of the accumulation model and traditional modes of hegemony was reflected by a political struggle within the power bloc and the State apparatus. The composition of the Mexican State must be demystified and appropriate political strategies implemented.

Postscript

The crisis surrounding the nationalization of the banks in 1982 was undoubtedly one of the most significant historical events in Twentieth Century Mexico. The nationalization signified many things to many people. For López Portillo, the nationalization of the banks will characterize his regime, a power struggle for national sovereignty. For ex-bankers and many businessmen, it was the end of a drawn-out confidence game. For the majority of Mexicans, the political struggle that characterized the nationalization was the initiation of political change and extensive economic sacrifice. For analysts and historians, the nationalization provided a rare opportunity to study the socioeconomic intricacies of the Mexican State, social classes, and social class fractions.

Significant developments occurred in the eight-year period following the nationalization of the banks. A consistent initiative to restrict the effects of the nationalization and to privatize the banks has characterized financial and regulatory policy. The nationalized bank system was partially reprivatized in 1983 with the sale of shares in nonbank financial institutions. Succeeding regulations allowed the financial fraction to create and institutionalize a private, parallel financial system, utilizing stock brokerage houses to capture and channel financial resources, that competed with the nationalized bank system. Rampant speculation transpired in the capital markets, amidst fraud and manipulation, and the State lost regulatory control of crucial financial instruments. Amidst the backdrop of financial innovation and increasing concentration and centralization of financial resources and wealth in the private capital markets, the nationalized bank system continued to perform traditional financial functions in a restricted market.

Nevertheless, according to some accounts, the nationalized bank system was a successful endeavor. As noted by Jaime Corredor, current ABM president and president of the Banco Internacional, the postnationalization bank system experienced positive growth. In terms of finance, profits and countable capital increased 200% in real terms, whereas expenses declined in real terms (Garcia del la Huerta, 1990). The postnationalized bank system also encouraged concentration and centralization.[1] But, as Carlos Tello noted, "The nationalized bank system functioned in essentially the same manner with the same practices as the prenationalization bank" (Quijano et al., 1984, p. 17). ABM president Corredor echoed Tello's sentiments, noting that the key professionals in key posts noticed no difference in the functioning of the bank before or after the nationalization of the banks.

Without a doubt, the most significant developments were the legislative changes in December 1989 and the reprivatization in 1990, two interconnected developments. The Salinas administration implemented radical new financial legislation in December 1989. The new legislation substantially modified the regulatory regime governing nonbank financial institutions. The most significant change concerned government concessions; that is, the language of the Constitution was changed so that constitutional phrasing deleted the concept of government concession and substituted the concept of government authorization of financial services to be provided by the private sector. In addition to this important change, there was a general deregulation of the financial intermediary sector and a provision for direct foreign investment in financial intermediaries. Another tremendously important development was the legal recognition of the existence of financial groups.[2] The December legislation provided an initial glimpse of the administration's ultimate goal: the reprivatization of the nationalized banks.

On the morning of May 2, 1990, the Salinas administration surprised and shocked the nation. The administration proposed to delete the fifth paragraph of the 28th Article of the Constitution, reserving, for the State, the bank concession. In other words, the administration proposed to reprivatize the nationalized bank system.

Public disclosure of the reprivatization initiative created a silent wave of public discussion and debate. Although the media and the Congress expended great amounts of time and money to support or condemn the presidential initiative, the majority of the people failed to launch any noticeable organized response. The measure was largely supported by the public. Not only was the initiative studied, discussed, and planned among a limited number of Salinas' advisers, it was carefully introduced to coincide with the visit of the Pope. The initiative was also submitted to the Chamber of Deputies at a time when several opposition parties were striking or abstaining from Chamber participation to protest PRI manipulation of the Banpesca bank scandal. In other words, the administration's timing on such a controversial piece of legislation was impeccably orchestrated.

There were many logical and rational explanations for the reprivatization. Selling the banks provided a large capital infusion to pay down debt and consolidate economic recovery. Additional capital from the sale of the banks would allow the State to invest in infrastructure development and augment social expenditures. In conjunction with the general deregulation of the financial sector, privatized banks would augment the development of financial groups and promote technological modernization and innovation. Privatization of the banks was also in line with the general redefinition of State and private sector relations. The bankless State reflected the conceptual definition of the minimalist neoliberal State. Reprivatization was also a political opportunity for the PRI. Because the privatization was also a long-term PAN agenda, the PRI opportunistically formed a cooperative alliance to isolate the opposition parties. However, undoubtedly the most important reason for nationalizing the banks was to regain private sector confidence and encourage capital repatriation and foreign investment. Above and beyond these empirical explanations for the reprivatization of the banks, there are some important theoretical issues that must be addressed.

Theoretically, privatization of the nationalized banks raises profound questions beyond the empirical explanation. One of the more significant questions is about finance capital. Finance capital, classically conceived in the style of Hilferding, ceased to exist when the State absorbed the nucleus of finance capital. Some analysts have asserted that finance capital continued to function as a class fraction even after the nationalization of the banks. However, due to the changes that occurred in the financial circuits and in the valorization processes vis-à-vis other fractions of capital, I have referred to the postnationalization ex-bankers as the financial fraction. In the postnationalization period, the financial fraction has augmented its political-economic power and has substantially transformed the financial circuits and valorization process. With the implementation of the December 1989 legislation, deregulating the financial sector and providing for the juridical recognition of the financial group (the financial fraction) as a fraction reflected a radical departure from previous developments. The stock brokerages, in conjunction with other financial intermediary institutions, were providing the axis for valorization and accumulation. The stock brokerages were functioning in a similar manner to the banks in terms of prenationalization finance capital. With the privatization of the banks now official, the stage is set for the reappearance of finance capital. *Within this context it is important to note that finance capital never really disappeared. The form and organization of the fraction relative to other fractions and vis-à-vis the valorization and accumulation processes was changed, thus the reason for renaming finance capital.* As details of the privatization unfold we will be able to better understand the new relationships that develop and the changes that occur with the financial circuits and the valorization process.

There are many other significant questions that must be addressed. Unfortunately, most of the questions will remain unanswered until the privatization process unwinds. So far, the details have remained highly confidential because of the political mechanics of the privatization. Undoubtedly, an important question will involve the role of the ex-bankers and foreign capital in regard to ownership of the privatized banks. Another important question will revolve around the role of the privatized banks vis-à-vis the newly constituted financial groups. The banks may play a very large role in consolidating Mexican finance capital on a national and international basis. Another important future question is the role foreign capital will play in the Mexican banking sector. Already, there is speculation that Banamex and Bancomer are interesting prospects for foreign investment banks looking to consolidate operations in Mexico. In essence, the function and role of the banks and the financial groups in the structural reorganization of the Mexican economy and the integration of the Mexican economy with the United States and Canada will be a very interesting development. For the time being, it appears that there has been a conciliation of interests between the State and the financial fraction and that the new accumulation model is becoming more apparent. The linkages with international production and finance are without a doubt extremely significant. In particular, Mexican finance capital will probably play an important role in the modernization and integration of the Mexican economy with the emerging American trade bloc.

NOTES

1. That is, the process of concentration and centralization also occurred in the national bank system. The rationale for this process was partly to reduce duplication and increase efficiency. However, concentration and centralization also occurred because several banks were financially "unhealthy."

2. A financial group is a financial organization that controls two or more financial intermediaries, with a 51% minimum capital participation.

Appendix

The spectrum of finance capital in Mexico encompassed three general forms (Castañeda, 1982).

The first form of finance capital is the integrated financial group. Grupo VISA, Grupo Vidriera, Grupo Chihuahua, and Grupo Somex are examples of integrated financial groups. A brief examination of these groups will illustrate the dynamism of the fusion or merger process and the different forms of finance capital.

Grupo VISA (Valores Industriales, S.A.) evolved from the Cervecería Cuauhtémoc (Garza-Sada family; Grupo Monterrey)[1] Cervecería Cuauhtémoc expanded its vertical and horizontal industrial capacity in the late 1890s and early 1900s (Fragoso, Concheiro, & Gutiérez, 1979; Nuncio, 1982; Saragoza, 1978). In this case industrial capital purchased and created their own banks and financial institutions to capture resources and convert money capital into productive capital (Fragoso et al., 1979, p. 58). Banco Serfín, the group's major financial institution, originated with the Garza-Sada investment in the Banco de Nuevo Léon. The Garza-Sadas also established additional financial institutions, including the Financiera Aceptaciones, Banco de Londres y México, Hipotecaria Serfín, Seguro Monterrey Serfín, Financiera Crédito de Monterrey, Banco de Juárez, Banco Azteca, Banco Veracruzano, and auxiliary credit institutions, for example, Almacenes y Silos, S.A. (Fragoso et al., 1979, p. 67). Financial operations were tightly integrated with industrial and commercial operations. The group specialized in the production and commercialization of food and drink products. Decision making was highly centralized, permitting coordinated command (Castañeda, 1982, p. 97). Interlocking directorates facilitated coordinated decision making. Eugenio Garza Lagüerra, for example, was president of Cervecería Cuauhtémoc, VISA, and Serfín. He was also a member of several administrative councils, including Banco de Londres y México, Banco Azteca, Financiera Aceptaciones, Seguros Monterrey Serfín, Hipotecaria Serfín, Financiera de Crédito Monterrey, Banco de Comercio (Bancomer), Banco Comercial Mexicano de Monterrey, Banco Comercial Mexicano de Chihuahua, Seguros la

Comercial, Mexicana de Cobre, and Transportación Martína Mexicana (Fragoso et al., 1979, p. 77).

Grupo Vidriera was another example of an integrated financial group.[2] Vidriera Monterrey created Financiera del Norte in 1937 and later acquired Banco de Nuevo Léon and the Banco del País.[3] Vidriera was incorporated as a *sociedad de fomento* (development society) in 1979 and was retitled Fomento de Industria y Comercio, S.A. (FIC). The group produces primarily glass and glass-related products (e.g., 85 percent of all glass in Mexico is produced by Vidriera). The group owns a controlling interest in more than fifty commercial and industrial subsidiaries and owns Banco del País (Banpaís) and 87 percent of the Grupo Financiero Banpaís.[4] As with the previous group, interlocking directorates are an organizational trait. For example, Rogelio Sada Zambrano (director of FIC) was a member of the board of directors for Vidriera Monterrey, Cristalería, Cristales Mexicanos, Financiera del Norte, Banco Banpaís, Financiera de País, and Hipotecaria Banpaís (Fragoso et al., 1979, p. 83).

A third example of the integrated financial group form of finance capital was the Grupo Chihuahua. The Grupo Chihuahua is a vertically and horizontally integrated organization, producing and commercializing wood and paper products, and consumer goods. From the Porfiriato until the 1930s, the Chihuahua group initially obtained capital from agriculture and cattle. During the 1930–1950 period the group began to expand into agro-industrial production and commercialization operations by using Chihuahua financial institutions (e.g., Financiera de Valores and Financiera y Fiduciaria de Chihuahua). In 1934, Elloy Vallina founded the Banco Commercial Mexicano to promote regional development. The group's expansion was enhanced during the latter 1940s by association with financial, business, and industrial interests in Mexico City. In the 1950s, Banco Comercial Mexicano began to absorb banks and insurance companies outside of Chihuahua. For example, in 1948, the group, in association with outside interests in Mexico City, created the Banco Capitalizador Comercial Mexicano. In 1951, the Compañia de Seguros La Comercial was purchased. The Financiera Comermex was established in 1962, specializing in bank services. In 1964, Inversa Mexicana (an investment capital institution) was established, and in 1965, the Hipotecaria Comermex was created. In 1979, the Grupo Chihuahua-Comermex formed a holding company (Castañeda, 1982, pp. 102–103; Fragoso et al., 1979, pp. 176–181; Hamilton, 1982, pp. 288–289).

The final example of an integrated financial group form of finance capital is Grupo Somex. Grupo Somex differs slightly from the previous examples of finance capital. Its shares are traded on the stock exchange and the State owns a controlling interest. Juridically, its structure is also different. The holding company is not the central controlling or organizational entity (e.g., FIC). Banco Mexicano Somex owns the capital of the holding company, Fisomex, and the holding company controls the shares of the companies constituting the group. Nevertheless, the decision-making structure is an integrated process, reflecting the interests of the entire group. Another differentiating factor is the diversified nature of Fisomex's holdings. The group's holdings include auto parts fabrication, petrochemicals, chemicals, domestic products, capital goods, urban development and real estate, tourism, and diverse industrial companies (e.g., transportation, bottling, etc.). The group's expansion strategy is also unique. It has tended to purchase insolvent private firms considered to be too important to liquidate. Second, it has established new firms in sectors the State considers strategic, for instance, areas of sufficient productive capacity (Castañeda, 1982, pp. 99–103).

A second form of finance capital in Mexico was characterized by a less clearly defined nexus between bank and industrial capital. The bank–industry relationship was not as integrated nor as centralized as the integrated financial group (e.g., Serfín). A brief examination of Grupo Cremi and Grupo ICA-Atlántico will illustrate the characteristics of this form of finance capital.

Grupo Cremi originated with the formation of industrial and commercial capital. It was initiated in the late 1890s, with the establishment of the brewery Cervecería Moctezuma and the department store El Palacio de Hierro. In 1934, the directors of these two companies founded the financiera Crédito Minero y Mercantil. Crédito Minero y Mercantil enabled the Bailleres family to expand the realm of the group's industrial activity. The relationship between financial and industrial sectors was heterogeneous. Operationally, the financial institution supported the group's mining activities in Industrias Peñoles.[5] The bank also controlled the majority interest in various companies, but there was no centralized financial coordinating policy. Grupo Cremi, therefore, does not constitute an integrated financial group, as in the example of Grupo Chihuahua (Comermex) (Castañeda, 1982, p. 104). Moreover, it didn't display a centralized, consortium type of organizational behavior; Grupo Cremi was a conglomeration of diverse industries (Fragoso et al., 1979, p. 210).

Grupo ICA-Atlántico was another example of a loosely integrated form of finance capital. Grupo ICA-Atlántico was a finance-construction consortium uniting Ingenieros Civiles Asociados (ICA) and Banco Atlántico. ICA, led by Bernardo Quintana, was founded in 1947 by 17 civil engineers. The company accumulated its capital primarily by contracting large public works projects, that is, infrastructure projects. The company expanded its operations by purchasing and establishing new businesses related to the production of construction materials, provision of technical and consulting services, and diverse commercial activities (e.g., telecommunications, liquor). Juridically, the ICA-Atlántico fusion was dominated by ICA. ICA had a decisive participation in Atlántico (Castañeda, 1982, p. 105). Quintana directed ICA and was a member of the board of directors of Atlántico. Banco Atlántico's role in the expansion of ICA was limited. In terms of promoting ICA's expansion, the banks' primary activity was the provision of credit for mortgages and real estate, the promotion of condominiums, and the management of subdivisions. The bank's promotion of ICA was also restricted by irregular growth in the latter 1970s. In 1976, for example, the bank's capture of fixed-rent resources decreased by 25 percent. Consequently, the bank obtained financing from rediscount operations and loans from other banks. The bank's profits also declined 64 percent in 1976 (Fragoso et al., 1979, p. 172).

The final form of finance capital was less integrated than the previous two types. Grupo Banamex and Grupo Bancomer were quintessential examples of a classical (a la Hilferding) fusion of bank and industrial capital. These two institutions were the largest and most powerful banks in the country and consolidated diversified holdings through tangible and intangible purchases.

Grupo Banamex has a long history, starting with the establishment of Banco Nacional de México in 1884. In 1977, Grupo Banamex was formed by the fusion of Banco Nacional de México, Financiera Banamex, and Hipotecaria Banamex. The fusion of these entities increased the group's capital and the amount of resources managed. For example, social capital was increased from 1.3 billion pesos to 2 billion pesos; total assets increased from 45 billion pesos to 80 billion pesos; and the number of shareholders was increased from 12,000 to 15,000. The administrative council was composed of prominent businessmen and bankers of diverse industrial and financial entities associated with the bank through stock ownership or the provision of credit (Fragoso et al., 1979, pp. 22–223). The bank's associations were numerous, including minority ownership of other national credit institutions (e.g., Fideresa); membership in an international banking consortium (Intermex); Banamex stock dispersed among international banking institutions (e.g., Societé Interprofessionalle pour la Compensation des Valeurs Mobilieres); and significant stock ownership in 167 diverse national autonomous companies and national companies associated with international capital, for example, Union Carbide Mexicana (21.7 percent owned by Banamex). Fideresa (Financiera de Desarrollo Regional) was a holding company, integrating nine regional banks and two financieras: Banco del Centro, Banco de Oriente, Banco Agrícola Industrial de Linares, Banco Ganadero y Agrícola, Banco de Tuxpan, Banco del Noroeste de México, Banco del Sureste, Banco Ganadero de Tampico, Financiera y Fidcuiaria del Golfo, and Financiera Peninsular.[6]

Grupo Bancomer was a second example of classical finance capital. Bancomer, originally the Banco de Comercio, was founded in 1932 by Salvador Ugarte, Raúl Bailleres, and Liberto Senderos. The bank purchased controlling interests of provincial banks and coordinated its activities with other banks (e.g., Crédito Minero y Mercantil) to form the BUDA group (Bailleres, Ugarte, Domínguez, and Amescua). The BUDA group's strategy of investing in existing financial institutions was the cornerstone of Banco de Comercio's investment strategy. The group eventually divided, and Banco de Comercio was controlled by the Jenkins group (William Jenkins, Manuel Espinosa Yglesias, and Maximino Avila Camacho). Eventually, Espinosa Yglesias controlled the majority of the bank's stock.

Bancomer's investment strategy, in relation to the previously examined examples of finance capital, was somewhat unique.[7] Bancomer's operations expanded very rapidly.[8] The bank also expanded its ownership of other types of financial institutions (e.g., Financiera Bancomer, Hipotecaria Bancomer, Asegurador Bancomer, Arrendadora Bancomer, and Casa de Bolsa Bancomer. The bank's participation in industrial firms, however, was relatively minimal. In 1980, for example, Bancomer owned 12 billion pesos worth of stock in 17 diverse companies (e.g., Bayer Industria de Ecatepec, Anderson Clayton, and Frisco).

Bancomer's minimal stock ownership and participation in industrial and commercial entities was exemplified by the limited participation of its director on the administrative boards of those companies in which Bancomer owned stock. Thus, for example, Espinosa Yglesias sat on only one outside administrative board (Frisco). Although Bancomer's fusion with industrial-commercial capital was relatively limited, it was still able to indirectly influence industry and commerce through the extension of credit. In comparison with the previous examples of finance capital, Bancomer was probably the least structured and possibly the least developed form of finance capital (i.e., in the classical sense).

NOTES

1. The Grupo Monterrey was originally created by the Garza-Sadas and was centered around the Cuauhtémoc brewery. In 1936, *Vidriera* (glass) group—vitro—was separated from the Cuauhtémoc group. In 1974, the group reorganized to form four separate entities: VISA, Vitro, CYDSA, and Alfa (Fragoso et al., 1979; Nuncio, 1982).

2. In the case of Vidriera, the fusion of finance capital was another example of the expansion of industrial capital.

3. Garza and Sada originally participated in the foundation of the Banco de Nuevo

Léon. The Banco de Nuevo Léon was therefore linked to the Cuauhtémoc group before the Vidriera division.

4. Grupo Financiero Banpaís is composed of Banpaís, Banco Comercial Peninsular, Almacenadora Banpaís, Arrendadora Banpaís, and Casa de Bolsa Banpaís. The holding company also owns between 25 and 50 percent of Industria Centroamericana de Tapas (Costa Rica), Distribuidora Industrial y Comercial de Centroamérica (Costa Rica and Nicaragua), and Brasividrio Limitada (Brazil; Castañeda, 1982, pp. 47–48).

5. Alberto Bailleres directed both entities.

6. Fideresa was also the largest holder of Banamex's free subscription stock (*serie de suscripción libre*) and received resource transfers and technical services from Banamex. Fideresa was also very profitable, increasing its social capital from 4 to 90 million pesos during 1970–1976 and its assets from 1.6 billion to 2.2 billion pesos for the same period (Castañeda, 1982, pp. 223–224). In 1980, the value of Banamex's net investment in the stocks of 167 companies equalled 12.4 billion pesos. The sectoral distribution of these investments was: insurance and finance institutions, 26.5 percent; support institutions, 18.3 percent; investment societies, 2.6 percent; automotive, 4.1 percent; consumer goods, 3.4 percent; electrical, 3.7 percent; metal, 2.1 percent; construction materials, 6.6 percent; mining, 11 percent; paper, 2.1 percent; chemicals, 4.2 percent; telecommunications, 1.3 percent; tourism, 10.1 percent; various, 3.4 percent (Castañeda, 1982, p. 110).

7. Ex-director Espinosa Yglesias once noted that inflation eroded intangible assets and that tangible assets constituted a primary investment objective, apart from credit operations. "In a world where inflation erodes the value of money, it is important that business capital is represented by goods that maintain their real value to obtain the stability of these goods, and to protect the capital of the shareholders. Therefore, Bancomer owns 223 buildings and as an additional protection, important participation in industrial and service businesses." (Castañeda, 1982, pp. 106–107)

8. Its total resources increased from 2 billion pesos in 1954 to 103 billion in 1976, that is, a 500 percent increase in twenty two years, approximately 22 percent per annum (Fragoso et al., 1979, p. 234). The number of affiliated banks increased from twenty to thirty seven.

Bibliography

Abedrop Dávila, Carlos, "Informe del Consejo," *Memoria,* 24(5), May 1979, 10–48.

Acosta, Carlos, "Exbanqueros Inconformos con Sólo Casas de Bolsa Proyectan un Banco," *Proceso,* 447, May 27, 1985, 25–26.

———, "La Pérdida de la Banca se Subsana con el Mercada Bursátil Más Próspero del Mundo," *Proceso,* 545, April 13, 1987, 10–13.

Acosta Lagunas, Augustín, "La Obra Pública Corresponde a Necesidades Sociales: Acosta Lagunas," *La Jornada,* July 4, 1984, p. 12.

Acosta Romero, Miguel, *La Banca Múltiple.* Mexico: Editorial Porrua, 1981.

Aguilar, Alonso, *Estado, Capitalismo y Clase en el Poder.* Mexico: Editorial Nuestro Tiempo, 1983.

Aguilar, Alonso, and Fernando Carmona, *México: Riqueza y Miseria.* Mexico: Editorial Nuestro Tiempo, 1984.

Aguilar, Alonso, Fernando Carmona, Arturo Guillén, and Ignacio Hernández, *La Nacionalización de la Banca.* Mexico: Editorial Nuestro Tiempo, 1982.

Aguilar Camin, Héctor, Carlos Monsiváis, Roberto Bouzas, José Manuel Quijano, José Blanco, Jaime Ros, Jorge Bustamante, and Sumiko Kushida, *Cuando los Banqueros se Van.* Mexico: Océano, 1982.

Aguilar García, Javier, "Nacionalización Bancaria y Movimiento Obrero en México," *Iztapalapa,* 4(8), January–June 1983, 144–150.

Aguilar Mora, Manuel, *El Bonapartismo Mexicano: I. Ascenso y Decadencia.* Mexico: Juan Pablo, 1982.

Aída, Mateos, and Enrique Quintana, "El Sistema Financiera Mexicano en la Coyuntura: 1980–1983," *Economía Informa,* 117, June 1984, 25–37.

Alcocer, Jorge, "Entrevista a Jorge Alcocer," *Momento Económico,* 2, 1984, 15–16.

———, Interview conducted by Russell White, 1986.

Alcocer, Jorge, and Isidro Cisneros, "Los Empresarios, entre los Negocios y la Política," in Jorge Alcocer (ed): *México: Presente y Futuro,* Mexico: Ediciones de Cultura Popular, 1985.

Alvarez, Alejandro, "Crisis Economía y Reforma Política en México." Paper presented at the Eleventh International Congress of the Latin American Studies Association, 1983.

Amin, Samir, *Unequal Development.* New York: Monthly Review Press, 1976.

Anda Gutierrez, Cuauhtemoc, *La Nacionalización de la Banca.* Mexico: Instituto Politecnico Nacional, 1982.

Anderson, Charles, "Bankers as Revolutionaries: Politics and Development Banking in

Mexico," in William Glade and Charles Anderson (eds): *The Political Economy of Mexico*. Madison: University of Wisconsin Press, 1968.

Anderson, Perry, "The Antinomies of Antonio Gramsci," *New Left Review*, 100, November 1976, 4–78.

Arriola, Carlos, and Juan Gustavo Galindo, "Los Empresarios y el Estado en México (1976–1982)," *Foro Internacional*, 25(2), October–December 1984, 118–137.

Ashcroft, Richard, "Marx and Weber on Liberalism as Bourgeois Ideology," *Comparative Studies in Society and History*, 24 March 1972, 130–168.

Báez, Francisco, "Nacionalización de la Banca, *Decisión Histórica*," 97, September 1982, n.p.

Banco de México, S.A., *Serie Historia del Sistema Bacario, Monetario y Crediticia, 1925–1978*. Mexico: Author.

Barkin, David, *The End to Food Self-Sufficiency in Mexico*. Unpublished manuscript, 1986.

Barnet, Richard, and Ronald Muller, *Global Reach*. New York: Simon and Schuster, 1974.

Bartra, Roger, *Estructura Agraria y Clases Sociales en México*. Mexico: Ediciones Era, 1974.

——, "Peasants and Political Power in Mexico," *Latin American Perspectives*, 2(2), (Summer), 1975a, 125–145.

——, "La Revolución Domesticada: Del Bonapartismo Pequeñoburgués a la Institucionalización de la Burguesía," *Historia y Sociedad*, segunda época (Summer), 1975b, 13–30.

——, *El Poder Despótico Burgués*. México: Serie Popular Era, 1978.

——, *Campesinado y Poder Política en México*. Mexico: Ediciónes Era, 1982a.

——, *El Reto de la Izquierda*. Mexico: Siglo Veintiuno, 1982b.

Basáñez, Miguel, *La Lucha por la Hegemonía en México, 1968–1980*. Mexico: Siglo Veintiuno, 1981.

——, "Notas para un Analisis de la Nacionalización," *Gaceta Mexicana de Administración Pública*, 7, July–September 1983, 49–58.

Basáñez, Miguel, and Roderic Camp, "La Nacionalización de la Banca y la Opinión Pública en México," *Foro Internacional*, 25(2), October–December 1984, 202–216.

Basave, Jorge, "Capital Financiero y Expropiación Bancaria en México," *Teoría y Política*, 9, January–March 1983, 117–140.

Basave, Jorge, Julio Moguel, Miguel Rivera, and Alejandro Toledo, "La Nacionalización de la Banca y la Situación Política Actual," *Teoría y Política*, 3(7 and 8), July–December, 1982, 47–63.

Basch, Antonin, *El Mercado de Capitales en México*. Mexico: CEMLA, 1968.

Bennett, Douglas, and Kenneth Sharpe, "The State as Banker and Entrepreneur," *Comparative Politics*, 12(2), 1980, 165–189.

Best, Michael, and William Connolly, "Politics and Subjects: The Limits of Structural Marxism," *Socialist Review*, 9(5), September–October 1979, 75–99.

Blanco, José Joaquín, "Progreso y Modernidad, las Dos Grandes Utopías," *Punto* (November 4, 1985), 9.

Blanco Mejía, José, "Bolentin de Prensa," *Economía Informa*, 97, September 1982.

Blanke, Bernard, Ulrich Jürgens, and Hans Kastendiek, "The Relationship Between the

Political and the Economic as a Point of Departure for a Materialistic Analysis of the Bourgeois State," *International Journal of Politics,* 4(4), Fall 1976, 68–126.

Bottomore, Tom, "Introduction to the Translation," in Rudolph Hilferding (ed): *Finance Capital.* London: Routledge & Kegan Paul, 1981.

Boulder Kapitalistate Collective, and Margaret Fay, "Hegel and the State," *Kapitalistate,* 4–5, Summer, 1976, 186–220.

Brading, David, *Miners and Merchants in Bourbon Mexico, 1763–1810.* Cambridge: Cambridge University Press, 1971.

Bravo, Victor, Ajuja Ruíz, and Marco Antonio Michel, "Alianza de Clases y Dominación: México 1930–1946," *Historía y Sociedad,* 9, 1976, 31–51.

Brandenburg, Frank R., *The Making of Modern Mexico.* Englewood Cliffs, NJ: Prentice-Hall, 1964.

Brewer, Anthony, *Marxist Theories of Imperialism.* London: Routledge and Kegan Paul, 1980.

Burris, Val, "Classes and Politics in Advanced Capitalism," *Socialist Review,* 9(6) November–December 1979, 135–142.

Calderon, José Maria, *Génesis de Presidencialismo en México.* Mexico: Ediciónes "El Caballito," 1972.

Carchedi, G., "Reproduction of Social Classes at the Level of Production Relations," *Economy and Society,* 4, November 1975, 361–417.

Cardero, María Elena, *Patrón Monetario y Acumulación en México: Nacionalización y Control de Cambios.* México: Siglo Veintiuno, 1984.

Cardoso, Ciro, *Formación y Desarrollo de la Burguesía en México, Siglo XIX.* Mexico: Siglo Veintiuno, 1981.

——, *México en el Siglo XIX (1821–1910), Historía Económica y de la Estructura Social.* Mexico: Editorial Nueva Imagen, 1983.

Carrillo Castro, Alejandro, *La Reforma Administrativa en Mexico.* Mexico, DF: Ediciónes INAP, 1978.

Carrión, Jorge, and Alonso Aguilar, *La Burguesía, la Oligarquía y el Estado.* Mexico: Editorial Nuestro Tiempo, 1980.

Castañeda, Jorge, *Los Últimos Capitalismos.* Mexico: Ediciónes Era, 1982.

Castañeda, Roberto, "Los Límites del Capitalismo en México," *Cuadernos Políticos,* 8, April–June 1976, 53–74.

Castillo, Heberto, "Un gran paso adelante," *Proceso,* 306, September 6, 1982, 35–38.

Ceceña, José Luis, *México en la Órbita Imperial.* Mexico: Ediciónes "El Caballito," 1970.

Cerutti, Mario, *Burguesía y Capitalismo en Monterrey, 1850–1910.* Mexico: Claves Latinoamericanas, 1983.

Chilcote, Ronald, *Theories of Comparative Politics.* Boulder, CO: Westview, 1981.

——, "Perspectives of Class and Political Struggle in the Portuguese Capitalist State," *Kapitalistate,* 8, 1980, 99–120.

Chilcote, Ronald, and Dale Johnson, *Theories of Development.* Beverly Hills, CA: Sage, 1983.

CIDE, "La Economía Mexicana: Evolución Reciente y Perspectivas," *Economía Mexicana,* 1, 1979, 1–25.

——, "La Evolución Reciente y las Perspectivas de la Economía Mexicana," *Economía Mexicana,* 2, 1980, 9–26.

———, "La Evolución Reciente y las Perspectivas de la Economía Mexicana," *Economía Mexicana*, 3, 1981, 9–22.

———, "Evolución Reciente y Perspectivas de la Economía Mexicana," *Economía Mexicana*, 4, 1982, 9–23.

Clarke, Simon, "State, Class Struggle, and the Reproduction of Capital," *Kapitalistate*, 10/11, 1983, 113–130.

———, "Marxism, Sociology and Poulantzas' Theory of the State," *Capital and Class*, 2, Summer 1977, 1–31.

Cockcroft, James, *Mexico*. New York: Monthly Review, 1982.

———, "Immiseration, Not Marginalization: The Case of Mexico," *Latin American Perspectives*, 10 (2 and 3, 37 and 38), 1983, 86–107.

Colmenares, David, Luis Angeles, and Carlos Ramírez, *La Nacionalización de la Banca*. Mexico: Terra Nova, 1982.

Concheiro, Elvira, "Conservar lo Importante," *Momento Económico*, 2, 1984, 7–12.

Conde, Raúl, Daniel Cataife, Atenea Flores, Margarita Galindo, Enrique Pino, Víctor Soria, and Gregoria Vidal, "Balance de Aspectos Centrales de la Política Económica del Actual Sexenio," *Iztapalapa*, 4(8), January–June 1983, 7–34.

Consejo Directivo de la ABM, "Informe del Consejo," *Revista Bancaria*, 30(6), June 1982, 16–42.

Cordera, Rolando, "Estado y Desarrollo en el Capitalismo, Tardio y Subordinado," *Investigación Económica*, 123(31), July–September 1971, 463–511.

Cordera, Rolando, and Carlos Tello (eds), *La Desigualdad en México*. Mexico: Siglo Veintiuno, 1984.

Cordero, Salvador, Rafael Santín, and Ricardo Tirado, *El Poder Empresarial en México*. Mexico: Terra Nova, 1983.

Córdova, Arnaldo, *La Formación del Poder Político en México*. Mexico: Serie Popular Era, 1972.

———, *La Ideología de la Revolución Mexicana*. Mexico: Ediciónes Era, 1973.

———, "Nocturno de la Democracia Mexicana, 1917–1984," *Nexos*, February 1986, 17–27.

Correa, Eugenia, "Política financiera y crisis: Análisis de las Condiciones Previas a la Nacionalización Bancaria," *Economia: Teoría y Práctica*, 6, Fall 1984, 75–96.

Cosio Villegas, Daniel, *Historía Moderna de México, el Porfiriato, Vida Económica*. Mexico: Editorial Hermes, 1974.

Cotrell, Allin, "On Classes in Contemporary Capitalism," *Bulletin of the Conference of Socialist Economists*, 5(1 and 2), May–October 1976, 1–9.

Couturier, Edith, "Pedro Romero de Terreros: ¿Comerciante o Empresario Capitalista del Siglo XVIII?" in *Origenes y Desarrollo de la Burguesía en América Latina, 1700–1955*. Mexico: Editorial Nueva Imagen, 1985.

Coyoacán, "Nacionalización de la Banca, Petróleo y Capital Financiero," *Coyoacan*, 5, January–June 1983, 15, 3–18.

Creel de la Barra, Enrique, Address before the XLVIII Convención Bancaria, *Revista Bancaria*, 30(6), June 1982, 96–100.

Dahrendorf, Ralf, *Class and Class Conflict in Industrial Society*. Stanford, CA: Stanford University Press, 1959.

de Albornoz, Alvaro, *El Sistema Bancario y la Inflación en México, Etapa de 1960 a 1970*. Mexico: Editora Galaxia, 1980.

de la Peña, Sergio, *La Formación del Capitalismo en México*. Mexico: Siglo Veintiuno, 1975.

Del Rio, Gabriel, "Nacionalización de la banca, es una luz mas de experanza," *Impacto*, 1698, September 15, 1982, 26.

Eckstein, Harry, and David Apter, *Comparative Politics, A Reader*. New York: Free Press of Glencoe, 1963.

Eckstein, Susan, *The Poverty of Revolution: The State and Urban Poor in Mexico*. Princeton, NJ: Princeton University Press, 1977.

Eraña García, Eugenio, "Informe del Consejo," *Memoria*, 26(3), March 1978, 13–43.

Esping-Anderson, Gosta, Roger Friedland, and Erik Olin Wright, "Modes of Class Struggle and the Capitalist State," *Kapitalistate*, 4 and 5, Summer 1976, 186–220.

Espino, Alma, and Ana Schvarz, *La Banca Nacionalizada*. Puebla, Mexico: UAP, 1983.

Esquerra Aragón, Manuel, "La Estatización de la Banca Mexicana y el Control de cambios," *Revista de la Universidad Autónoma de Guerrero*, 2(9), November–December 1983, 81–83.

Estévez, Jaime, and Rosario Green, "El Resurgimiento del Capital Financiero en los Setentas: Contribución a Su Analisis", *Economía Mexicana*, 4, 1980, 59–69.

Expansión, "Editorial: El Golpe del Estado," *Expansión*, (September 15), 1982a, n.p.

———, "Otras Reglas para Otro Juego," *Expansión*, (September 15), 1982b, 17–20.

———, "¿Tendrá Valor el Poder de Una Firma?" *Expansión*, (October 27), 1982c, 74–76.

Fanusie, Yaya, *Social Classes, the State and Public Policy in the Republic of Sierra Leone*. Ph.D. dissertation, University of California, Riverside, 1981.

Felipe Leal, Juan, *La Burguesía y el Estado Mexicano*. Mexico: Ediciónes "El Caballito," 1972.

———, *México: Estado, Burocracia y Sindicatos*. Mexico: Ediciónes "El Caballito," 1975.

Felipe Leal, Juan, and Mario Huacuja Rountree, *Economía y Sistema de Haciendas en México*. Mexico: Ediciónes Era, 1982.

Fernández-Vega, Carlos, "Empresa financiera de Bancomer y Abedrop," *La Jornada*, (May 23), 1985a, 6.

———, "Utilidades por 2 Mil Millones Obtuvieron Casas de Bolsa en 84," *La Jornada*, (April 25), 1985b, 11.

Fitzgerald, E.V.K., "The State and Capital Accumulation in Mexico," *Journal of Latin American Studies*, 10(2), 1978, 263–282.

———, "The Financial Constraint on Relative Autonomy: the State and Capital Accumulation in Mexico, 1940–82, in Christian Anglade and Carlos Fortin (eds): *The State and Capital Accumulation in Latin America*. Pittsburgh, PA: University of Pittsburgh Press, 1985.

Fortin, Carlos, "The Relative Autonomy of the State and Accumulation in Latin America," in Diane Tussie (ed): *Latin America in the World Economy*, Hampshire, England: Gower, 1983.

Foster-Carter, Aidan, "The Modes of Production Controversy," *New Left Review*, 107, January 1978, 47–77.

Fragoso, Juan Manuel, Elvira Concheiro, and Antonio Gutiérez, *El Poder de la Gran Burguesía*. Mexico: Ediciónes de Cultura Popular, 1979.

Frank, A. G., *Capitalism and Underdevelopment in Latin America*. New York: Monthly Review Press, 1967.

Frazier, Steve, "Mexico Starts $405 Million Sale of Stock Held by Banks Prior to Nationalization," *The Wall Street Journal*, (May 22), 1984a, 35.

———, "Mexico Unveils Plan to Reshape Financial System," *The Wall Street Journal*, (April 13), 1984b, 10.

Friedman, Daniel, "Marx's Perspective on the Objective Class Structure," *Polity*, 6, Spring 1974, 318–344.

Galaz, Lourdes, "Anuncian la Constitución de Ingeniería Financiera," *La Jornada*, May 29, 1985, 9.

Galindo, Magdalena, "Crisis y Nacionalización de la Banca," in *Iztapalapa*, 4(8) (Januuary–June), 1983a, 35–48.

———"El Proyecto Presidencial de MMH," *Iztapalapa*, 4(8) (January–June), 1983b, 49–56.

García de la Huerta, Carolina, "Privatizaciones Mexicanas Ahora le Toca a la Banca," *El Mercurio* (Santiago, Chile), May 20, 1990, F1.

García de León, Antonio, *Resistencia y Utopía, Memorial de Agravios y Crónica de Revueltas y Profecías Acaecidas en la Provincia de Chiapas durante los Últimos Quinientos Años de Su Historía*. Mexico: Ediciónes Era, 1985.

Garrido, Celso, and Enrique Quintana, "Reflexiones sobre la Reforma del Sistema Financiero Mexicano." Manuscript published in *El Cotidiano*, 3, as "Cambios en la Legislación Bancaria," 1985.

———, "En . . . Zimas de Poder," *El Cotidiano*, 2(9), January–February 1986, 27–35.

Genel, Julio Alfredo, *La Estrategia del Estado en el Desarrollo Financiero*. Mexico: CEMLA, 1977.

Gil Villegas Montiel, Francisco, "La Crisis de Legitimidad en la Última Etapa del Sexenio de José López Portillo," *Foro Internaciónal*, 25(2), October–December 1984, 190–201.

Gilly, Adolfo, *La Revolunción Interrumpida*. Mexico: Ediciónes "El Caballito," 1971.

———, *The Mexican Revolution*. London: Verso, 1983a.

———, *Por Todos los Caminos: I. Escritos sobre América Latina, 1956–1982*. Mexico: Editorial Nueva Imagen, 1983b.

———, "PRI: La Larga Travesía," *Nexos*, 91, July 1985, 15–29.

Gilly, Adolfo, Arnaldo Córduva, Armando Bartra, Manuel Aguilar Mora, and Enrique Semo, *Interpretaciónes de la Revolución Mexicana*. Mexico: Editorial Nueva Imagen, 1979.

Glade, William, and Charles Anderson, *The Political Economy of Mexico*. Madison: University of Wisconsin Press, 1963.

Gold, David, Clarence Lo, and Erik Olin Wright, "Recent Developments in Marxist Theories of the Capitalist State," *Monthly Review*, 27, October 1975, 29–43; November 1975, 36–51.

Goldsmith, Raymond, *The Financial Development of Mexico*. Paris: Development Centre of the Organization for Economic Co-Operation and Development, 1966.

González Casanova, Pablo, *El Estado y los Partidos Políticos en México* (4th ed.). Mexico: Ediciónes Era, 1985.

González Casanova, Pablo, and Enrique Florescano (eds), *México Hoy*. Mexico: Siglo Veintiuno, 1979.

González Méndez, Héctor, *Economías de Escala y Concentración Bancaria*. Mexico: Banco de México, 1980.

González Méndez, Ismael, "El Régimen Laboral Especial de los Trabajadores Bancarios en México y Sus Perspectivas de Organización," *Iztapalapa,* 4(8), January–June 1983, 151–162.

Gramsci, Antonio, *Selections From the Prison Notebooks*. New York: International Publishers, 1971.

Granados Chapa, Miguel Angel, *La Banca Nuestra de Cada Día*. Mexico: Oceano, 1982.

———, "Plaza Publica," *La Jornada,* January 10, 1985, 2.

Green, Rosario, *Estado y Banca Transnaciónal en México*. Mexico: Editorial Nueva Imagen, 1981.

Greenow, Linda, *Credit and Socioeconomic Change in Colonial Mexico*. Denver, CO: Westview, 1983.

Griffith-Jones, Stephany, "The Growth of Transnational Finance: Implications for National Development," in Diana Tussie (ed): *Latin America in the World Economy,* Hampshire, England: Gower, 1983.

Grossman, Henryk, "Marx, Classical Political Economy and the Problem of Dynamics," Pts. 1 and 2, *Capital and Class,* Summer and Autumn 1977, 2 and 3, 32–55 and 67–99.

Guadarrama Sistos, Roberto, "Estado Banca y Política Económica," *Estudios Políticos,* 2(1), January–March 1983, 30–37.

Guillén Romo, Héctor, *Orígenes de la Crisis en México*. Mexico: Ediciónes Era, 1984.

Habermas, Jürgen, *Legitimation Crisis*. Boston: Beacon Press, 1973.

Hamilton, Nora, "Mexico: The Limits of State Autonomy," *Latin American Perspectives,* 2(5), Summer 1975, 81–108.

———, *The Limits of State Autonomy*. Princeton, NJ: Princeton University Press, 1982.

———, "State–Class Alliances and Conflicts: Issues and Actors in the Mexican Economic Crisis." Unpublished Manuscript, 1983.

Hellman, Judith, *Mexico in Crisis* (2nd ed.). New York: Holmes and Meir, 1983.

Hilferding, Rudolf, *Finance Capital*. London: Routledge & Kegan Paul, 1981.

Hinojosa, Juan José, "Atropellamiento presidencial," *Proceso,* 306, September 6, 1982, 36–37.

Hiriart, Pablo, "Clase Politica," *La Jornada,* 2, March 23, 1986.

Hodges, Donald, and Ross Gandy, *Mexico, 1910–1982*. London: Zed Press, 1982.

Huerta, María Teresa, "En Torno al Origen de la Burguesía Porfirista: el Caso de Isidoro de la Torre" in Enrique Florescano (ed.): *Origenes y Desarrollo de la Burguesía en América Latina, 1700–1955*. Mexico: Editorial Nueva Imagen, 1985.

Hussein, Athar, "Hilferding's Finance Capital," *Bulletin of the Conference of Socialist Economists,* 5(1–2), May–October 1976, A.H. 1–A.H.18.

Ianni, Octavio, *El Estado Capitalista en la Época de Cárdenas*. Mexico: Serie Popular Era, 1977.

Ibarra Muñoz, David, Address presented before the XLIV Convención Bancaria, *Memoria,* 26(3), March 1978, 29–41.

International Currency Review, "World Banking Crisis, Case 1: The Mexican Calamity," *International Currency Review,* 14, October 1982, 37–48.

Jacobs, Eduardo, "La Evolución Reciente de los Grupos de Capital Nacional," *Economía Mexicana,* 3, 1981, 23–44.
Jacobs, Eduardo, and Wilson Peres Núñez, "Las Grandes Empresas y el Crecimiento Acelerado," *Economía Mexicana,* 4, 1982, 99–113.
——, "Tamaño de Planta y Financiamiento: Dos Problemas Centrales del Desarrollo Industrial," *Economía Mexicana,* 5, 1983, 79–110.
Jessop, Bob, *The Capitalist State.* New York: New York University Press, 1982.
——, "Accumulation Strategies, State Forms, and Hegemonic Projects," *Kapitalistate,* 10/11, 1983, 113–130.
Johnson, Dale, *Class and Social Development.* Beverly Hills, CA: Sage, 1982.
——, "Class Formation and Struggle in Latin America," *Latin American Perspectives,* 10(2 and 3, 37 and 38), 1983, 2–18.
Katz, Friedrich, *The Secret War in Mexico.* Chicago: University of Chicago Press, 1981.
Korth, Christopher, "International Financial Markets," in William Baughn and Donald Mandich (eds): *The International Banking Handbook.* Homewood, IL: Dow Jones-Irwin, 1983.
Krauze, Enrique, "El Timon y la Tormenta," *Vuelta,* 71, October 1982, 14–22.
——, *Caudillos Culturales en la Revolución Mexicana.* Mexico: SEP, 1985.
Krauze, Enrique, Jean Meyer, and Cayetano Reyes, *Historia de la Revolución Mexicana, 1924–1928: La Reconstrucción Económica,* Vol. 10. Mexico: El Colegio de México, 1977.
Laclau, Ernesto, *Politics and Ideology in Marxist Theory.* London: Verso, 1978.
La Jornada, "La Banca Ya No Podrá Participar con Capital en Casas de Bolsa," *La Jornada,* November 13, 1984, 1.
——, "Dentro y Fuera, Contra la Crisis," *La Jornada,* 1985a, 1.
——, "La Banca Nacionalizada en 1985," *La Jornada,* (January 8), 1985b, 19.
Landerreche Obregón, Juan, *Expropiación Bancaria y Control de Cambios.* Mexico: Editorial Jus, 1984.
Lavrin, Asunción, "El Capital Eclesiástico y las Élites Sociales en Nueva España a Fines del Siglo XVIII," in Enrique Florescano (ed): *Origines y Desarrollo de la Burguesía en América Latina, 1700–1955.* Mexico: Editorial Nueva Imagen, 1985.
Leriche, Christian, Enrique Quintana, and Pedro Bustos, "La Bolsa de Valores y la Agonía Financiera," *El Cotidiano,* 3(16), March–April 1987, 74–85.
Lieuwen, Edwin, *Mexican Militarism: The Political Rise and Fall of the Revolutionary Army.* Albuquerque: University of New Mexico Press, 1968.
Lissakers, Karin, "Dateline Wall Street: Faustian Finance," *Foreign Policy,* 51, Summer 1983, 160–175.
Loeffler, William, *Class, State, Hegemony: Theoretical Issues and Mexico.* Ph.D. dissertation, Rutgers University. Ann Arbor, MI: University Microfilms International, 1982.
López Portillo, José, *Plan Global de Desarrollo, 1980–1982.* Mexico: Talleres Gráficos de la Nación, 1980.
——, "Sexto Informe Presidencial," *Comercio Exterior,* 32(9), September 1982, 919–947.
——, *Mis Tiempos.* Mexico: Fernández, 1988.

Loyala Díaz, Rafael, *La Crisis Obregón-Calles y el Estado Mexicano.* Mexico: Siglo Veintiuno Editores, 1984.

Lugo Gil, Humberto, "La Nacionalización de la Banca Privada," *Gaceta,* 7, 1983, 123–125.

Mancera Aguayo, Miguel, Address before the XLVIII Convención Bancaria, *Revista Bancaria,* 30(6), June 1982, 62–67.

Manero, Antonio, *La Revolución Bancaria en México.* Mexico: Talleres de la Nación, 1957.

Marichal, Carlos, "Perspectivas históricas sobre el Imperialismo Financiero en América Latina," *Economía de América Latina,* 4, March 1980, 13–44.

Martínez Nova, Juan, *Conflicto Estado Empresarios en los Gobiernos de Cárdenas, Lopez Mateos y Echeverria.* Mexico: Editorial Nueva Imagen, 1984.

Marx, Karl, *Capital, Vol. 3.* New York: Vintage Books, 1981.

———, *The Civil War in France.* Peking: Foreign Languages Press, 1977.

———, *The Communist Manifesto.* New York: International Publishers, 1948.

———, *The Eighteenth Brumaire of Louis Bonaparte.* New York: International Publishers, 1963.

———, *The German Ideology.* New York: International Publishers, 1973a.

———, *Grundrisse.* New York: Vintage Books, 1973b.

Medina Macias, Ricardo, *La Expropiación de la Banca.* Mexico: EDAMEX, 1982.

Mendoza Pichardo, Gabriel, "Modificaciones bancarias: privatizadoras, monopolizadoras y desnacionalizadoras," *Coyuntura,* 10 (June, Pt. 2), 1990, 1.

Meneses, Manuel, and Carlos Fernández-Vega, "Falló en México el Modelo Democrático-Empresarial," *La Jornada,* (November 4), 1985a.

———, "Nuevo Rumbo con Justicia Social," *La Jornada,* (November 5), 1985b, 1.

Meyer, Jean, Enrique Krauze, and Cayetano Reyes, *Historia de la Revolución Mexicana, 1924–1928: Estado y Sociedad con Calles,* Vol. 11. Mexico: El Colegio de México, 1977.

Miliband, Ralph, *The State in Capitalist Society.* New York: Basic Books, 1969.

———, "Reply to Nicos Poulantzas," *New Left Review,* 59, January–February 1970, 53–60.

———, "Poulantzas and the Capitalist State," *New Left Review,* 82, November–December 1973, 83–92.

Moctezuma Cid, Julio, Address before the XLIII Convención Bancaria, *Memoria,* 25(3), March 1977, 28–31.

Molina Ochoa, Iván, and Luis Hernández Palacios, "La Crisis Fiscal del Estado Mexicano," *Iztapalapa,,* 4(8), January–June 1983, 128–143.

Morales, Cesáreo, "La Naturaleza de las Medidas del Primero de Septiembre," *Iztapalapa,* 4, January–June 1983, 80–99.

Morales, María Dolores, "El Comportamiento Empresarial de Dos Pioneros de Fraccionamientos en la Ciudad de México," in Enrique Florescano (ed): *Origenes y Desarrollo de la Burguesía en América Latina, 1700–1955.* Mexico: Editorial Nueva Imagen, 1985.

Morera Camacho, Carlos, "¿Apoyo a la Nacionalización de Una Alternativa Proletaria a la Crisis?" *Teoría y Política,* 9, January–March 1983, 143–168.

Morgan Guaranty Trust, "LDC Capital Flight," *World Financial Markets,* March 1986, 13–15.

Mouffe, Chantal, and Anne Showstack Sassoon, "Gramsci in France and Italy: A Review of the Literature," *Economy and Society,* 6(1), February 1977, 31–68.

Murray, Robin, "The Internationalization of Capital and the Nation State," *New Left Review,* 67, May–June 1971, 84–109.

Newell, Roberto, and Luis Rubio, *Mexico's Dilemma: The Political Origins of Economic Crisis.* Boulder, CO: Westview, 1984.

Nuncio, Abraham, *El Grupo Monterrey.* Mexico: Editorial Nueva Imagen, 1982.

Ochoa Campos, Moisés, *Calles el Estadista.* Mexico: Trillas, 1976.

Offe, Claus, "Political Authority and Class Structures," *International Journal of Sociology,* 11(1), Spring 1972, 73–10.

———, "The Theory of the Capitalist State and the Problem of Policy Formation," in Leon Lindberg et al. (eds): *Stress and Contradiction in Modern Capitalism,* London: Lexington Books, 1975.

———, "Crises of Crisis Management," *International Journal of Politics,* 6(3), Fall 1976, 29–67.

Ollman, Bertell, "Marx's Use of 'Class,'" *American Journal of Sociology,* 73, March 1968, 573–580.

Ortega, Maximino, and Sergio Kurzcyn, "Crisis Económica, Estatización y Sindicalización Bancaria," *Iztapalapa,* 4(8), January–June 1983, 117–127.

Ortiz, Guillermo, "Currency Substitution in México," *Journal of Money, Credit, and Banking,* 15(2), May 1983, 174–185.

Ortiz Mena, Antoñio, *Discursos y Declaraciónes,* Vol. 2. Mexico: SCHP, 1970.

Ortiz Pinchetti, Francisco, "El grupo Chihuahua se autopresto y perdio los fondos de Comermex," *Proceso,* 365, October 31, 1983, 17–19.

Ossowski, Stanislaw, *Class Structure in the Social Consciousness.* London: Routledge and Kegan Paul, 1963.

Othón de Mendizábal, Miguel, Nathan Whetten, José María Luis Mora, Angel Palerm Vich, Mariano Otero, Rodolfo Stavenhagen, Andrés Molina Enríquez, and Pablo González Casanova, *Las Clases Sociales en México.* Mexico: Editorial Nuestro Tiempo, 1968.

Pazos, Luis, *La Estatización de la Banca.* Mexico: Diana, 1982.

Pérez, Germán, and Rosa Maria Miron, "López Portillo: Un Sexenio de Auge y Crisis," in Christina Puga et al. (eds): *Evolución del Estado Mexicano,* Vol. 3. Mexico: Ediciónes "El Caballito," 1986.

Pérez, Germán, María del Carmen Solórzano, Christina Puga, David Torres, José Woldenberg, Samuel León Rolando Garcia, and Lucia Ocañia, "Comentarios politicos," *Estudios Politicos,* 2(1), January–March 1983, 65–76.

Potash, Robert. *Mexican Government and Industrial Development in the Early Republic: The Banco de Avio.* Amherst, MA: University of Massachusetts Press, 1983.

Poulantzas, Nicos, *Political Power and Social Classes.* London: Verso, 1973.

———, *Classes in Contemporary Capitalism.* London: Verso, 1978.

———, *Fascism and Dictatorship.* London: Verso, 1979.

———, *State, Power, Socialism.* London: Verso, 1980.

Puga, Cristina, Ricardo Tirado, Germán Pérez, Rocío Guadarrama, Paulina Fernández Christlieb, Luisa Béjar, José Woldenberg, Mario Huacuja, Rosa María Mirón, and Jaqueline Peschard, *Evolución del Estado Mexicano: Consolidación, 1940–1983,* Vol. 3. Mexico: Ediciónes "El Caballito," 1986.

———, "Austeridad (Tras)nacionalizada," *Punto Critico*, 127 (October), 1982d, 18–20.

———, "Estado Mexicano y Capital Imperialista," *Punto Critico*, 127 (October), 1982b, 6–7.

Punto Crítico, "Mexico: Class Struggle and 'Political Reform,'" *Contemporary Marxism*, 1, 1980, 73–79.

———, "El Patrioterismo Esconde los Programas de Austeridad del FMI," *Punto Critico*, 127 (October), 1982a, 3–6.

———, "Precarias Avances en la Disputa por la Nación," *Punto Critico*, 127 (October), 1982c, 8.

Quezada, Angélica, and Luis Acevedo, "No es Traidor el Sector Bancario: AMB," *Uno Más Uno*, September 1, 1982, 1.

Quijano, José Manuel, "Mexico: Crédito y Desnacionalización," *Economía Mexicana*, 3, 1979, 209–217.

———, *México: Estado y Banca Privada*. Mexico: CIDE, 1981.

Quijano, José Manuel, Guillermo Anaya, León Bendesky, María Elena Cardero, José Luis Manno, and Hilda Sánchez Martínez, *La Banca: Pasado y Presente (Problemas Financieros Mexicanos)*. Mexico: CIDE, 1983.

Quijano, José, and León Bendesky, "Cambios Recientes en el Sistema Financiero Internaciónal," in Jose Quijano et al. (eds): *La Banca*. Mexico: CIDE, 1983.

Quijano, José, Hilda Sánchez, and Fernando Antía, *Finanzas, Desarrollo Económico y Penetración Extranjera*. Puebla, Mexico: UAP, 1985.

Quijano, José, Carlos Tello, Arturo Warman, Adolfo Gilly, José Blanco, José Carreño Carlón, and Carlos Pereyra, "La banca que quedó," *Nexos*, 83, November 1984, 15–26.

Quintana, Enrique, "Crisis y Coyuntura Financiera," Unpublished manuscript, UCSD Center for U.S.–Mexican Studies, 1986.

———, "La Privatización Bancaria: ¿Revancha o Concertación?" *Cotidiano*, 36, July–August 1990, 3–8.

Quintero-Rivera, A. G., "Socialist and Cigarmaker: The Artisans' Proletarianization in the Making of the Puerto Rican Working Class," *Latin American Perspectives*, 10(2 and 3, 37 and 38), 1983, 2–18.

Ramírez, Carlos, "La Nacionalización de la Banca, Respuesta a la Demanda Popular," *Proceso*, 305, September 6, 1982, 6–14.

Ramírez Acosta, Ramón and Alejandro Mungaray Lagarda, "El Impacto de la Crisis Cambiaria de 1982 en las Relaciónes Económicas Fronterizas: El Caso Tijuana-San Diego," *Cuadernos de Economía*, 1, 1985, 2.

Ramírez Brun, Ricardo, *Estado y Acumulación de Capital en México, 1929–1979*. Mexico: UNAM, 1980.

Ramírez Gómez, Ramón, *La Moneda, el Crédito y la Banca a Traves de la Concepción Marxista y de las Teoría Subjectivas*. Mexico: UNAM, 1984.

Ranjel, J. Jesus, "Reorientación del Servicio de la Banca," *Excelsior*, August 10, 1982, 1.

Rey Romay, Benito, *La Ofensiva Empresarial Contra la Intervención del Estado*. Mexico: Siglo Veintiuno, 1984.

Reyes Esparza, Pedro, Enrique Olivares, Emilio Leyva, and Ignacio Hernández, *La Burguesía Mexicana*. Mexico: Editorial Nuestro Tiempo, 1981.

Reyna, José Luis, and Richard Weinert (eds), *Authoritarianism in Mexico*. Philadelphia, PA: Institute for the Study of Human Issues, 1977.

Rivera Ríos, Miguel, *Crisis y Reorganización del Capitalismo Mexicano*. Mexico: Ediciónes Era, 1986.

Robinson, Allan, "Portillo Pockets the Banks," *Euromoney,* October 1982, 47–53.

Rodríguez, Erwin, "La Transcendencia Económica y Política de la Expropiación de la Banca Privada en México," *Estudios Politicos,* 2(1), January–March, 1983, 38–43.

Ros, Jaime, "Crisis Económica y Política de Estabilización en México," *Investigación Económica,* 168, April–June 1984, 257–292.

Rosas, Javier, "Caciques y Caudillos en el Oriente Mexicano, 1919–1920: El Caso de Veracruz y Tabasco," *Estudios Politicos,* Nueva Epoca, 2(3), July–September 1983, 17–29.

Rosenzweig, Fernando, "Moneda y bancos," in Daniel Cosio Villegas (ed.): *Historia Moderna de Mexico*. Mexico: Editorial Hermes, 1974.

Rubel, Maximiliem, Hal Draper, Mauro Volpi, Livio Maritan, Alejandro Gaívez Cancino, Roberto L. Céspedes, and Dennis Berger, "Los Bonapartismos," *Criticas de la Economia Politica,* Edicion Latinoamericana, 25/25, October 1985.

Ruíz Durán, Clemente, "Inflación y Trabajadores (Notas sobre un Conficto de Clases)," *Economía Informa,* 97, September 1982, 5–8.

———, *90 Días de Política Monetaria y Crediticia Independiente*. Puebla, Mexico: UAP, 1984a.

———, "Entrevista a Clemente Ruíz Durán," *Momento Económico,* 2, 1984b, 13–14.

Sales Gutíerrez, Carlos, "No se Reprivatizó la Banca," *Excelsior,* January 1, 1983, 1.

Salinás, Irma, "Historia Intima del Grupo Monterrey," *El Buscón,* 11/12, 1984, 31–36.

Sánchez Martínez, Hilda, "El Sistema Monetario y Financiero Mexicano Bajo una Perspectiva História: El Porfiriato," in José Quijano, et al. (eds): *La Banca: Pasado y Presente*. Mexico: CIDE, 1983.

———, *Crisis y Política Económica*. Mexico: CIDE, 1984.

———, "La Revolución y la Etapa de Reconstrucción: Los Obstáculos a la Consolidación Financiera," *Finanzas, Desarrollo Económico y Penetración Extranjera*. Puebla, Mexico: UAP, 1985.

Saragoza, Alexander, *The Formation of a Mexican Elite: The Industrialization of Monterrey, Nuevo Leon, 1880–1920*. Unpublished Ph.D. dissertation, University of California, San Diego, 1978.

Schryer, Frans, Una Burquesía Campesina en la Revolución Mexicana: Los Rancheros de Pisaflores. Mexico: Ediciónes Era, 1986.

Schumpeter, Joseph, *History of Economic Analysis*. New York: Oxford University Press, 1980.

Schwaller, John Frederick, *Origins of Church Wealth in Mexico*. Albuquerque: University of New Mexico Press, 1985.

Secretaría de Programación y Presupuesto, *El sistema bancario y financiero en México, 1970–1982*. Mexico: SPP, 1984.

Seddon, David (ed), *Relations of Production*. London: Frank Cass, 1978.

Semo, Enrique, *História del Capitalismo en México*. Mexico: Ediciónes Era, 1973.

———, *História Mexicana: Economía y Luch a de Clases*. Mexico: Serie Popular Era, 1978.

Silva Herzog, Jesus, Address before the XLVIII Convención Bancaria, *Revista bancaria,* 30(6), June 1982, 70–78, and 124.

Solís, Leopoldo, *La Realidad Económica Mexicana*. 11th ed. Mexico: Siglo Veintiuno, 1981.

Solís, Leopoldo, and Dwight Brothers, *Evolución Financiera de México*. Mexico: CEMLA, 1967.

Soria, Vítor, "La Nacionalización de la Banca y la Crisis en México," *Iztapalapa*, 4(8), January–June 1983, 99–116.

Sweezy, Paul, *The Theory of Capitalist Development*. New York: Monthly Review Press, 1970.

Tello, Carlos, "La Banca Nacionalizada, Primeras Medidas Concretas," *Comercio Exterior*, 32(9), September 1982, 948–964.

———, Interview by Russell White, 1986.

———, *La Nacionalización de la Banca en México*. Mexico: Siglo Veintiuno, 1984.

———, *La Política Económica en México, 1970–1976*. Mexico: Siglo Veintiuno, 1979.

Ten Kate, Adriaan, and Robert Wallace, *Protection and Economic Development in Mexico*. West Meal, England: Gower, 1980.

Therborn, Göran, *The Ideology of Power and the Power of Ideology*. London: Verso, 1980.

Thomas, Clive, *The Rise of the Authoritarian State in Peripheral Societies*. New York: Monthly Review Press, 1984.

Thompson, John, *Inflation, Financial Markets, and Economic Development: The Experience of Mexico*. Greenwich, CT: JAI Press, 1979.

Tirado, Manlio, *La Nacionalización de la Banca Privada en México*. Mexico: Ediciónes Quinto Sol, 1982.

Torres Gaytán, Ricardo, *Un Siglo de Devaluaciónes de Pesos Mexicano*. Mexico: Siglio Veintiuno, 1980.

Turrent Díaz, Edwardo, *Historía del Banco de México*. Mexico: Banco de México, S.A., 1982.

———, La Nacionalización Bancaria en Mexico: Un enfoque de análisis histórico. Unpublished paper presented at the Eleventh International Congress of the Latin American Studies Association, 1983.

Uno Más Uno, "CCE: La Banca Mexicana, de las Más Profesionales y Responsables," *Uno Más Uno*, September 3, 1982, 6.

Urías, Margarita, "Militares y Comerciantes en México, 1830–1846," in Enrique Florescano (ed): *Origenes y Desarrollo de la Burgesía en América Latina, 1700–1955*. Mexico: Editorial Nueva Imagen, 1985.

Valdés, Leonardo, "La Nacionalización de la Banca, el Control de Cambios y la Política Económica de JLP," *Iztapalapa*, 4(8), January–June 1983, 57–80.

Valenzuela Feijóo, José, *El Capitalismo Mexicano en los Ochenta*. Mexico: Ediciones Era, 1986.

Vega Iñigues, Rolando, Address presented at the XLVI Convención Bancaria de ABM, *Memoria*, 28(6), June 1980, 10–19.

Vellinga, Menno, *Industrialización, Burguesía y Clase Obrera en México*. Mexico: Siglo Veintiuno, 1981.

Weber, Max, *The Theory of Social and Economic Organization*. New York: Oxford University Press, 1947.

Wirth, Margaret, "Towards a Critique of the Theory of State Monopoly Capitalism," *Economy and Society*, 6(3), 1977, 284–313.

Wood, Ellen, "The Separation of the Economic and the Political in Capitalism," *New Left Review,* 127, May–June 1981, 66–95.

Wright, Erik Olin, *Class, Crisis and the State.* London: Verso, 1979.

Wyman, Donald (ed.), *Mexico's Economic Crisis,* Monograph Series, No. 12. San Diego, CA: Center for U.S.–Mexican Studies, 1983.

Zeitlin, Maurice (ed.), *Classes, Class Conflict, and the State.* Cambridge, MA: Winthrop, 1980.

Zevada, Ricardo, *Calles: El Presidente.* Mexico: Editorial Nuestro Tiempo, 1971.

Zuñiga, Juan Antonio, "La Bolsa de Valores, al Servicio de Grandes Empresas, reduce el Papel de la Banca," *Proceso,* 365 (October 31), 1983a, 14–15.

———, "A los Exbanqueros, Indemnización Más Interes; en el Exterior, Plazos," 356 (August 29), 1983b, 31.

———, "Todo Como Antes: Los Banqueros Vuelven a la Banca," *Proceso,* 370 (December 5), 1983c, 14–17.

Index

Abedrop Dávila, Carlos, 110, 132, 143
ABM (Mexican Bankers Association),
     47, 63, 84, 86, 89, 108
ABM convention, 108–110
Accumulation, 14, 32, 47, 71, 79, 80,
     82, 100, 142, 145, 155
  primitive, 28
  subsidization of, 63, 98
Accumulation model, 11, 22, 29, 56, 60,
     66, 71, 75, 76, 78, 97, 100, 123,
     125, 127, 150, 156
Adjusted countable capital, 136
Adjustment programs, 106–108, 115,
     128
Agricultural banks, 46
Agricultural sector, 21, 22, 28, 29, 60,
     78
Agua Prieta coup (1920), 27
Alemán administration, 56, 58, 86
Alemán, Miguel, 86
Alfa, 85
Alliance for Production, 76, 81, 89, 99
Alvarez, Alejandro, 121
American trade bloc, 156
Anarchist, 7
Anaya, Carlos, 130
Artisans, 4, 10, 11
Assets, bank, 102
Atalaya 82, 107
Auxiliary credit organizations, 44, 62
Aviadores, 6
Avila Camacho, Maximino, 46, 86

Back-to-back loan guarantees, 75
Balance of payments, 98, 99, 111, 114
Banamex, 65, 73, 84, 85, 102, 103, 113,
     130, 132, 133
Banco Atlántico, 113
Banco Central Méxicano, 17, 18, 21
Banco de Empleados, 14

Banco de Fomentación, 20
Banco de Londres, 14, 15, 17, 18,
     20–22, 39, 47, 65
Banco de Montreal, 40, 44
Banco de México, 38, 39, 42, 43, 45,
     47, 57, 64, 109
Banco Hipotecario, 20
Banco Internacional, 47, 113, 153
Banco Internacional Hipotecario, 17, 19,
     20
Bancomer, 65, 73, 84–86, 102, 103,
     130, 133, 143
Banco Mexicano, 45, 46
Banco México de Comercio e Industria,
     20
Banco Nacional, 15–17, 18, 20, 21, 40,
     47
Banco Nacional de Crédito Rural, 73
Banco Nacional de México, 22
Banco Nacional de Transportes, 61
Banco Nacional Méxicano, 13
Banco Serfín, 55, 73
Banco Unico de Emisión, 35
Bank and Credit Public Service
     Regulatory Law, 137
Bank balance sheets, 105
Bank capital, 11, 12, 16, 21, 22, 38, 41,
     42, 47, 48, 55, 66, 67, 71, 74, 88,
     149, 150
Bank capital, fraction/strata, 14, 22
Bank capital and profits, 102
Bank concessions, 109, 116
Bank groups, 65
Bank liquidation, 34–36
Bank loan portfolios, 10
Bank practices, 105
Bank profits, 102, 106, 113, 129
Bank reform, 44, 46
Bank syndicates, 14
Bank system (1980–1982), 101–106
Bank-finance capital, 67

Banks, specialized, 103
Banobras, 46
Bartra, Roger, 121, 122
Bonapartist regime, 25, 27–29
Bourbon reforms, 4, 5
Bourgeoisie, 8, 11, 26, 29, 30, 63, 77,
    78, 88, 98, 108, 150
Bourgeoisie, proto, 28
Bourgeoisie, revolutionary, 29, 80
Brasil, 73

Caciques, 27, 28
Calles law, 43
Calles, Elías Plutarco, 29, 30, 38, 39, 42
CANACINTRA (Cámera Nacional de la
    Industria de Transformación,
    National Chamber of
    Manufacturing Industry), 86
Capital accumulation, 72, 98
Capital concentration, centralization,
    differentiation, 14
Capital flight, 77, 79, 86, 97–99, 101,
    105, 107, 111, 112
Capital formation, 80
Capital market, 47, 57, 67, 140, 145,
    153
Capitalist forms of production, 11
Capitalist mode of production, 22
Capitalist relations of production, 3, 72
Capitalist state, 7
Capitalists, revolutionary, 30
Cárdenas administration, 56, 76, 123,
    150
Cárdenas, Lázaro, 31, 33, 46, 47
Carranza, Venustiano, 27, 35, 41
Casas de moneda, 9
Casasús, Joaquín, 20
Caudillos, 27–29
CCE (Consejo Coordinador Empresarial,
    Management Coordinating
    Council), 79, 80, 111, 132, 133
Cedillo, Alfonso, 47
Central Bank, 64, 67, 107, 129, 130,
    142
Central Fraction of finance capital, 84,
    85; *See also* Class fractions;
    Finance capital
CETES (Certificados de Tesoria,
    Treasury Certificates), 83, 89,
    109, 142
Chiapas, 6

Chihuahua, 12, 14
Chile, 73, 78
Church, 3, 5, 9, 149
Church financial hegemony, 5
Church financial power, 5
Científicos, 21, 27
Civil society, 25
Class alliances, 27, 29, 31, 80
Class analysis, 120, 127
Class conflict, 7, 31
Class confrontations, intrastrata/fraction,
    19, 22, 100
Class contradictions, 83
Class forces, 63, 80
Class fractions, 72, 120, 149
Class struggles, intraclass and interclass,
    25, 72, 80, 123
Class struggles, political-economic, 10,
    56, 146
Classes, 123
Classes and class fractions, 6, 7, 22
Clouthier, Manuel, 132
Coincidence of interests, 99, 112, 124,
    150
Colonial system, 6
Combined and uneven articulation
    of modes of production, 4,
    149
Combined and uneven development of
    capitalism, 89
Comerciante financial power, 10
Comerciantes, 12
Comerciantes, speculative-usurious, 12
Comermex, 65, 86, 87; *See also* Class
    fractions; Finance capital
Commercial banks, 17, 57
Commercial capital, 3–6, 11, 22, 36
Commercial capital, usurious and
    speculative, 13
Commercial circuits, 9
Commercial code, 13, 21
Commercial emission banks, 16
Commercial hegemony, 15
Commercial house, 9, 10
Commercial oligarchy, 4
Commercial usury, 4
Commercial usury capital, 149
CONCAMIN (Confederación de Cámaras
    Nacionales de Comercio y
    Industria, Confederation of
    National Chambers of
Commerce and Industry), 63, 86, 111

CONCANACO (Confederación de Cámeras Nacionales de Comercio, Confederation of National Chambers of Commerce), 63, 86, 111
Concentration-centralization processes, 13, 19, 38, 64, 66, 67, 71, 79, 86, 87, 89, 153, 154
Concessions, 154
Conciliation of interests, 156
Confidence, crisis of, 63, 81, 82, 115, 145, 153
Confidence, re-establishment of, 135
Conjunctural crisis, 71
Conjunctural crisis/problems, 120, 145
Conservatives, 10, 111
Consolidation policy (1971), 76
Conspiracy theory, 117
Consumer credit, 62
Contradictions, 123, 130
  capitalism, 121
  classes/fractions, 149
COPARMEX (Confederación Patronal de la República Mexicana, Employers' Confederation of the Mexican Republic), 63, 79, 85
Corruption, 30
CPP (Costo Promedio de Pasivos, Average Cost of Debits), 102, 129
Corredor, Jaime, 153
Credit card policies, 130
Credit squeeze, 104
Crédito Hotelero, 46
Crédito Minero, 47, 55
Creel, Enrique, 37, 38
Creel de la Barra, Enrique, 110
Crisis (1884), 13
Crisis (1981), 106
Crisis (1982), 115
Crisis:
  cash, 106
  credit, 142
  financial and liquidity crisis, 155
  liquidity, 110, 124
  political, 80, 128, 144, 150
  political-economic, 84, 97, 113, 115, 117, 118, 121, 129, 134
  production, 129
CROM (Confederación Regional Obrera Mexicana, Regional Confederation of Mexican Workers), 28
Crown, 5

CTM (Confederación de Trabajadores de México, Confederation of Mexican Workers), 114
Currency exchange operations, 102, 105
Current account deficit, 83
CYDSA, 85; *See also* Grupo Monterrey

Debt, dollar-denominated, 106
Debt instruments, 142
Debt peons, 11
Debt service, 75, 100, 114
Deficits, 58, 77, 99
De-dollarization, 129
De la Madrid, administration/regime, 127, 137, 143
Democratic opening, 77
Deligitimating contradictions, 97
Deregulation, financial intermediaries, 154
Desarrollo compartido, 76
Devaluation, 59
Díaz, Jr., Porfirio, 19
Díaz Ordaz administration, 63
Díaz Serrano affair, 98
Disintermediation, 73, 89, 101, 105, 124
Dollar-denominated accounts, 112
Dollar-denominated debt, 129
Dominant bloc, 121
Dollarization, 61, 75, 100
Dual parity exchange, 111, 112
Durazo, Arturo, 117

Ecclesiastic property, nationalization of, 11
Echeverría administration, 76, 78, 80, 83
Economic development, 32, 33, 55
Economic disequilibrium, 64, 97, 107, 123
Economic groups, 72
Ecuador, 73
Ejidal bank, 47
El Banco de Londres y México, 12
El Banco de Santa Eulalia, 12
El Banco Mexicano, 12
Electoral process, 81
Emission banks, 12, 14–18, 34
Energy crisis, 97, 98
Escandón, Pablo, 20
Espinosa Yglesías, Manuel, 46, 133
Euromarket, 73

Evils, external and internal, 116
Exchange control, 112, 116
Exchange economy, 11
Exchange markets, 109, 112, 113
Exchange Regulatory Commission, 42
Expropriation, 121, 134

Fideicomisos, 60
Finance capital, 72, 76, 77, 83, 84–90,
    97, 100, 109, 125, 127, 149, 150,
    155, 157–161
Financial circuit(s), 5, 13, 19, 21, 22,
    36, 48, 55, 62, 66, 71, 74, 77, 97,
    124, 127, 135, 136, 145, 150, 155
Financial circuits, internationalization of,
    84, 87, 100
Financial contradictions, 74
Financial crisis, 123
Financial fraction, 123, 125, 127, 140,
    145, 150, 155, 156
Financial groups, 84, 86, 141, 154
Financial hegemony, 22
Financial-industrial groups, 47
Financial instruments, 78, 83, 89, 98,
    109, 141
Financial intermediary institutions, 155
Financial networks, 62
Financial policies, 130
Financial resources, 101
Financial service companies, 135
Financial valorization of capital, 74
Financieras, 44, 64, 66
Financiera Nacional Azucarera, 61
Fiscal policies, 106
Float, 13
Forces and relations of production, 72
Foreign banks, 44
Foreign capital, 4, 19–22, 27, 38, 40,
    56, 59
Foreign currency, 111, 124
Foreign currency reserves, 75
Foreign debt, 73, 74, 100
Foreign finance capital, 104
Forty Fraction, 86; *See also* Fracción
    Cuarenta
Foreign investment banks, 156
Fractions of finance capital, 84–89
Fracción cuarenta (Forty Fraction), 80,
    85
Free Mexico demonstrationss, 133
French, 12

Fusion, 13, 86, 88; *See also*
    Concentration-centralization
    processes

Garcia, Eraña, 89
Garza-Sada, 14, 85
Garza-Sada, Eugenio, 78
General Credit Law (1925), 38
General law of credit institutions (1897),
    15–17, 20, 21, 34
Global market, 11
Global economic crisis (1907), 18
Gold, 13, 43
Gómez Morín, Manuel, 44, 46
González, Carlos Hank, 86
González Cosio, Manuel, 20
Government bonds, 13
Grupo Banamex, 160, 161; *See also*
    Finance capital
Grupo Bancomer, 161; *See also* Finance
    capital
Grupo Chihuahua, 158; *See also* Finance
    capital
Grupo Comermex, 86; *See also* Finance
    capital
Grupo Cremi, 55, 84, 85, 143, 159, 160;
    See also Finance capital
Grupo DESC, 86; *See also* Finance
    capital
Grupo Garza-Sada, 55; *See also* Finance
    capital
Grupo ICA-Atlántico, 86, 159, 160; *See
    also* Finance capital
Grupo Industria y Comercio, 86; *See
    also* Finance capital
Grupo Monterrey, 85, 134, 157, 158; *See
    also* Finance capital
Grupo Pagliai-Alemán-Azcárraga, 86;
    See also Finance capital
Grupo Somex, 158, 159; *See also*
    Finance capital
Grupo Vidriera, 157, 158; *See also*
    Finance capital; Grupo Monterrey
Grupo Visa, 157; *See also* Finance
    capital; Grupo Monterrey
Guadalajara, 107

Hacendados, 9, 11, 12, 21
Hacienda, 6
Hegemonic crisis, 8, 9

Hegemonic fraction, 7, 29, 149
Hegemonic position, 84, 97, 150
Hegemonic project, 29
Hegemony, 27, 41, 84, 88, 146, 150
Henequeros, 14
Hidalgo, 33
Hipotecaria, 64
Historical-material analysis, 149
Historical perspective, 128, 149
Honduras, 73
Hot money, 75
Huerta, Victoriano, 19, 29, 34, 36

Ideology, revolutionary, 26
IFI (Ingeniería Financiera Internacional
    de México, International Financial
    Engineering), 143
IFNB (Instituciones Financieros
    No-Bancarios, Non-Bank Financial
    Institutions), 134, 153
IMF (International Monetary Fund), 79,
    82, 115, 118, 127, 130, 144
Incipient bourgeoisie, 56
Incipient industrialists, 14
Indemnization, 136
Industrial capital, 9, 10, 11
Industrialization myth, 56
Inflation, 58, 98, 100, 106, 107, 111,
    115, 129
Inflation and devaluation cycle, 115
Integral support program (Programa de
    Apoyo Integral), 106
Intendencias, 5
Interbank lending, 62, 65
Interlocking directorates, 19, 20,
    157–161
Internal regional markets, 11, 72
Interest rates, 40, 58, 78, 100, 102, 104,
    114, 115, 142
International banking syndicates, 73
International capital markets, 72, 74, 75
International division of labor, 11
International finance, 73
International reserves, 111, 115
Internationalization of production, 83
Investment banks, 57
ISI (Industrial Import Substitution)
    accumulation model, 64, 72, 76,
    83

Jenkins, William, 46

Keynesian stimulative policies, 108

Laissez-faire policies, 10
Landón y Escandón, Guillermo, 20
Latifundistas, 21
Latifundium, 6
Lazard, 143
Left, Mexican, 128, 146
Legislative reforms, 57, 62, 139, 154
Legorreta, Agústin, 85, 136, 143
Legorreta, Eduardo, 143
Liberal-oligarchic State, 10; *See also*
    State
Liberals, 10, 12
Limantour, Julio, 19
Liquidity, 58, 75, 104
London Bank of Mexico and South
    America, Ltd., 12
LOPPE (Ley Federal de Organizaciones
    Políticas y Procesos Electorales,
    Federal Law of Political
    Organizations and Electoral
    Processes), 81
López Mateos administration, 59, 62, 63,
    66, 130, 144
López Portillo administration, 76, 81–84,
    89, 98, 123, 128
López Portillo, José, 108, 110, 114, 115,
    117, 120, 122, 150, 153
Luxury tax, 78

Macedo, Pablo, 20, 38
Mancera, Gabriel, 20
Mancera Aguayo, Miguel, 108, 109,
    127, 130
Martínez del Río, Pablo, 20
Maximato, 29
Maximilian, 8
Mercantil Agricola e Hipotecario, 13
Merchant capital, 9
Mercantile capital, 11
Merchants, 4–6, 15
Mexican capitalism, 4; *See also*
    Capitalism
Mexdollar accounts, 104, 114; *See also*
    Dollarization
Mexican miracle, 71, 98
Military, 7, 28, 29
Miners, 9
Miñez, Roberto, 20

Mode of production, capitalist, 11; *See also* Combined and uneven activation of modes of production
Modernization, 26, 55, 59, 155, 156
Modes of production, articulation, 8
Monetary emission, 13, 14; *See also* Combined and uneven activation of modes of production
Monetary law, amendment to (1982), 112
Monetary reform (1905), 21
Money market, 57, 62
Monopolization, 67
Monopoly capital, 121
Monte de Piedad, 12, 13
Monterrey, 6, 9, 10, 14, 33, 133
Montes de Oca, Louis, 43, 47
Mortgage banks, 12, 16–18
Multibanks, 84, 86, 87, 103
Multinational banks, 73

Nafinsa, 46, 47, 66
National Agrarian Party (Partido Nacional Agrarista), 28
National Bank Commission, 38
National credit institutions, 42, 44, 46, 47, 61, 73, 101
National credit system, 16
National security, 117
Nationalization of the banks, 97–125
Nationalized bank system, developmentalist conception of, 130, 132
New Economic Policy (NEP), 29
Ninety days, 127, 129; *See also* Postnationalization
Nonfinancial service companies, 135
Northern Fraction, 85; *See also* Class fractions; Grupo Monterrey; Finance Capital

Obregón, Alvaro, 25, 27, 28, 29, 36, 41
Oligarchs, 9
Oligarchy, 80
Open market operations, 58
Orthodox paradigm, 128

PAN (Partido Acción Nacional, National Action Party), 121, 155

Pani, Alberto, 38, 40, 43, 44, 45
Paraestatales, 56, 63, 89
Parallel financial system, 153
Patronato del Ahorro Nacional, 61
PCM (Partido Comunista Mexicano, Mexican Communist Party), 81
PDM (Partido Democrática Mexicano, Mexican Democratic Party), 81
Peasantry, 11, 79
Peso, 13, 58, 104, 111
Peso capture, 106
Peso devaluation, 104
Petrodollars, 99
Petroleum, 75, 76, 82–84, 89, 97, 99, 100, 114, 115, 118, 123
Petrolization, 98
Petty-bourgeoisie, 25, 27–29; *See also* Class fractions
Piñeda, Rosendo, 20
Plan Global de Desarrollo, 99
PNFD (Programa Nacional de Financiamiento del Desarollo, National Program of Financial Development), 138
PNR (Partido Nacional Revolucionario, National Revolutionary Party), 29, 30
Political culture, 26
Political-economic contradictions, 88
Political instability, 7
Political parties, 30–32
Political reform, 81
Political vacuum, 124; *See also* Power vacuum
Porfiriato, 4, 12, 20, 22
Porfirian banking system, 9–22, 335
Positivism, 25
Postnationalization, 127–161
Power bloc, 20–22, 28, 29, 67, 76, 80, 84, 88, 89, 121, 124, 151
contradictory unity, 8
disintegration, 8
unproductive, 11
Power fragmentation, 10
Power vacuum, 6, 25
PRI (Partido Revolucionario Institucional, Institutional Revolutionary Party), 32, 155
Private credit institutions, 44, 55
Private sector investment, 77, 81
Privatization of the banks, 153–155

PRM (Partido de la Revolución
Mexicano, Party of the Mexican
Revolution), 30, 31
Production, 4
Productive structure, 78, 100, 123
Proletariat, 11, 27, 108
PST (Partido Socialista de Trabajadores,
Socialist Workers' Party), 81
Public interest, 118
Pubic sector investment, 78
Punto Crítico, 81, 119, 127

Qualitative credit controls, 45
Quasi-monetary instruments, 73

Rancheros, 33
Rediscount operations, 58
Redistribution, 76, 81
Refaccionario banks, 4, 17, 18
Reform (1850s), 8
Reform, liberal, 4, 11
Reforms, bank (1908), 18, 21, 22
Reforms, bank (1970, 1974), 87
Regulatory and Inspection Credit
Institution Commission, 34
Rhetoric, reactionary, 133
Rentierism, 83, 97
Reprivatization, 154
Republic, restoration of, 11, 12
Reserve requirements, 57, 74, 78, 109
Resource capture, 97, 101, 104, 153
Revolution, 33, 47, 100, 117, 123
(1910–1920), 25, 26
ideology, 124, 146
combined and uneven, 25
Revolutionary class coalition, 56
Revolutionary discourse, 99
Revolutionary nationalist rhetoric, 77,
99, 112; *See also* Revolution,
ideology
Rivero, Valentín, 14
Rodríguez, Abelardo, 30, 46
Rodríguez, Augustín, 45
Ruíz Crotínes, Adolfo, 58
Ruíz Durán, Clemente, 129
Rumors, 133

Sáenz, Aarón, 86
Salinas de Gortari, Carlos, 154

Salinas, Irma, 134
SAM (Sistema Alimentario Mexicano,
Mexican Alimentary System), 82
Savings, 109, 129
Savings and deposits banks, 64
Security market, 64
Selective reserve requirements, 58
Semifeudalism, 3
Silva Herzog, Jesús, 108, 109, 112, 113,
130
SNC (Sociedades Nacionales de Crédito,
National Credit Societies), 137
SNC directive councils, 137
Social classes, 27, 88, 125, 144, 149,
151
Social class contradictions, 55
Social forces, 124
Social formation, 3, 22, 72, 84
Social relations, 25, 123, 140
Social stabilization, 62
Social structure, 3, 4, 25
Social unrest, 62
Socioeconomic contradictions, 97
Socioeconomic structure, 6, 144
Sofimex, 47
Somex, *see* Grupo Somex
Sonora, 79
Spain, 6
Spanish capital, 13
Speculation, 6. 9, 42, 75, 77, 83, 86,
97, 100, 101, 104, 105, 107, 109,
111–114, 116–118, 121
Speculative profits, 106
Speculative rentier capitalism, 88, 97,
100
Stabilizing development, 63, 77, 82
Stabilizing devlopmental policies,
orthodox, 99
State and civil society, 7
State apparatus, 28, 29, 78, 82, 108,
109, 112, 124, 130, 144, 150, 151
State:
arena of class conflict, 7
autonomy, 10, 16, 22, 26, 31, 32, 41,
47, 67, 89, 119, 123
class character of, 97, 144, 145, 150
conception of, 7, 146
crisis of, 71, 72, 76, 88, 150
dependency, 10, 57, 67, 74
economic intervention, 66, 78, 82,
98, 127
fiscal crisis of, 71, 118

State (*Cont.*):
    formal juridical-political entity, 7
    historical materiality, 7
    instability, 10
    in the process of formation, 27–29,
        47, 150
    legitimacy, 77, 98, 119, 150
    liberal-oligarchic, 7, 8
    maneuverability, 97, 98, 123
    minimalist neo-liberal, 155; *See also*
        State, conception of
    political-financial dependency, 13; *See*
        also State/financial dependency
    regulatory role, 9
    relative autonomy, 7, 41, 71, 80, 88,
        97, 99, 121, 128, 150
    structural/instrumental conception, 7
State/capital alliance, 58, 80
State/capital crisis, 77, 79, 89, 113, 121,
    123
State/financial dependency, 142
State/financial fraction relationship, 135,
    143
State finance, 60, 66
    disequilibrium, 74
    privatization of, 61
State promoted private accumulation, 56;
    See also Accumulation;
    Accumulation model
Stock brokerage houses (casas de bolsa),
    139, 140–144, 153, 155

Stock exchange, 137
Stock index, 140
Strata, 11, 22; *See also* Class
    confrontations
Structural-class forces, 63, 83
Structural reorganization, 127, 134
Structural reorientation, 72
Structuralist-monetarist debate, 59
Suárez, Robert Guajardo, 80
Surplus value, 4, 71, 124
Swap line agreement, 107

Tello, Carlos, 79, 88, 104, 120, 127,
    128, 129, 144, 150, 154
Terms of trade, 98
Tierras baldías, 6
Transnationalization, 67, 72
Tributary despotism, 6

Unions, 108
U.S. Department of Commerce, 106

Vallina, Elloy, 137
Valorization process, 77, 150, 155
Vidriera, 85
VISA, 85

World Bank, 130
World War II, 56

About the Author

Russel N. White is President of Latin American Consulting, Inc. Latin American Consulting is an Export Management Company with representative offices in six Latin American Countries. As a consultant, he travels extensively throughout Mexico and South America.

Dr. White received his PhD from the University of California, Riverside in 1987. He was a University of California Fellow from 1984–1986. He is an Associate Editor with *Latin American Perspectives,* a theoretical and scholarly journal for discussion and debate on the political economy of capitalism, imperialism, and socialism in the Americas. He is a member of the Advisory Board to the World Trade Club, Seattle, and is Director of the Latin American Country Forum of the World Trade Club. He is also Chair of the Legislative Issues Committee for the World Trade Club.

From time to time, Dr. White lectures at different Universities. He recently lectured at the University of Puget Sound (Tacoma, Washington); Universidad Anahuac (Mexico City); Universidad de Occidente (Unidad Mazatlan, Sinaloa, Mexico). He has also worked in local politics, providing political analysis and consultation.

Russell resides in Kent, Washington on 20 acres of wetlands. He is an avid bicyclist, enjoys skiing, sailing, darts, music, wine, and local politics.